Byron and the Bible:

*A Compendium of Biblical Usage
in the Poetry of Lord Byron*

by

TRAVIS LOOPER

The Scarecrow Press, Inc.
Metuchen, N.J. & London
1978

PR
4392
B5
L6

Library of Congress Cataloging in Publication Data

Looper, Travis, 1937-
    Byron and the Bible.

    Bibliography: p.
    Includes index.
    1. Byron, George Gordon Noël Byron, Baron, 1788-
1824--Sources. 2. Bible. 3. Bible in literature.
I. Title.
PR4392.B5L6   821'.7   78-1518
ISBN 0-8108-1123-5

So thank your stars that matters are no worse,
And read your Bible, sir, and mind your purse.

--<u>Don Juan</u>, I

ACKNOWLEDGMENTS

In addition to acknowledging my many debts to Byron scholars and critics, which I have recognized in the notes, I am pleased to give special thanks to Clement T. Goode and other members of the Baylor University faculty for their assistance--Robert H. Ray, W. J. Wimpee, Robert G. Collmen; to John Murray, for his several courtesies; to Lucy I. Edwards of the Central Public Library, Nottingham; to Jerome J. McGann; to Leslie A. Marchand; to Doris Langley Moore; to Harold Ray Stevens; to H. Dale Hughes for his special encouragement; to Merritt Felmly for his assistance with the tables; to the staffs of the Moody Memorial Library and the Armstrong Browning Library, Baylor University; to the Humanities Research Center of the University of Texas at Austin; to the staffs of the Carl H. Pforzheimer Library, the Yale University Library, and the Pierpont Morgan Library; to Mrs. T. J. Stanberry, whose manuscript typing left nothing to be desired; and to Jo Ann, John, and Ruth Ann, who allowed me to steal time from them to complete this book.

T. D. L.

Waco, Texas

v

TABLE OF CONTENTS

Table of Contents   x

Part II. THE CROSS INDEX

Old Testament

New Testament

PREFACE

Earlier Studies

Inasmuch as a large portion of Byron's poetry is concerned with biblical themes and topics, a number of critics have probed into Byron's religious views and practices. Byron's personal religion has been examined frequently, but recent critics have been increasingly concerned with systematizing the theology evident in his poetry. A chronological examination of the literature regarding the relationship of the Bible to Byron's work may properly open with an investigation into studies that consider Byron's personal opinions and conduct, continue with a survey of theological studies, and then proceed to studies that are specifically biblical in nature.

Of those studies that consider Byron's personal opinions and conduct in the matters of religion, Gamaliel Bradford's chapter, "The Glory of Sin: Byron," in his Saints and Sinners (Boston: Houghton Mifflin, 1932, pp. 223-54), is representative of earlier simplistic attitudes. Bradford's major premise is that the poet was primarily interested in shocking people. Byron's beliefs need not be taken too seriously, even if determining them were possible. Bradford makes no serious attempt to ascertain the truth about Byron, assuming that one who did not conform to conventional religious patterns and viewpoints must have been indifferent. Bradford concludes that one can always, like Byron, play at rebellious defiance. This and similar studies add little to an understanding of Byron or of his work.

William J. Calvert, in Byron, Romantic Paradox (Chapel Hill: University of North Carolina Press, 1935), an early work that does detect the importance of religion to Byron, notes that Calvinism was an important influence on him as a child, but that as a

mature adult he displayed some decidedly non-Calvinistic attitudes.
He never completely overcame the restrictive qualities of Calvinism;
predestination, for example, allowed him to view himself as a part
of a grand cosmos filled with conflicting forces. Skepticism, on
the other hand, denied him the relatively easy solution offered by
unquestioning Calvinism; skepticism left the residue of a rigid divine
curse without any real consciousness of divine revelation, and this
rationalism brought the death of orthodoxy for Byron.

Edward Wayne Marjarum, in Byron as Skeptic and Believer
(Princeton, N.J.: Princeton University Press, 1938), an early full-
length study of Byron's religious position, rather like Calvert, postu-
lates the ambiguous nature of Byron's attraction to both spirit and
reason. Unlike later studies by Jerome J. McGann and Robert F.
Gleckner, who find a systematic and profound set of beliefs, Mar-
jarum concludes that Byron achieved no harmonious system of re-
ligion before his death. Although Marjarum denies in Byron's re-
ligious speculations any progressive development toward serenity,
he shows that the poet did move away from the forbidding theistic
Calvinism of his youth toward a skepticism influenced both by his
own mental vigor and by the natural science and rationalism of the
day. This skepticism proceeded from a modified form of deism to
rationalistic idealism, which Marjarum equates with agnosticism.

Hoxie Neale Fairchild, in the "Byron" section of Religious
Trends in English Poetry (5 vols., New York: Columbia University
Press, 1949, 3:388-451), minimizes the importance of childhood
training on Byron, astutely noting in the mature poet a tolerance
and latitudinarianism that are foreign to Calvinism. He sees Byron's
realistic acknowledgment of the limitations of evil in human nature
and his superstitiousness combining to prevent him "from denying
that Christianity, which he was unable to accept." Fairchild con-
cludes that Byron used religion primarily as a source for poetic
material, especially images and subject matter.

Leslie A. Marchand's three-volume Byron: A Biography
(New York: Knopf, 1957) considers Byron's religion a strange
amalgam of beliefs. The earliest contribution came from Calvinism

with its concepts of predestination, free will, and responsibility.
In a rationalistic reaction to this Calvinism, Byron later mingled
other religious concerns with his Calvinism to produce his view of
immortality, his rejection of orthodox beliefs concerning biblical in-
spiration, and his necessitarian view of the will. Byron's continu-
ing, serious interest in religious matters is made clear in Mar-
chand's lengthy discussion of Byron's relationship with Dr. James
Kennedy, the evangelical medical officer to the English garrison at
Cephalonia. Kennedy's lectures served to bring out Byron's aston-
ishing familiarity with the Bible and related books and commentaries.
Marchand, like Marjarum in Byron as Skeptic and Believer, resorts
to some pains to indicate that Byron, unlike his friends, was not
merely seeking an opportunity to taunt Kennedy, but was sincerely
interested.

C. N. Stavrou, in "Religion in Byron's Don Juan" (Studies
in English Literature 3 (1963): 567-94), notes that Calvert, Fair-
child, and Marchand have made a thorough study of the influence of
Calvinism on Byron. Stavrou, therefore, proceeds to discuss By-
ron's attacks on orthodox Christianity. Most of the poet's anti-
Christian comments are in his public verse. When Byron attacked
Christianity, he was assaulting a system that he considered to be
teaching as certain what was not so. He lived in hope that man-
kind was inclined to reject such a demeaning system, however cer-
tain, in favor of self-determination, however delusive. Stavrou
shows that Byron was not in opposition to Christianity itself, as the
privacy of his personal letters reveals pro-Christian attitudes.

Leslie A. Marchand, in Byron's Poetry: A Critical Introduc-
tion (Boston: Houghton Mifflin, 1965), demonstrates how serious
Byron's religious concern was. Not only was he familiar with the
standard concepts of Christianity, but he also gave deep thought to
unorthodox views popular at the time, such as Socinianism, a doc-
trine toward which Byron was favorably inclined. * Marchand empha-

---

*Socinianism refers to the doctrines of Faustus Socinus, who denied
the divinity of Jesus and the Trinity and who gave rationalistic ex-
planations of sin and salvation.

sizes Byron's tolerant consideration of all viewpoints by pointing
out that the poet had a

> ... strong leaning to Manicheanism, the belief in the
> struggle of equal forces of good and evil within the uni-
> verse (and within himself) ... [p. 86].

The above studies of Byron's religious views range from the
superficial to those which seriously examine his attitudes. Although
some disagreement exists as to the basic tenor of Byron's beliefs,
most of these critics discover a serious effort on Byron's part to
deal rationally with his conflicting attitudes.

Studies later than the above have been less concerned with
Byron's personal creed than with the idea of a unified theology in
Byron's poetry. Michael Kennedy Joseph, in Byron the Poet (Lon-
don: Gollancz, 1964), one of the first works to probe thoroughly
into the poet's theology, indicates that in Cain Byron examines tra-
ditional beliefs and finds no escape from the problems created by
Calvinism: Adam and Eve learned the truth, but man was not to
be free. Rather, man discovered the gulf, created by his own im-
potence and insignificance, between himself and God, whom Byron
viewed as "not actually malicious, but remote, indifferent and de-
structive." Although written about the same time as Cain, Heaven
and Earth makes little examination of the traditional doctrines of
Calvinism, even seeming to accept such at face value. The prob-
lems of Calvinism are never satisfactorily resolved in Byron's po-
etry because of the conflict between man's mean flesh and noble
spirit. Joseph suggests that the closest thing to a resolution is
found by Byron in the Cuvier myth. According to Joseph, Byron
conceived in his version of the myth a series of aboriginal calam-
ities--cosmic, social, historical--in which each new generation,
thrust out of Paradise as it were, looks back on a succession of
stronger predecessors. Each calamity is followed by waves of re-
currently new "creations" and "paradises"; but man is doomed to
repeat the pattern begun by Eden, enlightened only by folk myths.

Robert F. Gleckner in Byron and the Ruins of Paradise
(Baltimore: Johns Hopkins Press, 1967), one of the first studies

to deal in its entirety with Byron's theological thinking, formulates a coherent view of Byron's theology. He sees it as a personal theology of despair rather than a formal theology. Essential to Byron's view is his idea of the fall. Byron is not as concerned with the sin of Adam, or mankind, as with a universe that negates whatever tendency man possesses toward good and sentences him to eternal exile. Byron saw man's fall in terms of man's emotional and rational responses to a desolate universe. Man is doomed to "the hell of human existence" where he develops by learning to cope with mental creations of his own making, such as Eden and original innocence, in order to make life bearable.

Like Gleckner, Jerome J. McGann in Fiery Dust: Byron's Poetic Development (Chicago: University of Chicago Press, 1968), does not find a formal theology in Byron's poetry but does agree that Byron is systematic in his views. McGann takes an optimistic view of Byron's theology, however, and rejects Gleckner's negative view of despair. McGann does not place as much emphasis on Calvinism, the basis for Gleckner's rather negative viewpoint. He sees Byron as modifying orthodox Calvinism by adopting concepts from the Cuvier myth and from Socinianism, a rationalistic philosophy which denied such Christian concepts as the fall of man and the atonement of a divine Christ. Socinianism posited that as man learned to sin by imitating Adam, he learned to be righteous unto salvation by imitating a very human Jesus. Although, like the Socinians, Byron had no real hope for mankind's progressive development, he looked at man with a benevolent concern in spite of and largely because of man's fleshly weakness.

McGann shows that Byron's personal theological system developed from a Cuvier-based series of five falls. Although these falls seem at times to create an unpleasant world for man, McGann points out that a positive blessing comes ultimately. The first fall is the "fall into corporeality" which establishes material existence, or life, as the first imperative. The second fall is the fall into thought or consciousness, as manifested in Lucifer and countered by a split into antithetical principles. The third fall consists of Je-

hovah's creation of man, because of the imperative Love: Jehovah
sees this step as a unifying force, but Lucifer sees the enslave-
ment of man. The fourth fall is into Death, the result of Adam's
necessary duality. The recognition of death as a gift is the fifth
and final fall. Although the primordial One seems to shrink through-
out these falls, the end result is a death into life again so that
Heaven and Earth are a single order of reality and death is as im-
portant as life.

In his essay on Cain, "The Devout Stockade" (in Lord By-
ron's Cain: Twelve Essays and a Text with Variants and Annota-
tions; (Austin: University of Texas Press, 1968, pp. 26-34), Tru-
man Guy Steffan suggests that skepticism was the result of Byron's
concern for man, man at war with God. Steffan sees the skepticism
of Pierre Bayle and the generally anathematized commentaries of
Bishop William Warburton as significant sources for Byron's own
view. Byron appreciated these rationalists for their belief that hu-
man misery was a reflection upon the God of orthodoxy. Under the
influence of such skeptics Byron concluded that the wrath of God was
not justified by the depravity of man. The poet found an unbridge-
able gulf between an omnipotent God and his frail creation that pro-
hibited belief in the benevolence of God.

The above studies of Byron's theological position consider
the tension that Byron's paradoxical views lent his writings. These
critics view Byron's doubts and beliefs as part of a single pattern
formed by his effort to reconcile his conflicting opinions. He is
seen by some as a pessimist confronting a desolate universe and
by others as an optimist.

The first full-length study devoted to Byron's use of the
Bible, rather than to the theological evidences in his work, was
"Byron und die Bibel," a doctoral dissertation completed in 1906
at the University of Leipzig by Arthur Pönitz. Pönitz's pioneering
study attempts a rough compilation of Byron's allusions to the scrip-
ture, quoting some passages and merely listing reference informa-
tion for others. Other than listing his references according to
books of the Bible and dividing his material into the general cate-

gories of Old and New Testaments, he makes no effort at systematic classification or synthesis; consequently, his format is often chaotic, seriously handicapping usefulness of his volume as a reference tool. He lists the references according to the natural order of the books of the Bible and reaches general conclusions to the effect that Byron made considerable use of the Bible.

Heretofore the most significant study relating the work of Byron to the Bible has been Harold Ray Stevens' "Byron and the Bible: A Study of Poetic and Philosophic Development" (Ph.D. dissertation, University of Pennsylvania, 1964). Stevens analyzes the poetry in detail to demonstrate that the Bible was a continuing influence in much of Byron's poetry and thought. Stevens shows, first, that the Bible served as a source book for Byron's interest in theological doctrines. Second, the Bible suggested subjects and images for large portions of his poetry. Third, Stevens concludes that Byron used the Bible with seriousness and with aesthetic appreciation, and that the Bible helped Byron to understand problems such as the fall and election.

Murray Roston, in Prophet and Poet: The Bible and the Growth of Romanticism (Evanston, Ill.: Northwestern University Press, 1964), theorizes that poets of the Neo-Classical Period discovered the very "unclassical" style of biblical poetry and influenced Romantic poets to follow his freer biblical form. Roston declares that one can clearly see such biblical influence in Byron's poetry, especially in the following areas: Hebraic concepts, biblical settings, oriental luxuriance, idioms, and rhythms derived from biblical language.

Truman Guy Steffan's "The Re-Creation of Genesis," in the larger context of a series of essays rather than in a biblical study per se, examines "some of the artistic and dramatic principles in Cain that governed the poet's retention, modification, and omission of biblical incident, speech, and detail" (Lord Byron's Cain, p. 68). Of additional interest for this present study of biblical influences on Byron is Steffan's essay "A Medley of Language" (Lord Byron's Cain, pp. 91-108), wherein Steffan analyzes Byron's use of biblical

wording. Byron used a "motley of styles," combining the elevated
with the ludicrous. The poet made abundant use of biblical archa-
isms, particularly in the following areas: biblical pronouns, sec-
ond and third person verb forms, inversions, and compressions such
as "look'st" and "mean'st."

Need for Present Study

Studies of Byron and his work that take into account his theo-
logical views, such as those by Gleckner and McGann, have grown
more numerous and more thorough in recent years, arriving at a
level of sophistication. The study of Byron's writings as they relate
to the Bible itself, apart from merely religious and theological con-
cerns, is still in an embryonic state. Only Pönitz and Stevens have
seen fit to concern themselves with the vast amount of material in
Byron's work which is specifically biblical. Their studies, helpful
as they are, are merely indicative of the rich biblical ore in Byron;
neither Pönitz nor Stevens is by any means exhaustive.

Pönitz overlooks many significant quotations, references, and
allusions to the Bible in Byron's writings; and he neither categorizes
nor synthesizes the material that he finds. Also, his work is geared
to the Bible rather than to the writings of Byron; i.e., the refer-
ences Pönitz does have are listed according to the normal order of
the books of the Bible without any indexing system based on Byron's
writings. Many of the references are merely listed, without the in-
clusion of quotations and without any indication of the relationship
between Byron's passage and that in the Bible. Much of the pos-
sible value of such a study, then, has been lost because of the lack
of significant classification, effective synthesis, and true complete-
ness.

Stevens' study, while valuable for its explications of the po-
etry in the light of its biblical orientation, does not attempt to cate-
gorize, analyze, or systematically synthesize the various biblical
material in Byron's poetry. Stevens acknowledges (p. 4) that he
has "not attempted to give a statistical analysis of the frequency of
biblical allusions," "allusion" forming his general category for bib-

lical matter of all types. His index and appendix include listings
of Byron's allusions to the Bible, but his purpose is not to make a
compilation or compendium designed for reference purposes. Ste-
vens leaves the door open for a comprehensive catalogue by stating
that his compilation is "incomplete and artificial at best" (p. 2).

No satisfactory reference tool exists, then, to provide ready
access to the abundance of biblical material in Byron's work. This
present study is an attempt to meet this need for a comprehensive
reference compendium.

Procedure

Once having determined the need for the study, the research-
er's first step was to consider Byron's personal interest in the
Bible. The Bible was important to Byron throughout his life as he
once recognized:

> I am sure that no man reads the Bible with more pleasure
> than I do; I read a chapter every day, and in a short time
> shall be able to beat the Canters with their own weapons
> [Ernest J. Lovell, Jr., His Very Self and Voice: Col-
> lected Conversations of Lord Byron (New York: Macmil-
> lan, 1954), p. 569].

Byron's interest in the Bible began during the early period of his
childhood when he experienced the strong Scottish Calvinism of
Aberdeen. As a child he was taught to read the Bible by his nurse,
May Gray, who made an effort to instruct him in Calvinistic dogma
(Marchand, Byron, 1:33). Later, speaking of this period in his life,
he wrote John Murray that he had read the books of the Bible
"through and through" before he was eight years old, finding the
Old Testament to be more of a pleasure than the New (The Works
of Lord Byron: Letters and Journals, ed. Rowland E. Prothero, 6
vols. [London: John Murray, 1898-1901], 5:391 [hereafter cited as
L&J]).

Byron's interest in the Bible continued into his maturity.
He wrote Murray that as an adult he remained "a great reader and
admirer of those books" (ibid.), and he repeatedly refers to biblical
topics throughout his letters and journals. Byron's was a serious

interest; and his familiarity with the Bible, as well as with related
books and commentaries, frequently surprised his acquaintances.
He went to considerable inconvenience to participate with his friends
in the discussion of biblical matters with Dr. James Kennedy (Mar-
chand, Byron, 3:1104-5). As Byron was leaving Cephalonia for
Greece, Kennedy prevailed upon him to take certain religious books
and 322 Greek Testaments to Missolonghi for distribution (L&J 6:
314), although Byron later said the Greeks complained about the
quality of the translation of the Testaments (L&J 6:339). After the
poet's death in Missolonghi, Hobhouse recorded from Fletcher that
a Bible had been placed on Byron's breakfast table every morning
during his final sickness. Hobhouse adds that the dying Byron did
not make use of the Bible in this instance in a superstitious fashion:

> ... that is to say I am confident that although he might
> have a general belief in its contents he was not over-
> come by any religious terrors [John Cam Hobhouse diary
> entry of May 14, 1824, quoted in Marchand, Byron, 3:
> 1244-5].

An additional step in procedure was an attempt to ascertain
the Bibles actually owned by Byron. Byron owned various Bibles
or Testaments throughout his life. Some time before 1821 he re-
ceived the gift of a Bible from his half-sister, Augusta Leigh. He
wrote that

> ... as it was the last gift of my Sister (whom I shall
> probably never see again), I can only use it carefully, and
> less frequently, because I like to keep it in good order
> [L&J 5:391].

Dr. Kennedy, evidently speaking of this "little pocket-bible," said
that Byron had a finely bound pocket Bible with an unusual arrange-
ment of titles and chapters (Lovell, His Very Self and Voice, p.
437). On October 9, 1821, Byron wrote to Murray and asked for
an additional Bible, "a common Bible, of a good legible print (bound
in Russia)" [L&J 5:391].* Murray answered on November 14: "The

---

*This order for a bound Bible is also interesting because of Black's
statement that until the 1820 edition of the Rhemes New Testament,
bound in black cloth, "... English editions were either sold unbound,

bible I have sent you is one with a selection of the best commen-
taries" [L&J 5:392n].   The posthumous sale catalog of Byron's li-
brary mentions both a Testament and a Bible.   The Testament,
item 246, purchased by one "Wiltshire" for seven shillings, is de-
scribed as "Novum Testamentum Graecum, russia, Oxon., 1805"
(A. N. L. Munby, ed., Sale Catalogues of Libraries of Eminent
Persons, 6 vols. [London: Mansell with Sotheby Parke: Bernet Pub-
lications, n.d.], vol. 1:   Poets and Men of Letters, p. 223).
The Bible, item 198, was purchased by "Brumby" for £3.8.   It was
the "Biblia Sacra Armena, with Lord Byron's autograph, 1805"
(ibid., p. 247).   One must wonder exactly which translation of the
Bible was read to Byron by May Gray.   Which translation did Au-
gusta give him?   What translation did John Murray send in 1821?

The Geneva Bible had been the Bible of Calvinism (A. Dakin,
Calvinism [Philadelphia: Westminster Press, 1946], p. 151) in the
days of Shakespeare (F. F. Bruce, The Books and the Parchments
[London: Pickering & Inglish, 1950], p. 215), but after the middle
of the seventeenth century (Black, Cambridge History of the Bible,
3:362) the King James Version became what The Cambridge History
of the Bible refers to as "the Bible par excellence wherever the
English tongue ..." was spoken (Bruce, Books and Parchments, p.
217).   Other translations existed at the time, the most important
of which were those by Wycliffe, Tyndale, Coverdale, and that
known as the Bishop's Bible; but these Bibles were soon replaced
in popular usage by the King James Version because of its excel-
lence.   A few private translations or paraphrases of the Bible ap-
peared during the seventeenth and eighteenth centuries--notably
those by Henry Ainsworth (1571-1623); Dr. Henry Hammond (1605-
1660), who was chaplain to Charles I; Abraham Woodhead (1609-
1678); and Dr. Edward Harwood (1729-1794) (Black, Cambridge His-
tory..., 3:363-4)--but these were relatively insignificant attempts,
and the influence of such versions was negligible.   Parliament, in

_____

(cont.) or in the lower grades of leather, like roan and calf."   Mat-
thew Black, ed., The Cambridge History of the Bible, vol. 3 (Cam-
bridge, England: Cambridge University Press, 1963), p. 467.

fact, attempted in 1653 to restrain those who did seek to publish private translations. Ira Maurice Price sums up the real dominance of the King James Version from the seventeenth century on:

> For almost three centuries the Authorized, or King James Version, has been the Bible of the English-speaking world. Its simple, majestic Anglo-Saxon, its clear, sparkling style, its directness and force of utterance have made it the model in language, style and dignity of some of the choicest writers of the last two centuries. Its phrasing is woven into much of our noblest literature; and its style, which to an astonishing degree is merely the style of the original authors of the Bible, has extended very great influence in moulding that ideal of simplicity, directness, and clarity which now dominates the writing of English [The Ancestry of Our English Bible (New York: Harper, 1956), pp. 276-7].

Previous studies have assumed that Byron's Bible was the King James Version, and every reasonable indication supports this assumption.

With Byron's interest in the Bible and his possession of various Bibles and Testaments confirmed, and with the establishment of the King James translation as the version he was most likely to have used historically, the next step in the researcher's procedure was an attempt to locate any Bibles or Testaments that actually belonged to Byron. To that end a correspondence was initiated with authorities who might be of assistance. John Murray, present head of the house which published Byron's work, replied (in a personal letter, 7 November 1974) that

> ... the record of the whereabouts of Byron's Bibles and Testaments is very thin....* We have in the library here a Bible which is said to have been Byron's and probably was, but it is a difficult point to prove.

The Bible referred to is the King James Version published at Cambridge in 1795, according to a copy of the title page sent by Murray.

---

*The Bible in John Murray's possession includes the Apocrypha between the Testaments. The Cambridge History of the Bible, pp. 168-69, points out that all Protestant versions of the Bible after Coverdale, except for a few King James Versions published in the 1630's and 1640's, place the Apocrypha in such a block.

The Bible, however, may have been handed down to Byron after having "... belonged to Mrs. Catherine Byron" (Virginia Murray, personal letter, 21 March 1975), the poet's mother, as suggested by the inscription "C Byron." Doris Langley Moore wrote (in a personal letter, 16 March 1975),

> I telephoned Mr. Murray to know whether the Bible ordered from his ancestor was the King James Version. Murray did not actually publish Bibles, ... but the present head of the house thinks he would have sent the King James Version....

No other personal Bibles that belonged to Byron were located. The King James Version certainly was not the only version which he possessed nor with which he was familiar. As has been indicated, he owned a New Testament that was in the original Greek. Byron himself translated portions of an Armenian scripture (L&J 5:391). With his Catholic sympathies he no doubt had some familiarity with --may even have owned--the Douay Bible, a translation published in 1609-1610 to provide for Catholics a counterpart to the increasing number of Protestant revisions (Price, Ancestry of Our English Bible, p. 266).* But no firm indication exists to suggest that Byron's writings were significantly influenced by versions other than the King James Bible.

The compendium itself amply supports the supposition that Byron's Bible was indeed the King James Version. The great number of exact quotations, some of them rather lengthy, provides considerable evidence. The long quotation from Genesis 6:1-2 in the motto for Heaven and Earth serves as an excellent example. Although a definitive estimate may not be possible until Byron's per-

---

*Byron's admiration for Catholicism found frequent expression in his letters. For instance, he wrote that Catholicism "is by far the most elegant worship, hardly excepting the Greek mythology. What with incense, pictures, statues..., confession, absolution,--there is something sensible to grasp at. Besides, it leaves no possibility of doubt" (L&J 6:39). Byron's appreciation of Catholicism culminated in the training of his daughter Allegra: "I am educating my natural daughter a strict Catholic in a convent of Romagna; for I think people can never have enough of religion, if they are to have any" (L&J 6:32).

sonal Bibles are identified, one must conclude that all available evidence suggests that Byron's Bible was the King James Version.

With the most likely biblical version that Byron actually used established, the next step in the researcher's procedure was to determine the most suitable edition of Byron's works to be used for the compendium. The edition used should employ useful line numbering, should be readily available in one volume, and should be considered "standard." Major editions considered included the seven volumes of Byron's Poetry, edited by Ernest Hartley Coleridge, in The Works of Lord Byron, 1898-1904; the one-volume edition of The Poetical Works of Lord Byron, edited by Coleridge in 1905; and The Complete Poetical Works of Byron, edited by Paul E. More in 1905. The seven-volume edition was considered unwieldy for reference purposes and would rarely be available outside of large libraries; in addition, the line numbering would be inadequate for use in a reference tool such as the compendium because lines for Don Juan are not numbered. Coleridge's one-volume edition would have the obvious advantage of compactness; but it is an English publication, not readily available in the United States, and has no line numbering for Don Juan. The edition of the poetry that seemed best for meeting all the requirements for the compendium was that by Paul E. More; it is a one-volume edition, and it is readily available. Virtually all of the lines of poetry are numbered, including those in Don Juan. Most important, the work is considered "standard"; Jerome J. McGann says of it:

> Of the three editions done by Coleridge and More, the text offered by More is most to be preferred, primarily because it is the cleanest of the three. Both of Coleridge's editions are full of misprints.... More's edition is more complete and more careful than any edition before or since ... ["Editing Byron's Poetry," The Byron Journal 1 (1973): 5-6].

All references in the compendium to Byron's poetry, then, are keyed to Paul E. More's 1905 edition of The Complete Poetical Works of Byron, published by the Riverside Press of Houghton Mifflin and known as the "Cambridge Edition."

The actual research procedure for the compendium began

with a detailed examination of the six volumes of Byron's letters
and journals.   This initial study revealed that Byron wrote freely
on biblical topics and used biblical phraseology, facts supporting
suggestions that the Bible had been a shaping influence on the poet
and his work.

Examination of Byron's prose was followed by intensive, pro-
tracted study of the Bible and of Byron's poetry.   The Old Testa-
ment was considered in seven historical or topical segments: Gene-
sis, Exodus-Deuteronomy, Joshua-Esther, Psalms, Job and Wisdom
Literature, Major Prophets, Minor Prophets.   The New Testament
was analyzed in three historical or literary segments: the Gospels
and Acts, the Epistles of Paul, James-Revelation.   Each of the ten
segments of the Bible was studied carefully for subject matter,
themes, imagery, language, and rhythms reminiscent of Byron's
poetry.   At the conclusion of the study of each segment of the Bible,
all of Byron's poetry was read (for a total of ten readings) in an
effort to find any debt the poet may have owed to that particular
portion of the Bible.   Each poetic relation to the Bible was trans-
ferred to a card with the corresponding passage from the Bible.
Finally, each parallel was considered in an effort to discover the
exact relationship of the poetry to the Bible so that each could be
categorized according to the system given below.

Methodology

This study is an attempt to register the passages from By-
ron's poetry that depend upon the Bible for material.   The study
aims also at categorizing the various methods used by Byron in
weaving such biblical matter into his poetry.   The instances in
which Byron incorporates the Bible into his poetry seem to fall into
eight primary types.

The most obvious method Byron employs with biblical ma-
terial is apparent in the classification "Quote: Exact."   Byron fre-
quently quotes the Bible precisely, with perfect biblical wording or
with only insignificant changes.   In the compendium, material of
this sort normally consists of three or more consecutive words

quoted from the Bible, unless a word or short phrase is unequivocal-
ly biblical.   An appropriate example of the "Quote: Exact" cate-
gory is found in the following:

> He [Lord Henry] was all things to all men.
> Don Juan 16. 610-11

The line cites I Corinthians 9:22, "I am made all things to all men,
that I might by all means save some."

At times, however, Byron's quotations from the Bible are
not exact; so a category of "Quote: Approximate" seemed necessary.
Some restructuring of quotations by Byron for rhythmic or gram-
matical purposes occurs.   At other times he changes the biblical
passage to provide more emphasis, frequently satirical, to a con-
cept.   Alteration of this type is evident in the following adaptation
of Genesis 4:15, "And the Lord set a mark upon Cain":

> Ay, there it is; 'tis like a mother's curse
> Upon my soul--the mark is set upon me.
> The Two Foscari 3. i. 186-7

Sometimes a word or two is deliberately altered, or non-biblical
words may be included within the quotation so that the quotation is
given a double edge, one cutting with the traditional biblical conno-
tation and the other with Byron's wit.   Following is an example
employing part of Matthew 12:25-26, "Every city or house divided
against itself shall not stand":

> Venice, and all that she inherits, are
> Divided like a house against itself.
> Marino Faliero 4. i. 376-7

Familiarity with Byron's poetry would lead one to expect the
poet's frequent use of the Bible in ways that are satirical or parod-
ic. *   The manner in which Byron puts biblical matter to humorous

*Joseph Twadell Shipley recognizes three types or levels of parody
in Dictionary of World Literature, p. 424: "... (1) Verbal, in
which the alteration of a word makes the piece trivial, e.g., 'the
short and simple flannels of the poor'.... (2) Formal, in which
the style and mannerisms of a writer are used for a ludicrous sub-
ject.   These two levels are humorous only.   (3) Thematic, in which
the form, usually a typical subject, and the spirit of the writer are

use in a certain context may be of more significance than the mere
fact that the Bible is quoted. As a result, the compendium includes
a classification, "Quote: Parodic," for those passages in which
Byron quotes the Bible, but for purposes of direct ridicule, mim-
icry, or burlesque of the Bible or of some subject within the con-
text of the poetry. An example is found in the following passage:

> Few will twice
> Lift up their lungs when fairly overcrow'd.
> The Vision of Judgment 11.757-8

This quotation parodies Isaiah 24:14: "They shall lift up their voice,
they shall sing for the majesty of the Lord."

A classification, "Reference: Subject," is included in the
compendium for those passages in which Byron significantly devel-
ops a biblical topic. These passages do not normally include quo-
tations--only the words essential for identifying the topic itself.
Frequently, however, Byron does seem to have in mind a specific
biblical passage. Such is the case with the general reference to the
destruction of Pharaoh in the Red Sea, as related in Exodus 14:19-
31:

> Her sandy ocean, and the sea waves' sway
> Roll'd over Pharaoh and his thousands,--why,
> Mountains and waters, do ye not as they?
> The Prophecy of Dante 2.109-11

On occasion Byron clearly burlesques* some biblical subject.
The passage taken from the Bible may be very brief, even a mere
word; but the context is clearly parodic.† Instances of this nature

---

(cont.) transposed.... On its [parody's] third level, it is search-
ing and effective criticism of a poet by a poet."
     Byron seems primarily to have used levels one (e.g., "Let
there be darkness") and three (e.g., Cain).

*The Oxford English Dictionary defines burlesque as "that species
of literary composition, or of dramatic representation, which aims
at exciting laughter by caricature of the manner or spirit of seri-
ous works, or by ludicrous treatment of their subjects." The verb
form of the word means "to turn into ridicule by grotesque parody
or imitation; to caricature, travesty."

†The Oxford English Dictionary: parody is "a composition in prose

are referred to in the compendium by the term "Reference: Parod-
ic" and are typified by the following reference:

> Eve's slip ... tumbled all mankind into the grave,
> Besides fish, beasts, and birds. "The sparrow's fall
> Is special providence."
>
> Don Juan 9.147-50

While burlesquing Genesis, the passage quotes parodically from
Matthew 10:29: "Are not two sparrows sold for a farthing? and one
of them shall not fall on the ground without your Father."

Byron does not always use the Bible in ways that are obvi-
ous; often he makes slight, undeveloped, nearly incidental use of the
Bible. Instances of such usage are termed "Allusions"* in the com-
pendium. These instances are direct but may involve only a word
or phrase that clues the reader to the biblical reference, with no
specific mention of the subject involved. Such usage is apparent in
the following:

> His [the monarch's] slaves
> Will take the crumbs he deigns to scatter from
> His royal table at the hour.
>
> Sardanapalus 2.1.112-14

The allusion is to Matthew 15:27 (and Mark 7:28): "And she [a wom-
an of Canaan] said, Truth, Lord: yet the dogs eat of the crumbs
which fall from their masters' table."

When these allusions to the Bible in Byron's poetry are part
of a humorous or satirical context, they are referred to in the com-
pendium as "Allusion: Parodic." An illustration of this category
is evident in the following passage:

(cont.) or verse in which the characteristic turns of thought and
phrase in an author or class of authors are imitated in such a way
as to make them appear ridiculous, especially by applying them to
ludicrously inappropriate subjects."

*H. W. Fowler in A Dictionary of Modern English Usage, p. 16,
says an allusion "... is never an outright or explicit mention."
Harry Shaw in Dictionary of Literary Terms, p. 14, defines allu-
sion as "a reference, usually brief, often casual, occasionally in-
direct, to a person, event or condition presumably familiar but
sometimes obscure to the reader."

> Sweet is old wine in bottles, ale in barrels.
>   Don Juan 1.1005

The passage places a humorous twist on Matthew 9:17: "Neither do men put new wine into old bottles: else the bottles break, ... but they put new wine into new bottles."

In a less obvious method Byron occasionally employs biblical rhythms. In these cases precise reference or quotation may not be made. Such use of biblical language is referred to in the compendium by the term "parallelism,"* as seen in Don Juan (11.657-72), where the refrain "I have seen" echoes over and over from some six passages in Ecclesiastes.

The compendium is composed of two sections. The larger portion alphabetizes Byron's works, cataloging in sequence all biblical references from that work. Each reference is given its own number with the corresponding biblical equivalent succeeding it. For lengthy biblical passages the reference and a brief summary are given in lieu of quotation. All references are classified according to one of the eight categories given above.

The smaller portion of the compendium is a Cross Index, alphabetized by the books of the Bible and providing only enough information for reference to the main entry.

This arrangement for the compendium was inevitable. To serve as a useful reference tool, the compendium had to be cross-indexed for both biblical and poetical listings. For instance, a reader of The Giaour who wanted further information on a biblical source for lines 62-65 could turn to the poetical listing for The Giaour in the main portion of the compendium and find a reference to Isaiah 14:12. A reader searching for Byron's uses of the Lucifer image of Isaiah 14:12 and unaware of the Giaour passage could begin his search with the biblical portion of the compendium and find the reference to The Giaour.

---

*Among the many definitions for parallel in the Oxford English Dictionary is the statement that it means "the placing of things mentally or descriptively side by side so as to show their correspondence; comparison, or a comparison; esp. a comparison of things as being alike, a statement of parallelism or analogy, a simile."

Also, the texts of both the biblical and poetic quotations, rather than simple line and verse references, were felt to be necessary for a useful compendium. With the quotations readily available, one using the compendium may determine instantly the nature and content of both biblical and poetical material without time-consuming consultations of additional books.

The method of specific categorization of all references was meant to provide the reader, especially the reader either unfamiliar with the Bible or unfamiliar with Byron, with an insight into the relationship between the biblical passages and those of Byron. Such categorizations should be generally helpful, but they are especially so with allusions that are often tangential at best. At times, however, Byron's reference is so general, perhaps to an entire chapter of the Bible or to a long narrative, that brevity was required. In such cases, and they are relatively few, the biblical reference is stated and a description of the passage given, without the lengthy quotation otherwise required.

To simplify the biblical Cross Index and to serve as a convenience to future researchers, each separate reference is given its own number. Users of the compendium are then spared detailed notation of the poem, act, scene, line, and biblical passage that may be involved.

Although the compendium is intended to be a comprehensive aid to biblical references in Byron's poetry, no attempt was made to catalog references to the biblical Aprocrypha. Byron does not seem to use the language of the Apocrypha frequently and does not use it as the framework for significant poems. The reader will not find here any references to variant readings or to poetry not included in the More edition. Words that may have been biblical echoes in Byron's mind but are too general to trace to a specific source are not included. "Dust," for example, appears frequently in Byron's poetry. In a number of instances the word refers to a specific passage, as Genesis 2:7, "And the Lord God formed man of the dust of ground"; or Genesis 3:19, "For dust thou art, and unto dust shalt thou return." Such is the case when Byron says,

> To dust if I return, from dust I sprung,
> And then, at least, my heart can ne'er be moved.
>   "Stanzas to the Po" 11.51-2

But other uses of "dust" are too general or highly questionable, such as Byron's use of "dust" in this passage:

> If chance some bard, though once by dunces fear'd,
> Now prone in dust, can only be revered.
>   English Bards and Scotch Reviewers 11.365-6

Therefore, limiting the references or allusions to items that have the highest probability of a significant biblical source seemed wisest.

GUIDE TO THE USE
OF THE COMPENDIUM

The compendium consists of two major parts: Part I, the Compendium proper; and Part II, the Cross Index. Part I is divided into two larger sections of Old and New Testament materials that are found in Byron's poetry. The listing within each category is alphabetical by poem title.

In Part I a given notation, with its own number, consists of two essential parts: the line reference and quotation from Byron's poem, and the corresponding biblical reference and material. For each notation a usage classification (the eight specific categories are defined in detail on pages 15-19 of the Preface) is indicated opposite the line reference and underlined. When a line of poetry quotes exactly from the Bible, the quotation is drawn to the attention by single quotation marks. When a biblical passage is too long to quote, perhaps an entire chapter, indication is made by "Rf." (i.e., "Reference") followed by a short summary of biblical content.

Part II of the compendium, the Cross Index, lists the material according to the books of the Bible in their standard order, rather than alphabetically according to Byron's poem. Each entry consists of a specific biblical passage followed by the numbered reference to Byron's poetic passages.

Part I

The Compendium

OLD TESTAMENT

THE AGE OF BRONZE

---

1 <u>Line 111</u>   <u>Allusion</u>
    The rocky isle that holds or held his dust.
<u>Genesis 3:19</u>
    For dust thou art, and unto dust shalt thou return.

2 <u>Lines 161-62</u>   Reference: Subject
    Poland! o'er which the avenging angel past, / But left thee
    as he found thee, still a waste.
<u>Exodus 11:4-12:36</u>
    Rf. the destroyer of the firstborn in Egypt

3 <u>Lines 254-56</u>   Quote: Exact
    A tyrant's grave-- / 'The king of kings,' and yet of slaves
    the slave, / Who bursts the chains of millions to renew.
<u>Ezra 7:12</u>
    Artaxerxes, 'king of kings.'

4 <u>Lines 254-56</u>   Parallelism
    A tryant's grave-- / The king of kings, and yet 'of slaves
    the slave,' / Who bursts the chains of millions to renew.
<u>Ezra 7:12</u>
    Artaxerxes, 'king of kings.'

5 <u>Lines 336-37</u>   Reference: Subject
    The faith's red "auto," fed with human fuel, / While sate
    the catholic Moloch, calmly cruel.
<u>Amos 5:26</u>
    But ye have borne the tabernacle of your Moloch and Chiun
    your images, the star of your god, which ye made to your-
    selves.

6 <u>Lines 548-51</u>   Allusion: Parodic
    Even this thy genius, Canning! ... never, even in that dull
    House, couldst tame / To 'unleaven'd prose' thine own poetic
    flame.

Exodus 12:39
And they baked unleavened cakes of the dough ... for it was
not leavened.

7   Lines 642-43   Allusion: Parodic
Lo! Mother Church, while all religion writhes, / Like
Niobe, weeps o'er her offspring, Tithes.
Leviticus 27-30
And all the tithe of the land, whether of the seed of the land,
or of the fruit of the tree, is the Lord's: it is holy unto
the Lord.

8   Lines 642-43   Allusion: Parodic
Lo! Mother Church, while all religion writhes, / Like
Niobe, weeps o'er her offspring, Tithes.
Jeremiah 31:15
Rahel [Rachel] weeping for her children refused to be com-
forted for her children, because they were not.

9   Line 646   Allusion: Parodic
Church, state, and faction wrestle in the dark.
Genesis 32:24-25
Rf. Jacob's wrestling with God.

10 Lines 646-47   Allusion: Parodic
Church, state, and faction wrestle in the dark, / Toss'd
by the deluge in their common ark.
Genesis 6-9
Rf. the flood and Noah's ark.

11 Lines 648-49   Allusion: Parodic
Shorn of her bishops, banks, and dividends, / Another Babel
soars--but Britain ends.
Genesis 11:4, 9
And they said, Go to, let us build us a city and a tower,
whose top may reach unto heaven; ... [and] the name of it
called Babel.

12 Lines 663-64   Allusion: Parodic
More wealth than Britain ever had to lose, / Were all her
atoms of unleaven'd ore.
Exodus 12:39
And they baked unleavened cakes of the dough ... for it was
not leavened.

13 Lines 668-70   Quote: Exact
How rich is Britain! not indeed in mines, / Or peace or
plenty, corn or oil, or wines; / No land of Canaan, full of
'milk and honey.'
Exodus 3:8, 17
A land flowing with 'milk and honey.'

14 Lines 668-70   Quote: Exact
    How rich is Britain! not indeed in mines, / Or peace or
    plenty, corn or oil, or wines; / No 'land of Canaan,' full of
    milk and honey.
    Leviticus 14:34
    When ye be come into the 'land of Canaan,' which I give to
    you for a possession.

BEPPO

---

15 Lines 601-602   Quote: Exact
    Of these same we see several, and of others, / 'Men of the
    world,' who know the world like men.
    Psalm 17:14
    From men which are thy hand, O Lord, from 'men the
    world,' which have their portion in this life.

16 Lines 633-34   Quote: Parodic
    Oh, Mirth and Innocence! Oh, 'Milk and Water!' / Ye
    happy mixtures of more happy days!
    Exodus 3:8
    And to bring them up out of that land unto a good land and
    a large, unto a land flowing with 'milk and honey.'

THE BLUES

---

17 Eclogue First, 129-30   Quote: Parodic
    I have heard people say / That it [Journal de Trevoux]
    threaten'd to 'give up the ghost' t'other day.
    Job 10:18
    Oh that I had 'given up the ghost,' and no eye had seen me!

18 Eclogue Second, 11-13   Reference: Subject
    For although we are two, / Yet she somehow contrives that
    all things shall be done / In a style which proclaims us
    eternally one.
    Genesis 2:24
    Therefore shall a man leave his father and his mother, and
    shall cleave unto his wife: and they shall be one flesh.

THE BRIDE OF ABYDOS

19   Canto I, 158-61   Reference: Subject
      Fair as the first that fell of womankind, / When on that dread
      yet lovely serpent smiling, / Whose image then was stamp'd
      upon her mind-- / But once beguiled and ever more beguil-
      ing.
      Genesis 3:1-24
      Rf. serpent's temptation of Eve.

20   Canto II, 88-90   Quote: Approximate
      Which none save noblest Moslem wear, / To guard from
      'winds of heaven' the breast.
      Daniel 7:2
      Daniel spake and said, I saw in my vision by night, and, be-
      hold, the four 'winds of the heaven' strove upon the great sea.

21   Canto II, 388   Allusion
      Ay! let me like the ocean-Patriarch roam.
      Genesis 6-9
      Rf. Noah and the flood.

22   Canto II, 645-46   Reference: Subject
      And, oh! that pang where more than Madness lies! / The
      worm that will not sleep--and never dies.
      Isaiah 66:24
      Look upon the carcases of the men that have transgressed
      against me: for their worm shall not die.

23   Canto II, 652-53   Reference: Subject
      Vainly thou heap'st the dust upon thy head, / Vainly the
      sackcloth o'er thy limbs dost spread.
      Lamentations 2:10
      They have cast up dust upon their heads, they have girded
      themselves with sackcloth.

CAIN

24   Entire work   Reference: Subject
      Genesis 1-4
      Rf. Cain after the fall of Adam and Eve

25   Act I, i. 105-106   Quote: Exact
      The 'tree of life' / Was withheld from us [Cain and Abel]
      by my father's folly.

Genesis 3:24
> So he [God] drove out the man; and he placed ... Cheru-
> bims, ... to keep the way of the 'tree of life. '

26 Act I. i. 126-27   Reference: Subject
> One who aspired to be what made thee, and / Would not
> have made thee what thou art.

Isaiah 14:12
> How art thou fallen from heaven, O Lucifer, son of the morn-
> ing!

27 Act I. i. 130   Reference: Subject
> He conquer'd; let him reign!

Isaiah 14:12
> Rf. God's defeat of Lucifer

28 Act I. i. 131-32   Quote: Exact
> Lucifer: Thy sire's Maker and the earth's. Cain: And hea-
> ven's / 'And all that in them is. '

Exodus 20:11
> For in six days the Lord made heaven and earth, the sea,
> 'and all that in them is. '

29 Act I. i. 204-206   Quote: Exact
> He / Who would not let ye live, or he who would / Have
> made ye 'live for ever' in the joy / And power of knowledge?

Genesis 3:22-23
> And the Lord God said, Behold, the man is become as one
> of us, to know good and evil: and now, lest he put forth
> his hand, and take also of the tree of life, and eat, and
> 'live for ever': Therefore the Lord God sent him forth from
> the garden of Eden.

30 Act I. i. 263   Quote: Parodic
> Lucifer. Ask 'the Destroyer. '

Exodus 12:23
> The Lord will pass over the door, and will not suffer 'the
> destroyer' to come in unto your houses to smite you.

31 Act I. i. 263-64   Reference: Subject
> The Maker--call him / Which name thou wilt: he makes but
> to destroy.

Job 4:17
> Shall a man be more pure than his maker?

32 Act I. i. 322   Quote: Exact
> Cain. To cull some first-fruits.

Exodus 23:16
> And the feast of harvest, the firstfruits of thy labours.

33 Act I. i. 392-94   Reference: Subject
> Oh, my mother! thou / Hast pluck'd a fruit more fatal to
> thine offspring / Than to thyself.

Genesis: 3:6
And when the woman saw that the tree was good for food,
and that it was pleasant to the eyes, ... she took of the
fruit thereof, and did eat.

34 Act I. i. 479-80   Quote: Approximate
Ask of your sire, the exile fresh from Eden; / Or of his
'first-born son': ask your own heart.
Exodus 4:22
Thus saith the Lord, Israel is 'my son, even my firstborn.'

35 Act I. i. 498-99   Quote: Exact
And yon bright star / Is leader of the host of heaven.
I Kings 22:19
I saw the Lord sitting on his throne, and all the host of hea-
ven standing by him on his right hand and on his left.

36 Act I. i. 501-502   Quote: Exact
Lucifer: Hast thou seen him?   Adam: Yes--in his works.
Psalm 104:31
The glory of the Lord shall endure for ever: the Lord shall
rejoice in his works.

37 Act II. i. 83-85   Reference: Subject
What are they which dwell / So humbly in their pride as to
sojourn / With worms in clay?
Job 19:26
After my skin worms destroy this body.

38 Act II. i. 148-50   Quote: Approximate
Thou / 'Shalt soon return to earth and all its dust': / 'Tis
part of thy eternity, and mine.
Ecclesiastes 12:7
Then 'shall the dust return to the earth' as it was: and the
spirit shall return unto God who gave it.

39 Act II. ii. 261-64   Reference: Subject
They bear not / The wing of seraph, nor the face of man, /
Nor form of mightiest brute, nor aught that is / Now breath-
ing.
Ezekiel 1:5-14
Rf. vision of four creatures.

40 Act II. ii. 279-80   Quote: Approximate
Cain: Ah me! and did they perish?   Lucifer: Yes, from
their earth, as thou wilt fade from thine.
Job 18:17
His remembrance shall perish from the earth, and he shall
have no name in the street.

41 Act II. ii. 304-307   Reference: Parodic
[Your] scarcely-yet shaped planet, ... A Paradise of Ignor-
ance, from which / Knowledge was barr'd as poison.

Genesis 3:1-24
   Rf.   Eden and the tree of knowledge

42   Act II. ii. 311-12   Quote: Approximate
     For ever! Since / I must one day 'return here from the
     earth. '
     Ecclesiastes 12:7
     Then shall the dust 'return to the earth' as it was.

43   Act II. ii. 438-39   Quote: Exact
     Then 'my father's God' did well / When he prohibited the
     fatal tree.
     Exodus 15:2
     He is my God, and I will prepare him an habitation; 'my fa-
     ther's God, ' and I will exalt him.

44   Act II. ii. 528-29   Quote: Approximate
     Thou lovest it, because 'tis beautiful, / As was 'the apple
     in thy mother's eye. '
     Deuteronomy 32:10
     He found him in a desert land, and in the waste howling wild-
     erness; he led him about, he instructed him, he kept him as
     'the apple of his eye. '

45   Act II. ii. 571   Allusion
     Show me where Jehovah dwells.
     Psalm 83:18
     Men may know that thou, whose name alone is Jehovah, art
     the most high over all the earth.

46   Act II. ii. 579-80   Allusion
     And the 'Jehovah' and thyself [Lucifer] have thine [element]-- /
     Ye do not dwell together?
     Psalm 83:18
     Men may know that thou, whose name alone is 'Jehovah' art
     the most high over all the earth.

47   Act II. ii. 636-37   Reference: Subject
     I battle it against him, as I battled / In highest heaven.
     Isaiah 14:12
     How art thou fallen from heaven, O Lucifer, son of the morn-
     ing!

48   Act II. ii. 641-44   Quote: Approximate
     And world by world, / And star by star, and universe by
     universe, / Shall 'tremble in the balance, ' till the great /
     conflict shall cease, if ever it shall cease.
     Daniel 5:27
     Thou art 'weighed' in the balances, and art found wanting.

49   Act III. i. 77   Quote: Approximate
     'Thou hast not spoken well. '

Exodus 10:29
And Moses said, 'Thou hast spoken well, ' I will see thy face
again no more.

50 Act III. i. 101-103   Reference: Subject
A meek brow, whose base humility / Shows more of fear
than worship, as a bribe / To 'the Creator'?
Ecclesiastes 12:1
Remember now 'thy Creator. '

51 Act III. i. 107-108   Quote: Approximate
These are a goodly offering to the Lord, / Given with 'a
gentle and a contrite spirit. '
Psalm 51:17
The sacrifices of God are a broken spirit: 'a broken and a
contrite heart, ' O God, thou wilt not despise.

52 Act III. i. 113-15   Reference: Subject
For what must I be grateful? / For being dust, and grovel-
ling in the dust, / Till I return to dust?
Genesis 3:19
For dust thou art, and unto dust shalt thou return.

53 Act III. i. 117-18   Reference: Subject
For what should I / Be contrite?
Psalm 51:17
The sacrifices of God are ... a broken and a contrite heart.

54 Act III, i. 120-21   Reference: Subject
To be more than expiated by / The ages prophesied, upon
'our seed. '
II Samuel 22:51
He ... sheweth mercy to his anointed, ... and to 'his seed'
for evermore.

55 Act III. i. 169-70   Quote: Exact
And friend to man. / Has 'the Most High' been so--if so you
term him?
II Samuel 22:14
The Lord thundered from heaven, and 'the Most High' uttered
his voice.

56 Act III. i. 190-91   Reference: Subject
Abel, I pray thee, sacrifice alone-- / Jehovah loves thee
well.
Genesis 4:4-5
And the Lord had respect unto Abel and to his offering: But
unto Cain and to his offering he had not respect.

57 Act III. i. 209-210   Quote: Exact
If it must be so--well, then / 'What shall I do'?
Job 7:20
I have sinned; 'what shall I do' unto thee ... ?

58   Act III. i. 248   Quote: Approximate
     Jehovah upon earth!   and 'God in heaven'!
     Deuteronomy 3:24
     For what 'God' is there 'in heaven' or in earth, That can do
     according to thy works?

59   Act III. i. 259-63   Quote: Exact
     Or if the sweet and blooming fruits of earth / And milder
     seasons ... seem / 'Good to thee. '
     Jeremiah 40:4
     If it seem 'good unto thee' to come with me into Babylon,
     come.

60   Act III. i. 267-68   Reference: Subject
     And altar without gore, may win thy favour, / Look on it!
     and for him who dresseth it.
     Leviticus 1-7
     Rf. preparations for sacrifices.

61   Act III. i. 281-82   Reference: Parodic
     Abel: Thy fruits are scatter'd on the earth.   Cain: 'From
     earth they came, to earth let them return. '
     Genesis 3:19
     In the sweat of thy face shalt thou eat bread, till thou return
     unto the ground; 'for out of it wast thou taken: for dust thou
     art, ' and unto dust shalt thou return.

62   Act III. i. 282   Reference: Subject
     From earth they came, to earth let them return.
     Ecclesiastes 12:7
     Then shall the dust return to the earth as it was.

63   Act III. i. 282-83   Reference: Subject
     From earth they came, to earth let them return; / Their
     seed will bear fresh fruit there ere the summer.
     Ezekiel 17:8
     It was planted in a good soil by great waters, that it might
     bring forth branches, and that it might bring forth branches,
     and that it might bear fruit, that it might be a goodly vine.

64   Act III. i. 283-85   Quote: Parodic
     See / How heav'n 'licks up the flames' when thick with blood!
     I Kings 18:38
     Then the fire of the Lord fell, and consumed the burnt sac-
     rifice, and the wood, and the stones, and the dust, and 'lick-
     ed up the water' that was in the trench.

65   Act III. i. 381   Quote: Exact
     What do I see? --'Tis true!   My son!   my son!
     II Samuel 18:33
     O my son Absalom, my son, my son Absalom!   would God I
     had died for thee, O Absalom, my son, my son!

66   Act III. i. 388-89   Quote: Approximate
      Was it some more hostile angel, / Who 'walks not with Je-
      hovah'?
      Genesis 5:22
      And Enoch 'walked with God. '

67   Act III. i. 432-33   Quote: Exact
      May the clear rivers 'turn to blood' as he / Stoops down to
      stain them with his raging lip!
      Exodus 7:17
      The waters which are in the river, ... they shall be 'turned
      to blood. '

68   Act III. i. 441-42   Reference: Subject
      May the grass wither from thy feet! the woods / Deny thee
      shelter! earth a home!
      Psalm 102:11
      And I am withered like grass.

69   Act III. i. 465-66   Reference: Subject
      I must not speak of this--it is between thee / And the great
      God.
      II Chronicles 2:5
      For great is our God above all gods.

70   Act III. i. 468-82   Quote: Exact/Approx-
                                                    imate
      Angel: 'Where is thy brother Abel? Cain: Am I then / My
      brother's keeper? Angel: Cain! what hast thou done? / The
      voice of thy slain brother's blood cries out, / Even from the
      ground, unto the Lord!-- / Now art thou / Cursed from the
      earth, which open'd late her mouth / To drink thy brother's
      blood from thy rash hand. / Henceforth, when thou shalt
      till the ground, it shall not / Yield thee her strength; a fugi-
      tive shalt thou / Be from this day, and vagabond on earth!
      Adah: This punishment is more than he can bear. / Behold,
      thou drivest him from the face of Earth, / And from the
      face of God shall he be hid. / A fugitive and vagabond on
      earth, / 'T will come to pass, that whoso findeth him / Shall
      slay him. '
      Genesis 4:9-14
      'And the Lord said unto Cain, Where is Abel thy brother?
      And he said, I know not: Am I my brother's keeper? And
      he said, What hast thou done? the voice of thy brother's
      blood crieth unto me from the ground. And now art thou
      cursed from the earth, which hath opened her mouth to re-
      ceive thy brother's blood from thy hand; When thou tillest
      the ground, it shall not henceforth yield unto thee her strength;
      a fugitive and a vagabond shalt thou be in the earth. And
      Cain said unto the Lord, My punishment is greater than I
      can bear. Behold, thou hast driven me out this day from the
      face of the earth; and from thy face shall I be hid; and I
      shall be a fugitive and a vagabond in the earth; and it shall

come to pass, that every one that findeth me shall slay me. '

71   Act III. i. 503   Quote: Exact
     Stern hast thou been and stubborn 'from the womb. '
     Judges 13:5-7
     For the child shall be a Nazarite unto God 'from the womb. '

72   Act III. i. 554-55   Reference: Subject
     Lead! thou shalt be my guide, and may our God / Be thine!
     Now let us carry forth our children.
     Ruth 1:16
     Thy people shall be my people, and thy God my God.

CHILDE HAROLD'S PILGRIMAGE

---

73   Canto I, 37-38   Quote: Approximate
     For he through Sin's long labyrinth had run, / Nor made
     atonement when he did amiss.
     Numbers 25:13
     Because he was zealous for his God, and made an atonement
     for the children of Israel.

74   Canto I, 212-15   Reference: Subject
     And when the Almighty lifts his fiercest scourge / 'Gainst
     those who most transgress his high command, / With treble
     vengeance will his hot shafts urge / Gaul's locust host, and
     earth from fellest foemen purge.
     Exodus 10:1-20
     Rf. the plague of locust on Egypt.

75   Canto I, 223-24   Quote: Parodic
     Who lick yet loathe the hand that waves the sword / To save
     them from the wrath of Gaul's unsparing Lord.
     Psalm 78:31
     The wrath of God came upon them.

76   Canto I, 225-27   Quote: Exact
     But whoso entereth within this town, / That, sheening far,
     celestial seems to be, / Disconsolate will wander up and
     down.
     Psalm 59:15
     Let them wander up and down for meat, and grudge if they
     be not satisfied.

77   Canto I, 231-33   Reference: Parodic
     Ne personage of high or mean degree / Doth care for clean-
     ness of surtout or shirt, / Though shent with Egypt's plague,
     unkempt, unwash'd, unhurt.

Exodus 7-11
    Rf. the plagues on Egypt when the Israelites fled.

78 Canto I, 236   Allusion
        Lo! Cintra's glorious Eden intervenes.
    Genesis 2:1-24
        Rf. garden of Eden.

79 Canto I, 295-96   Quote: Parodic
        And sundry signatures adorn the roll, / Whereat the Urchin
        points, and laughs 'with all his soul. '
    Deuteronomy 11:13
        To love the Lord your God, and to serve him with all your
        heart and 'with all your soul. '

80 Canto I, 297-98   Quote: Parodic
        Convention is the dwarfish demon styled / That foil'd the
        knights in Marialva's dome. / Of brains (if brains they had)
        he them beguiled, / And turn'd a nation's shallow joy to
        gloom.
    Job 41:22
        In his neck remaineth strength, and sorrow is turned into
        joy before him.

81 Canto I, 340-41   Quote: Approximate
        Men forget the blood which she hath spilt, / And 'bow the
        knee to Pomp' that loves to varnish guilt.
    I Kings 19:18
        Yet I have left me seven thousand in Israel, all 'the knees
        which have not bowed unto Baal. '

82 Canto I, 384   Quote: Approximate
        Here 'ceased the swift their race, ' here sunk the strong.
    Ecclesiastes 9:11
        I returned, and saw under the sun, that 'the race is not to
        the swift, ' nor the battle to the strong.

83 Canto I, 400-401   Parallelism
        Pride! bend thine eye from heaven to thine estate, / See
        'how the Mighty shrink' into a song!
    II Samuel 1:19
        The beauty of Israel is slain upon thy high places: 'how are
        the mighty fallen. '

84 Canto I, 428-29   Allusion
        And at his iron feet / Destruction covers to mark what deeds
        are done.
    Daniel 2:33-42
        Thou, O king, sawest, and behold a great image ... His legs
        of iron, his feet part of iron and part of clay.

85 Canto I, 436-37   Quote: Approximate
        What gallant War-hounds rouse them from their lair, / And

gnash their fangs, loud yelling for the prey.
Lamentations 2:16
　　All thine enemies have opened their mouth against thee:　they
　　hiss and gnash the teeth.

86　Canto I, 607-608   Quote:　Parodic
　　Match me those Houries, whom ye scarce allow / To taste
　　the gale lest Love should 'ride the wind. '
　　Job 30:22
　　　Thou liftest me up to 'the wind'; thou causest me 'to ride
　　　upon it, ' and dissolvest my substance.

87　Canto I, 625-26   Reference:　Subject
　　When I recount thy worshippers of yore / I tremble, and can
　　only bend the knee.
　　Isaiah 45:23
　　　Unto me every knee shall bow, every tongue shall swear.

88　Canto I, 644-45   Reference:　Subject
　　Now to my theme--but from thy holy haunt / Let me 'some
　　remnant, ' some memorial bear.
　　Leviticus 2:2-3
　　　And the priest shall burn the memorial of it upon the altar,
　　　to be an offering made by fire, of a sweet savour unto the
　　　Lord:　And 'the remnant' of the meat offering shall be Aa-
　　　ron's and his sons.

89　Canto I, 657-58   Quote:　Exact
　　Fair is proud Seville; let her country boast / Her strength,
　　her wealth, her site 'of ancient days. '
　　Isaiah 23:7
　　　Is this your joyous city, whose antiquity is 'of ancient days'?

90　Canto I, 684-85   Reference:　Subject
　　The Sabbath comes, a day of blessed rest; / What hallows
　　it upon this Christian shore?
　　Exodus 20:8-10
　　　Remember the sabbath day, to keep it holy.　Six days shalt
　　　thou labour, ... But the seventh day is the sabbath of the
　　　Lord thy God.

91　Canto I, 684-86   Quote:　Exact
　　The Sabbath comes, a day of blessed rest; / What hallows
　　it upon this Christian shore? / Lo! it is sacred to 'a sol-
　　emn feast. '
　　Deuteronomy 16:15
　　　Seven days shalt thou keep 'a solemn feast' unto the Lord thy
　　　God.

92　Canto I, 693-97   Reference:　Parodic
　　The seventh day this, the jubilee of man. / London, right
　　well thou know'st the day of prayer: / Then thy spruce cit-
　　izen, wash'd artisan, / And smug apprentice gulp their week-

ly air; / Thy coach of hackney, whiskey, one-horse chair.
Genesis 2:2
 And on the seventh day God ended his work which he had
 made; and he rested on the seventh day from all his work
 which he had made.

93 Canto I, 693-94   Reference: Subject
 The seventh day this, the jubilee of man. / London, right
 well thou know'st the day of prayer.
Exodus 20:8-10
 Remember the sabbath day, to keep it holy.   Six days shalt
 thou labour, ... But the seventh day is the sabbath of the
 Lord thy God.

94 Canto I, 942-43   Quote: Approximate
 And Fancy hover o'er thy bloodless bier, / Till my frail
 frame 'return to whence it rose.'
Ecclesiastes 12:7
 Then shall the dust 'return to the earth' as it was.

95 Canto I, 943-44   Quote: Approximate
 Till my frail frame 'return to whence it rose,' And mourn'd
 and mourner lie united in repose.
Ecclesiastes 12:7
 Then shall the dust return to the earth as it was: and the
 spirit shall 'return unto God who gave it.'

96 Canto II, 10   Quote: Exact
 'Ancient of days!' august Athena!
Daniel 7:9 (7:22)
 I beheld till the thrones were cast down, and the 'Ancient of
 days' did sit, whose garment was white as snow.

97 Canto II, 10-11   Quote: Exact
 Ancient of days! august Athena! where, / Where are thy 'men
 of might'? thy grand in soul?
Psalm 76:5
 And none of the 'men of might' have found their hands.

98 Canto II, 19   Quote: Exact
 'Son of the morning,' rise! approach you here!
Isaiah 14:12
 How art thou fallen from heaven, O Lucifer, 'son of the
 morning'!

99 Canto II, 24-26   Reference: Subject
 Other creeds / Will rise with other years, till man shall
 learn / Vainly his incense soars, his victim bleeds.
Isaiah 1:13
 Bring no more vain oblations; incense is an abomination unto
 me; the new moons and sabbaths, the calling of assemblies,
 I can not away with; it is iniquity, even the solemn meeting.

100   Canto II, 27   Reference: Subject
      Poor child of Doubt and Death [man], whose hope is built
      on reeds.
      Isaiah 36:6
      Lo thou trustest in the staff of this broken reed.

101   Canto II, 44-45   Reference: Parodic
      Is that a temple where a God may dwell? Why ev'n the
      worm at least disdains her shatter'd cell!
      Exodus 25:8
      And let them make me a sanctuary; that I may dwell among
      them.

102   Canto II, 143-44   Quote: Parodic
      But Harold felt not as in other times, / And left without a
      sigh 'the land of war and crimes. '
      Exodus 3:8
      And I am come down to deliver them ... unto 'a land flow-
      ing with milk and honey. '

103   Canto II, 205   Reference: Parodic
      Alas, when mingling souls forget to blend.
      Genesis 2:24
      Therefore shall a man leave his father and his mother, and
      shall cleave unto his wife: and they shall be one flesh.

104   Canto II, 219   Allusion
      Where [forest] things that own not man's 'dominion' dwell.
      Genesis 1:26-28
      And God said, Let us make man in our image, after our
      likeness: and let them have 'dominion' over the fish of the
      sea, and over the fowl of the air, and over the cattle, and
      over all the earth, and over every creeping thing that creep-
      eth upon the earth.

105   Canto II, 424-25   Quote: Exact
      Monastic Zitza, from thy shady brow, / Thou small, but
      favour'd spot of 'holy ground'!
      Exodus 3:5
      Put off thy shoes from off thy feet, for the place whereon
      thou standest is 'holy ground. '

106   Canto II, 503   Quote: Approximate
      'Within, ' a palace, ' and without, ' a fort.
      Genesis 6:14
      Rooms shalt thou make in the ark, and shalt pitch it 'within
      and without' with pitch.

107   Canto II, 563-65   Reference: Subject
      But crimes that scorn the tender voice of Ruth, / Beseem-
      ing all men ill but most the man / In years, have mark'd
      him with a tiger's tooth.

Ruth 1:9
And they [Ruth and Naomi] lifted up their voice, and wept.

108 Canto II, 655-56   Quote: Approximate
To the wolf and the vulture he leaves his wild flock, And
descends to the plain like the 'stream from the rock. '
Deuteronomy 8:15
Who brought thee forth 'water out of the rock' of flint.

109 Canto II, 695-96   Reference: Subject
Who now shall lead thy scatter'd children forth, / And long
accustom'd bondage uncreate?
Nehemiah 5:5, 18
Rf. Babylonian captivity of Israel.

110 Canto II, 828   Quote: Exact
Where'er we tread 'tis haunted, 'holy ground. '
Exodus 3:5
Put off thy shoes from off thy feet, for the place whereon
thou standest is 'holy ground. '

111 Canto II, 884-85   Quote: Exact
Soon shall thy voice be lost amid the throng / Of louder
minstrels 'in these later days. '
Numbers 24:14
Come therefore, and I will advertise thee what this people
shall do to thy people 'in the latter days. '

112 Canto III, 6-7   Quote: Exact
The waters heave around me, and on high / The winds 'lift
up their voices. '
Isaiah 42:11
Let the wilderness and the cities thereof 'lift up their voice. '

113 Canto III, 74-75   Quote: Approximate
But he fill'd again, / And from a purer fount, on 'holier
ground. '
Exodus 3:5
Put off thy shoes from off thy feet, for the place whereon
thou standest is 'holy ground. '

114 Canto III, 88-90   Quote: Exact
Searching through the crowd to find / Fit speculation, such
as 'in strange land' / He found in wonder--works of God
and Nature's hand.
Exodus 2:22
For he said, I have been a stranger 'in a strange land. '

115 Canto III, 90   Allusion
He found in wonder-works of God and Nature's hand.
Genesis 1:1
In the beginning God created the heaven and the earth.

116   Canto III, 107-108   Allusion
       Proud though in desolation; which could find / A 'life within
       itself, to 'breathe' without mankind.
       Genesis 2:7
       And the Lord God formed man of the dust of the ground,
       and 'breathed' into his nostrils the 'breath of life'; and man
       became a living soul.

117   Canto III, 118-20   Reference: Subject
       Like the Chaldean he could watch the stars, / Till he had
       peopled them with beings bright / As their own beams.
       Genesis 15:5
       [God to Abram] Look now toward heaven, and tell the stars,
       if thou be able to number them: and he said unto him, So
       shall thy seed be.

118   Canto III, 208   Quote: Exact
       Ah! then and there was hurrying 'to and fro. '
       Genesis 8:7
       And he sent forth a raven, which went forth 'to and fro. '

119   Canto III, 281-82   Allusion
       The tree will wither long before it fall.
       Psalm 1:3
       And he shall be like a tree planted by the rivers of water,
       that bringeth forth his fruit in his season; his leaf also
       shall not wither; and whatsoever he doeth shall prosper.

120   Canto III, 303-304   Reference: Subject
       Like to the apples on the Dead Sea's shore, / All ashes to
       the taste.
       Deuteronomy 32:32
       For their vine is of the vine of Sodom, and of the fields of
       Gomorrah.

121   Canto III, 345-46   Quote: Approximate
       Which, be it wisdom, coldness, or deep pride, / Is 'gall
       and wormwood' to an enemy.
       Lamentations 3:19
       Remembering mine affliction and my misery, the 'wormwood
       and the gall. '

122   Canto III, 487-89   Reference: Subject
       And there was one soft breast, as hath been said, / Which
       unto his was bound by stronger ties / Than the church links
       withal; and, though unwed.
       Genesis 2:24
       Therefore shall a man leave his father and his mother, and
       shall cleave unto his wife: and they shall be one flesh.

123   Canto III, 500-501   Quote: Exact
       And hills all rich with blossom'd trees, / And fields which
       promise 'corn and wine. '

Genesis 27:28
Therefore God give thee of the dew of heaven, and the fat-
ness of the earth, and plenty of 'corn and wine.'

124   Canto III, 506-508   Allusion
And peasant girls, with deep blue eyes / And hands which
offer early flowers, / Walk smiling o'er this paradise.
Genesis 2-3
Rf. the garden of Eden.

125   Canto III, 549-50   Quote: Exact
For he was Freedom's champion, one of those, / The 'few
in number,' who had not o'erstept.
Genesis 34:30
And I being 'few in number,' they shall gather themselves
together against me, and slay me.

126   Canto III, 634   Allusion
And held within their urn one mind, one heart, one dust.
Genesis 3:19
Till thou return unto the ground; for out of it wast thou ta-
ken: for dust thou art, and unto dust shalt thou return.

127   Canto III, 659-60   Parallelism
We may deplore and struggle with the coil, / In wretched
interchange of 'wrong for wrong.'
Exodus 21:23-25
Thou shalt give life for life, 'eye for eye, tooth for tooth,
hand for hand, foot for foot, burning for burning, wound
for wound, stripe for stripe.'

128   Canto III, 662-65   Quote: Parodic
There, in a moment, we may plunge our years / In fatal
penitence, and in the blight / Of our own soul 'turn all our
blood to tears,' / And colour things to come with hues of
Night.
Exodus 7:17
Behold, I will smite with the rod that is in mine hand upon
the 'waters' which are in the river, and they shall be 'turn-
ed to blood.'

129   Canto III, 666-67   Quote: Approximate
The race of life becomes a hopeless flight / To those that
'walk in darkness.'
Ecclesiastes 2:14
But the fool 'walketh in darkness.'

130   Canto III, 692-94   Reference: Subject
For some sin, to sorrow I was cast, / To act and suffer
but remount at last / With a fresh pinion.
Isaiah 40:31
But they that wait upon the Lord shall renew their strength;
they shall mount up with wings as eagles.

131   Canto III, 697   Reference: Subject
        Spurning the clay-cold bonds which round our being cling.
      Genesis 2:7
        And the Lord God formed man of the dust of the ground

132   Canto III, 702-703   Reference: Subject
        When elements to elements conform, / And dust is as it
        should be.
      Genesis 3:19
        Till thou return unto the ground; for out of it wast thou ta-
        ken: for dust thou art, and unto dust shalt thou return.

133   Canto III, 839-41   Allusion
        Where not a beam nor air nor leaf is lost, / But hath a
        part of being, and a sense / Of that which is of all Crea-
        tor and defence.
      Genesis 1:1
        In the beginning God created the heaven and the earth.

134   Canto III, 840-41   Reference: Subject
        And a sense / Of that which is of all Creator and defence.
      Psalm 59:9
        For God is my defence.

135   Canto III, 903-904   Reference: Subject
        Are ye like those within the human breast, / Or do ye find
        at length, like eagles, some high nest?
      Jeremiah 49:16
        Make thy nest as high as the eagle, I will bring thee down.

136   Canto III, 981-85   Reference: Subject
        They were gigantic minds, and their steep aim / Was, Ti-
        tan-like, on daring doubts to pile / Thoughts which should
        call down thunder and the flame / Of Heaven, again assail'd,
        if Heaven the while / On man and man's research could
        deign do more than smile.
      Isaiah 14
        Rf. Lucifer's rebellion.

137   Canto III, 989-990   Allusion: Parodic
        Historian, bard, philosopher, combined. He multiplied him-
        self among mankind.
      Genesis 1:22, 28
        And God blessed them, saying, Be fruitful, and multiply,
        and replenish the earth.

138   Canto III, 1004-1010   Reference: Subject
        Yet, peace be with their ashes for by them, / If merited,
        the penalty is paid / ... By slumber, on one pillow,--in
        the dust, / Which, thus much we are sure, must lie de-
        cay'd.
      Genesis 3:19
        Till thou return unto the ground; for out of it wast thou

taken: for dust thou art, and unto dust shalt thou return.

139   Canto III, 1013-14   Allusion
      But let me quit man's works again to read / His Maker's,
      spread around me.
      Genesis 1-2 (note 1:1)
      In the beginning God created the heaven and the earth.

140   Canto III, 1049-51   Quote: Parodic
      I have not loved the world, nor the world me; / I have not
      flatter'd its rank breath, nor 'bow'd' / To its idolatries 'a
      patient knee. '
      Genesis 41:43
      And he made him to ride in the second chariot which he
      had; and they cried before him, 'Bow the knee': and he
      made him ruler over all the land of Egypt.

141   Canto III, 1050-51   Reference: Subject
      I have not flatter'd its rank breath, nor 'bow'd' / To its
      idolatries 'a patient knee. '
      I Kings 19:18
      Yet I have left me seven thousand in Israel, all the 'knees
      which have not bowed' unto Baal.

142   Canto III, 1050-52   Quote: Exact
      I have not flatter'd its rank breath, nor bow'd / To its
      idolatries a patient knee, / Nor coin'd my cheek to smiles,
      nor 'cried aloud. '
      I Kings 18:28
      And they 'cried aloud, ' and cut themselves.

143   Canto III, 1055-56   Quote: Approximate
      In a shroud / Of 'thoughts which were not their thoughts. '
      Isaiah 55:8
      For 'my thoughts are not your thoughts, ' neither are your
      ways my ways.

144   Canto IV, 192-93   Parallelism
      Some, with hope replenish'd and rebuoy'd, / 'Return to
      whence they came. '
      Ecclesiastes 12:7
      Then shall the dust 'return to the earth as it was': and
      the spirit shall 'return unto God who gave it. '

145   Canto IV, 194-96   Reference: Subject
      Some, bow'd and bent, / Wax gray and ghastly, withering
      ere their time, / And perish with the 'reed on which they
      leant. '
      II Kings 18:21
      Now, behold, thou trustest upon the staff of this bruised
      'reed, ' even upon Egypt, 'on which if a man lean, ' it will
      go into his hand, and pierce it.

146   Canto IV, 296-97   Reference: Subject
      Vanity can give / No hollow air; alone--man with his God
      must strive.
      Genesis 32:24-32
      And Jacob was left alone; and there wrestled a man with
      him until the breaking of the day ... And Jacob called the
      name of the place Peniel: for I have seen God face to face,
      and my life is preserved.

147   Canto IV, 300-302   Quote: Exact
      In melancholy bosoms, such as were / Of moody texture
      from their earliest day / And loved 'to dwell in darkness'
      and dismay.
      Psalm 143:3
      He hath made me 'to dwell in darkness,' as those that have
      been long dead.

148   Canto IV, 305-306   Reference: Parodic
      [Demons] making the sun like blood, the earth a tomb, / The
      tomb a hell, and hell itself a murkier gloom.
      Joel 2:31
      The sun shall be turned into darkness, and the moon into
      blood, before the great and the terrible day of the Lord
      come.

149   Canto IV, 377-78   Quote: Approximate
      Awe the robbers back, who press / To shed thy blood and
      'drink the tears' of thy distress.
      Psalm 80:5
      Thou feedest them with the bread of tears; and givest them
      'tears to drink' in great measure.

150   Canto IV, 478-80   Reference: Subject
      In Santa Croce's holy precincts lie / Ashes which make it
      holier, dust which is / Even in itself an immortality.
      Genesis 3:19
      Till thou return unto the ground; for out of it wast thou ta-
      ken; for dust thou art, and unto dust shalt thou return.

151   Canto IV, 483-83   Allusion
      The particle of those sublimities / Which have relapsed to
      chaos.
      Genesis 1:2
      And the earth was without form, and void.

152   Canto IV, 486   Reference: Subject
      Here Machiavelli's earth return'd to whence it rose.
      Ecclesiastes 12:7
      Then shall the dust return to the earth as it was.

153   Canto IV, 500-502   Reference: Subject
      Their bones, distinguish'd from our common clay / In death
      as life? Are they resolved to dust, / And have their coun-
      try's marbles nought to say?

Genesis 3:19
Till thou return unto the ground; for out of it was thou ta-
ken; for dust thou art, and unto dust shalt thou return.

154 Canto IV, 509   Quote: Exact
'Their children's children' would in vain adore.
Genesis 45:10
And thou shalt dwell in the land of Goshen, and thou shalt
be near unto me, thou, and thy children, and 'thy children's
children,' and thy flocks, and thy herds, and all that thou
hast.

155 Canto IV, 572-73   Allusion
Reck'd not of the awe / Which reigns when mountains trem-
ble.
Habakkuk 3:10
The mountains saw thee, and they trembled.

156 Canto IV, 584-85   Allusion
And Sanguinetto tells ye where the dead / Made the earth
wet and turn'd the unwilling waters red.
Exodus 7:17
Behold, I will smite with the rod that is in mine hand upon
the waters which are in the river, and they shall be turned
to blood.

157 Canto IV, 683-84   Quote: Approximate
If free to choose, I cannot now 'restore / Its health'; but
what it then detested, still abhor.
Jeremiah 30:17
For I will 'restore health' unto thee.

158 Canto IV, 741-43   Reference: Subject
Thy country's foes ere thou wouldst pause to feel / The
wrath of thy own wrongs, or reap the due / Of hoarded
vengeance till thine eagles flew / O'er prostrate Asia.
Jeremiah 48:40
Behold, he shall fly as an eagle, and shall spread his wings
over Moab.

159 Canto IV, 825-28   Reference: Parodic
And blood of earth flow on as they have flow'd / An univer-
sal deluge, which appears / Without an ark for wretched
man's abode / And ebbs but to reflow!--Renew thy rainbow,
God!
Genesis 6-9
Rf. Noah, the flood, and the rainbow of promise.

160 Canto IV, 831-32   Allusion
Life short, and truth a gem which loves the deep, / And
all things weigh'd in custom's falsest scale.
Daniel 5:27
Thou art weighed in the balances and found wanting.

161   Canto IV, 847-48   Allusion
      I speak not of men's creeds--they rest between / Man and
      his Maker--but of things allow'd.
      Genesis 2:7
      And the Lord God formed man of the dust of the ground,
      and breathed into his nostrils the breath of life.

162   Canto IV, 865   Quote: Approximate
      But France got 'drunk with blood' to vomit crime.
      Isaiah 49:26
      And they shall be 'drunken with their own blood' as with
      sweet wine.

163   Canto IV, 963   Reference: Subject
      Behold the Imperial Mount! 'tis thus the mighty falls.
      II Samuel 1:19
      How are the mighty fallen.

164   Canto IV, 1022-23   Allusion
      While the tree / Of freedom's wither'd trunk puts forth a
      leaf.
      Psalm 1:3
      And he shall be like a tree planted by the rivers of water,
      that bringeth forth his fruit in his season; his leaf also
      shall not wither; and whatsoever he doeth shall prosper.

165   Canto IV, 1052-53   Quote: Approximate
      The sweetness of the violet's deep blue eyes, / Kiss'd by
      'the breath of heaven,' seems colour'd by its skies.
      Genesis 2:7
      And the Lord God ... breathed into his nostrils 'the breath
      of life'; and man became a living soul.

166   Canto IV, 1072-73   Reference: Subject
      Alas! our young affections run to waste, / Or water but
      the desert.
      Isaiah 35:6
      For in the wilderness shall waters break out, and streams
      in the desert.

167   Canto IV, 1077-80   Reference: Parodic
      And trees whose gums are poison;--such the plants / Which
      spring beneath her steps as Passion flies / O'er the world's
      wilderness, and vainly pants / For some celestial fruit for-
      bidden to our wants.
      Genesis 2:17
      But of the tree of the knowledge of good and evil, thou
      shalt not eat of it: for in the day that thou eatest thereof
      thou shalt surely die.

168   Canto IV, 1104-1105   Quote: Approximate
      The fatal spell, and still it draws us on, / 'Reaping the
      whirlwind' from 'the oft-sown winds.'

Hosea 8:7
For they have 'sown the wind, ' and they shall 'reap the whirlwind. '

169   Canto IV, 1122-23   Allusion: Parodic
And Circumstance, that unspiritual god / And miscreator.
Genesis 1:1
In the beginning God created the heaven and the earth.

170   Canto IV, 1126-32   Reference: Subject
Our life is a false nature, 't is not in / The harmony of things,--this hard decree, / This uneradicable taint of sin, / This boundless upas, this all-blasting tree / Whose root is earth, whose leaves and branches be / The skies which rain their plagues on men like dew-- / Disease, death, bondage--all the woes we see.
Genesis 3:1-24
Rf. the tree of knowledge of good and evil, and the fall of man.

171   Canto IV, 1131-32   Reference: Subject
The skies which rain their plagues on men like dew-- / Disease, death, bondage--all the woes we see.
Exodus 6-13
Rf. the plagues on Egypt.

172   Canto IV, 1137-38   Quote: Exact
Our right of thought, our last and only 'place / Of refuge'--this, at least, shall still be mine.
Isaiah 4:6
And there shall be a tabernacle ... for a 'place of refuge. '

173   Canto IV, 1169   Allusion
Time, the avenger!
Numbers 35:12
And they shall be unto you cities for refuge from the avenger; that the manslayer die not until he stand before the congregation in judgment.

174   Canto IV, 1187-88   Reference: Parodic
Thy former realm, I call thee from 'the dust'! / 'Dost' thou not hear my heart?--Awake! thou shalt, and must.
Genesis 2:7
And the Lord God formed man of 'the dust' of the ground.

175   Canto IV, 1189-92   Reference: Subject
It is not that I may not have incurr'd / For my ancestral faults or mine the wound / I bleed withal, and, had it been conferr'd / With a just weapon, it had flow'd unbound.
Genesis 3
Rf. the effect of the fall on mankind.

176 Canto IV, 1193-95   Reference: Subject
        But now my blood shall not sink in the ground: / To thee
        I do devote it--'thou' shalt take / The vengeance, which
        shall yet be sought and found.
      Genesis 4:10
        And he said, What hast thou done? the voice of thy brother's
        blood crieth unto me from the ground.

177 Canto IV, 1214-15   Allusion
        Because not altogether of such clay / As rots into the
        souls of those whom I survey.
      Genesis 2:7
        And the Lord God formed man of the dust of the ground, and
        breathed into his nostrils the breath of life.

178 Canto IV, 1225   Quote: Approximate
        But I have lived, and have 'not lived in vain.'
      Isaiah 65:23
        They shall 'not labour in vain,' nor bring forth for trouble.

179 Canto IV, 1235-36   Quote: Approximate
        Nameless, yet thus omnipotent, which here / 'Walk'st in
        the shadow of' the midnight hour.
      Psalm 23:4
        Yea, though I 'walk through the valley of the shadow' of
        death, I will fear no evil.

180 Canto IV, 1274-75   Quote: Exact
        Here, where the Roman millions' blame or praise / Was
        'death or life,' the playthings of a crowd.
      II Samuel 15:21
        Surely in what place my lord the king shall be, whether in
        'death or life,' even there also will thy servant be.

181 Canto IV, 1296   Allusion
        Heroes have trod this spot--'tis on their dust ye tread.
      Genesis 2:7
        And the Lord God formed man of the dust of the ground,
        and breathed into his nostrils the breath of life.

182 Canto IV, 1304   Reference: Subject
        Rome and her Ruin past Redemption's skill.
      Leviticus 25:51
        He shall give again the price of his redemption out of the
        money.

183 Canto IV, 1310-11   Reference: Subject
        Arch, empire, each thing round thee, and man plods / His
        way through thorns to ashes--glorious dome!
      Genesis 3:18-19
        Thorns also and thistles shall it bring forth to thee ... for
        dust thou art, and unto dust shalt thou return.

184 Canto IV, 1333   Quote: Approximate
      Full swells 'the deep pure fountain of young life.'
      Psalm 36:9
      For with thee is 'the fountain of life': in thy light shall we
      see light.

185 Canto IV, 1340-41   Reference: Parodic
      She sees her little bud put forth its leaves-- / What may
      the fruit be yet?--I know not, Cain was Eve's
      Genesis 4:1-2
      And Adam knew Eve his wife; and she conceived, and bare
      Cain, and said, I have gotten a man from the Lord.

186 Canto IV, 1385-86   Reference: Subject
      Power, Glory, Strength, and Beauty, all are aisled / In
      this eternal ark of worship undefiled.
      Exodus 26:10-22
      Rf. the ark of the covenant.

187 Canto IV, 1392-94   Quote: Exact
      And thou / Shalt one day, if found worthy, so defined, / See
      thy God 'face to face.'
      Exodus 33:11
      And the Lord spake unto Moses 'face to face.'

188 Canto IV, 1394   Quote: Exact
      'See' thy 'God face to face' as thou dost now.
      Genesis 32:30
      And Jacob called the name of the place Peniel: for I have
      'seen God face to face,' and my life is preserved.

189 Canto IV, 1394-95   Reference: Subject
      See thy God face to face as thou dost now / His 'Holy of
      Holies,' nor be blasted by his brow.
      Exodus 26:33
      And the vail shall divide unto you between the holy 'place'
      and the 'most holy.'

190 Canto IV, 1522-23   Reference: Subject
      Of sackcloth was thy wedding garment made; / Thy bridal's
      fruit is ashes.
      Esther 4:1
      Rf. sackcloth and ashes.

191 Canto IV, 1531   Quote: Exact
      'Woe unto us,' not her; for she sleeps well.
      I Samuel 4:7-8
      'Woe unto us!' for there hath not been such a thing hereto-
      fore. 'Woe unto us!'

192 Canto IV, 1623-26   Reference: Parodic
      And monarchs tremble in their capitals, / The oak levia-

thans, whose huge ribs make / Their 'clay creator' the
vain title take / Of lord of thee and arbiter of war.
Genesis 2:7
And the Lord God formed man of the dust of the ground.

193 Canto IV, 1638   Allusion
Such as creation's dawn beheld, thou [the ocean] rollest now.
Genesis 1
Rf. the creation of the world.

THE CORSAIR

---

194 Canto I, 563-64   Allusion
Receive these tablets and peruse with care, / Words of
high trust and truth are graven there.
Exodus 24:12
And the Lord said unto Moses, Come up to me into the
mount, and be there: and I will give thee tables of stone,
and a law, and commandments which I have written.

195 Canto II, 203-204   Quote: Parodic
Remember we have wives. / On them such outrage 'Ven-
geance will repay. '
Deuteronomy 32:35
'To me belongeth vengeance, ' and recompence.

196 Canto III, 204-207   Allusion
Still half unconscious, heedless of his wrath, / Again she
ventured on the dangerous path, / Again his rage repell'd--
until arose / That strife of thought, the source of woman's
woes!
Genesis 3:6, 23
And when the woman saw that the tree was good for food,
and that it was pleasant to the eyes, and a tree to be de-
sired to make one wise, she took of the fruit thereof, and
did eat, and gave also unto her husband with her.

197 Canto III, 368   Quote: Approximate
Now fare thee well--more 'peace be with thy' breast!
Genesis 43:23
And he said, 'Peace be to you, ' fear not.

198 Canto III, 544-45   Quote: Exact
If he had driven her from 'that resting-place, ' / His had
been more or less than mortal heart.
Numbers 10:33
And the ark of the covenant of the Lord went before them
in the three days' journey, to search out 'a resting place'
for them.

THE CURSE OF MINERVA

199   Lines 155-56   Reference: Subject
    As once of yore in some obnoxious place, / Ten names
(if found) had saved a wretched race.
Genesis 18:1-33
    And the Lord said, Because the cry of Sodom and Gomor-
rah is great, and because their sin is very grievous; I will
go down now ... And Abraham drew near, and said, Wilt
thou also destroy the righteous with the wicked ... ?   And
he said, Oh let not the Lord be angry, and I will speak yet
but this once: Peradventure ten shall be found there.   And
he said, I will not destroy it for ten's sake.

200   Line 162   Quote Approximate
    'Hear and believe,' for Time will tell the rest.
Exodus 19:9
    Lo, I come unto thee in a thick cloud, that the people may
'hear' when I speak with thee, 'and believe' thee for ever.

201   Line 199   Allusion
    Oh, loathed in life nor pardon'd in the dust.
Genesis 3:19
    For dust thou art, and unto dust shalt thou return.

202   Lines 311-12   Quote: Exact
    The law of heaven and earth is 'life for life,' / And she
who raised, in vain regrets, the strife.
Exodus 21:23
    And if any mischief follow, then thou shalt give 'life for
life.'

203   Line 312   Quote: Approximate
    And she who 'raised,' in vain regrets, 'the strife.'
Habakkuk 1:3
    For spoiling and violence are before me: and there are
that 'raise up strife' and contention.

THE DEFORMED TRANSFORMED

204   Part I. i. 25-27   Allusion
    For if I brought thee forth, it was / As foolish hens at
times hatch vipers, by / Sitting upon strange eggs.
Isaiah 59:5
    They hatch cockatrice eggs, and weave the spider's web:

he that eatheth of their eggs dieth, and that which is crush-
ed breaketh out into a viper.

205   Part I. i. 263-64   Quote: Exact
      I'll animate the ideal marble, till / Your soul be recon-
      ciled to her 'new garment. '
      I Kings 11:29
      And he had clad himself with a 'new garment. '

206   Part I. i. 292-95   Reference: Subject
      Would you so far / Outstep these times, and be a Titan?
      Or / (To talk canonically) wax a son / of Anak?
      Numbers 13:28-33
      Rf. the children of Anak, inhabitants of Canaan.

207   Part I. i. 295-298   Reference: Parodic
      Glorious ambition! / I love thee most in dwarfs! A mortal
      of / Philistine stature would have gladly pared / His own
      Goliath down to a slight David.
      I Samuel 17
      Rf. David's slaying of the Philistine giant, Goliath.

208   Part I. i. 456-57   Reference: Subject
      Clay thou art; and unto spirit / All clay is of equal merit.
      Ecclesiastes 12:7
      Then shall the dust return to the earth as it was: and the
      spirit shall return unto God who gave it.

209   Part I. i. 466-67   Reference: Subject
      Where nor fish, beast, nor worm, / Save 'the worm which
      dieth not. '
      Isaiah 66:24
      For 'their worm shall not die, ' neither shall their fire be
      quenched.

210   Part I. i. 501-502   Allusion: Parodic
      And scarce a better to be found on earth, / Since Sodom
      was put out.
      Genesis 13-14; 18-19
      Rf. destruction of Sodom and Gomorrah.

211   Part I. ii. 578-81   Allusion
      Arnold: How old? What! are there / New worlds / Caesar:
      To you. You'll find there are such shortly, / By its rich
      harvests, new disease, and gold; / From one half of the
      world named a whole new one.
      Isaiah 66:22
      For as the new heavens and the new earth, which I will
      make, ... so shall your seed and your name remain.

212   Part I. ii. 608-11   Reference: Subject
      Christ ascended from the cross, / Which his blood made a
      badge of glory and of joy (as once of torture unto him, / God

and God's Son, man's sole and only 'refuge').
Psalm 9:9
The Lord also will be a 'refuge' for the oppressed, a 'refuge' in times of trouble.

213   Part II. i. 79-80   Quote: Approximate
When the first 'o'erleapt thy wall,' / Its foundation mourn'd thy fall.
II Samuel 22:30
For by thee I have run through a troop: by my God have I 'leaped over a wall.'

214   Part II. iii. 256-67   Quote: Approximate
You know that "'Vengeance is the Lord's' ": / You see he loves no interlopers.
Deuteronomy 32:35
'To me belongeth vengeance,' and recompence.

215   Part II. iii. 317-18   Quote: Approximate
But 'get ye hence,' / And thank your meanness, other God you have none.
I Kings 17:3
'Get thee hence,' and turn thee eastward.

216   Part II. iii. 318   Reference: Subject
And thank your meanness, other God you have none.
Exodus 20:3
Thou shalt have no other gods before me.

217   Part II. iii. 325   Reference: Subject
Rebel in hell--you shall obey on earth!
Isaiah 14:12
How art thou fallen from heaven, O Lucifer, son of the morning!

218   Part II. iii. 425   Reference: Subject
Like stars, no doubt; for that's a metaphor / For Lucifer and Venus.
Isaiah 14:12
How art thou fallen from heaven, O Lucifer, son of the morning!

219   Part III. i. 7-8   Quote: Approximate
The spring is come; the violet's gone, / 'The first-born child of the early sun.'
Exodus 13:13
And all 'the firstborn of man' among thy children shalt thou redeem.

220   Part III. i. 58-60   Quote: Approximate
While man was in stature / As towers in our time, / 'The first-born of Nature.'
Exodus 13:13
And all 'the firstborn of man' among thy children shalt thou redeem.

221   Part III. i. 58-61   Allusion
      While man was in stature / As towers in our time, / The
      first-born of Nature, / And, like her, sublime!
      Genesis 6:4
      There were giants in the earth in those days.

DOMESTIC PIECES

"The Dream"

222   Lines 124-25   Reference: Subject
      So cloudless, clear, and purely beautiful, / That 'God' a-
      lone was to be seen 'in Heaven.'
      II Chronicles 36:23
      All the kingdoms of the earth hath the Lord 'God of heaven'
      given me.

"Epistle to Augusta"

223   Line 5   Quote: Exact
      Go where I will, to me 'thou art the same.'
      Psalm 102:27
      But 'thou art the same,' and thy years shall have no end.

224   Lines 55-56   Quote: Exact
      And even at moments I could think I see / Some 'living
      thing' to love--but none like thee.
      Genesis 1:28
      And God said ... have dominion over ... every 'living thing'
      that moveth upon the earth.

"Fare Thee Well"

225   Lines 47-48   Quote: Aproximate
      All my hopes, 'where'er thou goest,' / Wither, yet with
      thee 'they go.'
      Ruth 1:16
      And Ruth said ... 'whither thou goest, I will go.'

"Lines: On Hearing That Lady Byron Was Ill"

226   Lines 23-24   Quote: Approximate
      Thou hast 'sown in my sorrow,' and must 'reap' / The bit-
      ter harvest 'in a woe' as real!
      Psalm 126:5
      They that 'sow in tears' shall 'reap in joy.'

227   Lines 37-38   Quote: Approximate
      (The moral Clytemnestra of thy lord!); / And 'hew'd down'
      with an unsuspected sword.

Deuteronomy 12:3
And ye shall 'hew down' the graven images of their gods.

"A Sketch"

228   Lines 85-88   Reference: Subject
May the strong curse of crush'd affections light / Back on
thy bosom with reflected blight! / And make thee, in thy
leprosy of mind, / As loathsome to thyself as to mankind!
Job 7:5
My flesh is clothed with worms and clods of dust; my skin
is broken and become loathsome.

"Stanzas to Augusta: Through the day of my destiny"

229   Lines 5-6   Quote: Approximate
Though thy soul 'with my grief was acquainted,' / It shrunk
not to share it with me.
Isaiah 53:3
He is ... a man of sorrows, and 'acquainted with grief.'

230   Lines 45-46   Reference: Subject
In the desert a fountain is springing, / In the wide waste
there still is a tree.
Isaiah 35:1-6
The wilderness and the solitary place shall be glad for them;
and the desert shall rejoice, ... for in the wilderness shall
waters break out, and streams in the desert.

DON JUAN

---

231   Dedication, 31-32   Reference: Subject
And he who understands it would be able / To add a story
to the Tower of Babel.
Genesis 11:1-9
Go to, let us build us a city and a tower, whose top may
reach unto heaven ... Therefore is the name of it called
Babel.

232   Dedication, 81-83   Reference: Subject
Think'st thou, could he--the blind Old Man--arise / Like
Samuel from the grave, to freeze once more / The blood
of monarchs with his prophecies.
I Samuel 28
Rf. Samuel's visit from the dead to speak to Saul.

233   Dedication, 125-26   Quote: Exact
Thy clanking chain, and Erin's yet green wounds, / Have

voices, to 'cry aloud' for me.

I Kings 18:27

And it came to pass at noon, that Elijah mocked them, and said, 'Cry aloud': for he is a god.

234 Canto I, 71-72   Reference: Parodic
Than Jose, who begot our hero, who / Begot--But that's to come--Well, to renew.
Genesis 5, 10, 11, 36, 46
Rf. "begat" chapters.

235 Canto I, 118-19   Quote: Exact
Whose suicide was almost an anomaly-- / One sad example more, that " 'All is vanity.' "
Ecclesiastes 1:2
Vanity of vanities, saith the Preacher, vanity of vanities; 'all is vanity.'

236 Canto I, 139-44   Reference: Parodic
Where our first parents never learn'd to kiss / ... Where all was peace, and innocence, and bliss / (I wonder how they got through the twelve hours), / Don José, like a lineal son of Eve, / Went plucking various fruit without her leave.
Genesis 3:1-24
Rf. Eve and the forbidden fruit.

237 Canto I, 140   Reference: Parodic
They [Adam and Eve] were exiled from their earlier bowers.
Genesis 3:23-24
Therefore the Lord God sent him forth from the garden of Eden, ... So he drove out the man.

238 Canto I, 459-60   Allusion
For from a root the ugliest in Old Spain / Sprung up a branch as beautiful as fresh.
Job 14:7-8
For there is hope of a tree, if it be cut down, that it will sprout again, and that the tender branch thereof will not cease. Though the root thereof wax old in the earth, and the stock thereof die in the ground.

239 Canto I, 499-501   Quote: Approximate
Who cannot leave alone our helpless clay, / But will keep baking, broiling, burning on, / That howsoever people 'fast and pray.'
Nehemiah 1:4
I sat down ... and 'fasted, and prayed' before the God of heaven.

240 Canto I, 518   Quote: Parodic
And not exactly either 'one' or two.

Genesis 2:23-24
And Adam said, This is now bone of my bones, and flesh
of my flesh: she shall be called Woman, because she was
taken out of Man.   Therefore shall a man leave his father
and his mother, and shall cleave unto his wife: and they
shall be 'one' flesh.

241   Canto I, 609-10   Quote: Exact
She now determined that 'a virtuous woman' / Should rather
face and overcome temptation.
Proverbs 31:10
Who can find 'a virtuous woman'? for her price is far a-
bove rubies.

242   Canto I, 1010-16   Reference: Parodic
Is first and passionate love--it stands alone, / Like Adam's
recollection of his fall; / The tree of knowledge has been
pluck'd--all's known-- / And life yields nothing further to
recall / Worthy of this ambrosial sin, so shown, / No
doubt in fable, as the unforgiven / Fire which Prometheus
filch'd for us from heaven.
Genesis 3:1-24
Rf. Adam and the forbidden fruit.

243   Canto I, 1073   Allusion
'Twas, as the watchmen say, a cloudy night.
Isaiah 21:11
Watchman, what of the night?   Watchman, what of the night?

244   Canto I, 1165-66   Quote: Exact
Is't wise or fitting, causeless to explore / For facts against
'a virtuous woman's' fame?
Proverbs 31:10
Who can find 'a virtuous woman'? for her price is far above
rubies.

245   Canto I, 1187-88   Quote: Parodic
Did not his countryman, Count Corniani, / Call me the only
'virtuous wife' in Spain?
Proverbs 31:10
Who can find a 'virtuous woman'? for her price is far above
rubies.

246   Canto I, 1203-1205   Quote: Parodic
Your attorney, / Whom I see standing there, and looking
sensible / Of 'having play'd' the fool?
I Samuel 26:21
Behold, I 'have played the fool, ' and have erred exceedingly.

247   Canto I, 1255   Reference: Subject
'God grant you' feel not then the bitterest grief!
I Samuel 1:17
And the 'God' of Israel 'grant thee' thy petition.

248 Canto I, 1279-80   Quote: Exact
     And ne'er believed in negatives, till these / Were proved
     by competent 'false witnesses. '
     Psalm 27:12
     Deliver me not over unto the will of mine enemies: for
     'false witnesses' are risen up against me.

249 Canto I, 1294   Reference: Parodic
     Alfonso saw his wife, and thought of Job's.
     Job 2:9
     Then said his wife unto him, Dost thou still retain thine in-
     tegrity / curse God, and die.

250 Canto I, 1299-1300   Allusion
     The anvil of his speech received the hammer, / With "Pray,
     sir, leave the room, and say no more. "
     Isaiah 41:7
     And he that smootheth with the hammer [encourages] him
     that smote the anvil.

251 Canto I, 1330-31   Reference: Subject
     He had no business to commit a sin, / Forbid by heavenly,
     fined by human laws.
     Leviticus 5:15
     If a soul commit a trespass, and sin.

252 Canto I, 1337-44   Reference: Parodic
     Of his position I can give no notion: / 'Tis written in the
     Hebrew Chronicle, / How the physicians, leaving pill and
     potion, / Prescribed, by way of blister, a young belle, /
     When old King David's blood grew dull in motion, / And
     that the medicine answer'd very well; / Perhaps 'twas in a
     different way applied, / For David lived, but Juan nearly
     died.
     I Kings 1:1-2
     Now King David was old and stricken in years; and they cov-
     ered him with clothes, but he gat no heat. Wherefore his
     servants said unto him, Let there be sought for my lord
     the king a young virgin: and let her stand before the king,
     ... and let her lie in thy bosom, that my lord the king may
     get heat.

253 Canto I, 1437-40   Reference: Parodic
     He stood like Adam lingering near his garden, / With use-
     less penitence perplex'd and haunted, / Beseeching she no
     further would refuse, / When, lo! he stumbled o'er a pair
     of shoes.
     Genesis 3:23-24
     Rf. expulsion of Adam from Eden.

254 Canto I, 1485-88   Reference: Parodic
     Juan contrived to give an awkward blow, / And then his only
     garment quite gave way; / He fled, like Joseph, leaving

it / but there, / I doubt, all likeness ends between the
pair.
Genesis 39:10-13
    As she spake to Joseph day by day, ... he hearkened not
    unto her, to lie by her, or to be with her ... And she
    caught him by his garment, saying, Lie with me: and he
    left his garment in her hand, and fled, and got him out.

255   Canto I, 1625-28   Reference: Parodic
    If ever I should condescend to prose, / I'll write poetical
    commandments, which / Shall supersede beyond all doubt
    all those / That went before.
Exodus 20:1-17; Deuteronomy 5:1-21
    Rf. the Ten Commandments.

256   Canto I, 1641-42   Quote: Parodic
    'Thou shalt not covet' Mr. Sotheby's Muse, / 'His Pegasus,
    nor anything that's his.'
Exodus 20:17
    'Thou shalt not covet' thy neighbour's house, thou shalt not
    covet thy neighbour's wife, nor his manservant, nor his
    maidservant, nor his ox, 'nor his ass, nor any thing that
    is thy neighbour's.'

257   Canto I, 1643   Quote: Exact
    'Thou shalt not bear false witness' like "the Blues."
Exodus 20:16
    'Thou shalt not bear false witness' against thy neighbour.

258   Canto I, 1705-1706   Reference: Subject
    No more--no more--Oh! never more on me / The freshness
    of the heart can fall like dew.
Proverbs 19:12
    The king's wrath is as the roaring of a lion; but his favour
    is as dew upon the grass.

259   Canto I, 1739-40   Allusion: Parodic
    Some liken it to climbing up a hill, / Whose summit, like
    all hills, is lost in vapour.
Exodus 19:16, 18
    There were thunders and lightnings, and a thick cloud upon
    the mount, ... And mount Sinai was altogether on a smoke.

260   Canto I, 1756-57   Quote: Approximate
    And 'flesh' (which Death mows down to hay) 'is grass'; /
    You've pass'd your youth not so unpleasantly.
Isaiah 40:6
    The voice said, Cry. And he said, What shall I cry? 'All
    flesh is grass,' and all the goodliness thereof is as the flo-
    wer of the field.

261   Canto I, 1769-70   Quote: Parodic
    Go, little book, from this my solitude! / I 'cast thee on the
    waters'--go thy ways!

Ecclesiastes 11:1

'Cast thy bread upon the waters': for thou shalt find it after many days.

262 Canto II, 10-11   Quote: Approximate

In the third form, or even in the fourth, / His 'daily task' had kept his fancy cool.

Exodus 5:13

And the taskmasters hasted them, saying, Fulfill your works, your 'daily tasks,' as when there was straw.

263 Canto II, 21-22   Quote: Exact

That's quite natural, / Or else the thing had hardly 'come to pass.'

Exodus 4:8

And it shall 'come to pass.'

264 Canto II, 53-54   Quote: Parodic

Oh love! 'when I forget you,' may I fail / To--say my prayers.

Psalm 137:5

'If I forget thee,' O Jerusalem, let my right hand forget her cunning.

265 Canto II, 62-64   Reference: Parodic

As if a Spanish ship were Noah's ark, / To wean him from the wickedness of earth, / And send him like a dove of promise forth.

Genesis 6-9 (esp. 8:6-12)

Noah opened the window of the ark which he had made ... he sent forth a dove from him, to see if the waters were abated.

266 Canto II, 121-22   Reference: Parodic

So Juan wept, as wept the captive Jews / By Babel's waters, still remembering Sion.

Psalm 137:1

By the rivers of Babylon, there we sat down, yea, we wept, when we remembered Zion.

267 Canto II, 145-46   Quote: Parodic

And, oh! 'if e'er I should forget,' I swear-- / But that's impossible, and cannot be.

Psalm 137:5

'If I forget' thee, O Jerusalem, let my right hand forget her cunning.

268 Canto II, 289-91   Quote: Exact

The good old gentleman was quite aghast, / And made a loud and pious lamentation; / Repented 'all his sins.'

Ezekiel 18:21

But if the wicked will turn from 'all his sins.'

269   Canto II, 355-56   Reference: Subject
    Some 'cursed the day on which they saw the sun,' / And
gnash'd their teeth.
Jeremiah 20:14
    'Cursed by the day' wherein I was born.

270   Canto II, 452-53   Allusion: Parodic
    O'er the cutter's edge he tried to cross, / And so he found
a wine-and-watery grave.
Isaiah 1:22
    Thy silver is become dross, thy wine mixed with water.

271   Canto II, 538-39   Quote: Approximate
    For on the third day there came on a calm, / And though
at first 'their strength it might renew.'
Isaiah 41:1
    Keep silence before me, O islands; and let the people 're-
new their strength.'

272   Canto II, 538, 553   Quote: Parodic
    For on 'the third day' there came on a calm / ... 'The
fourth day' came ... / 'The fifth day' ... / 'On the sixth
day' ... / 'The seventh day,' and no wind.
Genesis 1:13-2:2
    And the evening and the morning were 'the third day' ...
'the fourth day' ... 'the fifth day' ... 'the sixth day' ... And
on 'the seventh day' God ended his work.

273   Canto II, 730-31   Quote: Aproximate
    The airy child of vapour and the sun, / 'Brought forth' in
purple, cradled in vermilion.
Genesis 1:21
    And God created ... every living creature that moveth, which
the waters 'brought forth' abundantly.

274   Canto II, 755-60   Reference: Parodic
    Because the tackle of our shatter'd bark / Was not so safe
for roosting as a church; / And had it been the dove from
Noah's ark, / Returning there from her successful search, /
Which in their way that moment chanced to fall, / They
would have eat her, olive-branch and all.
Genesis 8:8-12
    Also he sent forth a dove from him, to see if the waters
were abated from off the face of the ground; But the dove
found no rest for the sole of her foot, and she returned un-
to him into the ark ... And the dove came in to him ... and,
lo, in her mouth was an olive leaf.

275   Canto II, 813-14   Allusion
    By night chill'd, by day scorch'd, thus one by one / They
perish'd.
Genesis 31:40
    In the day the drought consumed me, and the frost by night.

276 Canto II, 993-94

Quote: Approximate

A fisherman he had been 'in his youth,' / And still a sort
of fisherman was he.

Leviticus 22:13

And is returned unto her father's house, as 'in her youth,'
she shall eat of her father's meat.

277 Canto II, 1125-28

Reference: Subject

Like to a torrent which a mountain's base, / That over-
powers some Alpine river's rush, / Checks to a lake, whose
waves in circles spread; / Or the Red Sea--but the sea is
not red.

Exodus 14:21

Rf. Moses' parting of the Red Sea.

278 Canto II, 1250-53

Quote: Parodic

And he saw / A sight on which he had not lately gazed, /
As all his latter meals had been quite raw, / Three or four
things, for which 'the Lord he praised.'

I Chronicles 16:25

For great is 'the Lord,' and greatly to 'be praised.'

279 Canto II, 1324-25

Quote: Parodic

Like other men, too, may have had my passion-- / But
that, like other things, has 'pass'd away.'

Psalm 37:36

Yet he 'passed away,' and, lo, he was not.

280 Canto II, 1505-1506

Quote: Approximate

They fear'd no eyes nor ears on that lone beach, / They
felt no 'terrors from the night.'

Psalm 91:5

Thou shalt not be afraid for the 'terror by night.'

281 Canto II, 1511-12

Reference: Subject

Of nature's oracle--first love,--that all / Which Eve has
left her daughters since her fall.

Genesis 3:1-24

Unto the woman he said, I will greatly multiply thy sorrow
and thy conception ... and thy desire shall be to thy hus-
band, and he shall rule over thee.

282 Canto II, 1538-40

Reference: Parodic

Till then never, / Excepting our first parents, such a pair /
Had run the risk of being damn'd for ever.

Genesis 3:1-24

But of the fruit of the tree which is in the midst of the gar-
den, God hath said, Ye shall not eat of it, neither shall ye
touch it, lest ye die.

283 Canto II, 1557

Quote: Approximate

And now and then 'her eye to heaven' is cast.

Deuteronomy 4:19
    And lest thou 'lift up thine eyes unto heaven.'

284   Canto II, 1585-86   Quote: Exact
        Alas! 'the love of women!' it is known / To be a lovely
        and a fearful thing.
    II Samuel 1:26
        Thy love to me was wonderful, passing 'the love of women.'

285   Canto II, 1695-96   Reference: Parodic
        With one or two small senses added, just / To hint that
        flesh is form'd of fiery dust.
    Genesis 2:7
        And the Lord God formed man of the dust of the ground,
        and breathed into his nostrils the breath of life; and man
        became a living soul.

286   Canto II, 1699-1700   Reference: Parodic
        In the same object graces quite as killing / As when she
        rose upon us like an Eve.
    Genesis 3:6, 20
        Rf. temptation of Eve.

287   Canto III, 79-80   Reference: Parodic
        But Dante's Beatrice and Milton's Eve / Were not drawn
        from their spouses, you conceive.
    Genesis 2:21-22
        And the Lord God caused a deep sleep to fall upon Adam,
        and he slept: and he took one of his ribs, and closed up
        the flesh instead thereof; And the rib, which the Lord God
        had taken from man, made he a woman, and brought her
        unto the man.

288   Canto III, 101-102   Quote: Parodic
        When we have what we like, 't is hard to miss it, / At
        least 'in the beginning,' ere one tires.
    Genesis 1:1
        'In the beginning' God created the heaven and the earth.

289   Canto III, 281-82   Quote: Parodic
        Ah! 'what is man?' what perils still environ / The happiest
        mortals even after dinner.
    Psalm 8:4
        'What is man,' that thou art mindful of him?

290   Canto III, 382   Quote: Exact
        His angry word once o'er, he 'shed no blood.'
    Genesis 37:22
        And Reuben said unto them, 'Shed no blood,' but cast
        him into this pit.

291   Canto III, 454-55   Reference: Parodic
        There wanted but the loss of this to wean / His feelings

from all milk of human kindness.
Isaiah 28:9
Whom shall he teach knowledge? ... them that are weaned
from the milk, and drawn from the breasts.

292 Canto III, 513-18   Reference: Parodic
These Oriental writings on the wall, / Quite common in
those countries, are a kind / Of monitors adapted to re-
call, / Like skulls at Memphian banquets, to the mind / The
words which shook Belshazzar in his hall, / And took his
kingdom from him.
Daniel 5:17-31
Rf. the handwriting on the wall before Belshazzar.

293 Canto III, 623-24   Quote: Parodic
He being paid to satirize or flatter, / As the psalm says,
" 'inditing a good matter.' "
Psalm 45:1
My heart is 'inditing a good matter': I speak of the things
which I have made touching the king.

294 Canto III, 851-52   Reference: Parodic
But Wordsworth's poem, and his followers, like / Joanna
Southcote's Shiloh, and her sect.
Joshua 18:1-10
Rf. Shiloh, the temporary location of the Hebrew ark of
the covenant.

295 Canto III, 855-56   Allusion: Parodic
And the new births of both their stale virginities / Have
proved but dropsies, taken for divinities.
Isaiah 7:14
Therefore the Lord himself shall give you a sign; Behold,
a virgin shall conceive, and bear a son, and shall call his
name Immanuel.

296 Canto III, 917-18   Quote: Approximate
Ave Maria! oh that face so fair! / Those downcast eyes be-
neath 'the Almighty dove.'
Genesis 17:1
The Lord appeared to Abram, and said unto him, I am 'the
Almighty God.'

297 Canto III, 927-28   Allusion
All that springs from the great Whole, / Who hath produced,
and will receive the soul.
Genesis 2:7; 3:19
And the Lord God formed man of the dust of the ground ...
For dust thou art, and unto dust shalt thou return.

298 Canto IV, 4-8   Reference: Subject
And down we tend, / Like Lucifer when hurl'd from heaven
for sinning; / Our sin the same, and hard as his to mend, /

Being pride, which leads the mind to soar too far, / Till
our own weakness shows us what we are.

Isaiah 14:12

How art thou fallen from heaven, O Lucifer, son of the
morning!

299 Canto IV, 73-74   Allusion
They were alone once more; for them to be / Thus was
another Eden.

Genesis 2-3

Rf. Adam and Eve in Eden.

300 Canto IV, 83-84   Reference: Parodic
The precious porcelain of human clay, / Break with the
first fall.

Genesis 3:1-24

Rf. fall of Adam and Eve.

301 Canto IV, 239-40   Reference: Parodic
Strange state of being! (for 'tis still to be) / Senseless to
feel, and with seal'd eyes to see.

Isaiah 6:10

Make their ears heavy, and shut their eyes; lest they see
with their eyes, ... and understand with their heart, and
convert, and be healed.

302 Canto IV, 316-17   Quote: Approximate
And drawing from his belt a pistol, he / Replied, 'Your
blood be then on your own head. '

Leviticus 20:9

He hath cursed his father or his mother; 'his blood shall
be upon him. '

303 Canto IV, 365   Quote: Approximate
Not I have 'made this desolation. '

Joshua 8:28

And Joshua burnt Ai, and 'made' it an heap for ever, even
'a desolation' unto this day.

304 Canto IV, 431-32   Allusion
Her mother was a Moorish maid, from Fez, / Where all is
Eden, or a wilderness.

Genesis 2:8

And the Lord God planted a garden eastward in Eden; and
there he put the man whom he had formed.

305 Canto IV, 516-17   Reference: Subject
On him her flashing eyes a moment bent, / Then to the
wall she turn'd.

II Kings 20:2

Then he turned his face to the wall, and prayed.

306 Canto IV, 557-60   Reference: Subject
And went down to the grave unborn, wherein / Blossom and

bough lie wither'd with one blight; / In vain the dews of
Heaven descend above / The bleeding flower and 'blasted
fruit' of love.

II Kings 19:26
They were as the grass of the field, ... and as 'corn blast-
ed' before it be grown up.

307- Canto IV, 559-60   Quote Exact
      In vain 'the dews of Heaven' descend above / The bleeding
      flower and blasted fruit of love.
      Genesis 27:28
          Therefore God give thee of 'the dew of heaven,' and the fat-
          ness of the earth.

308   Canto IV, 841-42   Allusion: Parodic
      Yet there will still be bards: though fame is smoke, / Its
      fumes are frankincense to human thought.
      Exodus 30:34
          And the Lord said unto Moses, Take unto thee ... these
          sweet spices with pure frankincense.

309   Canto V, 111-12   Quote: Approximate
      She has served me also much the same as you, / Except
      that I have found it 'nothing new.'
      Ecclesiastes 1:9
          And that which is done is that which shall be done: and
          there is 'no new thing' under the sun.

310   Canto V, 121-22   Allusion: Parodic
      "Have you no friends?"--"I had--but, 'by God's blessing,' /
      Have not been troubled with them lately."
      Psalm 129:8
          The 'blessing of the Lord' be upon you: we bless you in
          the name of the Lord.

311   Canto V, 174-75   Quote: Parodic
      Ambition, Avarice, Vengeance, Glory, glue / The glittering
      lime-twigs of 'our latter days.'
      Numbers 24:14
          Come therefore, and I will advertise thee what this people
          shall do to thy people in 'the latter days.'

312   Canto V, 351-52   Reference: Parodic
      Besides, I'm hungry, and just now would take, / Like Esau,
      for my birthright a beef-steak.
      Genesis 25:30-34
          And Esau said to Jacob, Feed me, I pray thee, with that
          same red pottage; for I am faint ... And Jacob said, Sell
          me this day thy birthright.

313   Canto V, 470   Reference: Subject
      And huge tombs worse--mankind, since Adam fell.

Genesis 3:1-24
Rf. fall of Adam.

314   Canto V, 471-74   Reference: Parodic
Methinks the story of the tower of Babel / Might teach them
this much better than I'm able. / Babel was Nimrod's hunt-
ing-box, and then / a town of gardens, walls, and wealth
amazing.
Genesis 10:10; 11:1-9
Nimrod: He began to be a mighty one in the earth. He
was a mighty hunter before the Lord. ... And the beginning
of his kingdom was Babel.

315   Canto V, 475-76   Reference: Parodic
Where Nabuchadonosor, king of men, / Reign'd till one
summer's day he took to grazing.
Daniel 4:33
The same hour was the thing fulfilled upon Nebuchadnezzar:
and he was driven from men, and did eat grass as oxen.

316   Canto V, 477-78   Reference: Parodic
And Daniel tamed the lions in their den, / The people's
awe and admiration raising.
Daniel 6:21-22
Then said Daniel ... My God hath sent his angel, and hath
shut the lions' mouths, that they have not hurt me.

317   Canto V, 489-504   Reference: Parodic
But to resume,--should there be (what may not / Be in
these days?) some infidels, who don't, / Because they can't
find out the very spot / Of that same Babel, or because
they won't / (Though Claudius Rich, Esquire, some bricks
has got, / And written lately two memoirs upon't).
Genesis 11:1-9
Rf. tower of Babel.

318   Canto V, 644-46   Reference: Parodic
No trifling, sir; for when / I say a thing, it must at once
be done. / What fear you? think you this a lion's den?
Daniel 6:16
Then the king commanded, and they brought Daniel, and
cast him into the den of lions.

319   Canto V, 670-72   Reference: Parodic
"Keep your good name; though Eve herself once fell." / "Nay,"
quoth the maid, "the Sultan's self shan't carry me, / Unless
his highness promises to marry me."
Genesis 3:1-24
Rf. fall of Eve.

320   Canto V, 865-68   Reference: Parodic
Her form had all the softness of her sex, / Her features
all the sweetness of the devil, / When he put on the cherub

to perplex / Eve, and paved (God knows how) the road to
evil.
Genesis 3:1-24
Now the serpent was more subtil than any beast of the
field ... And the serpent said unto the woman, Ye shall
not surely die ... ye shall be as gods, knowing good and
evil.

321 Canto V, 1042   Reference: Parodic
The spouse of Potiphar, the Lady Booby.
Genesis 39:7-20
Rf. Joseph's temptation by Potiphar's wife.

322 Canto V, 1097-1101   Reference: Subject
It teaches them that they are flesh and blood, / It also
gently hints to them that others, / Although of clay, are
yet not quite of mud; / That urns and pipkins are but fra-
gile brothers, / And works of the same pottery, bad or
good.
Jeremiah 18-19
Rf. the potter and the clay.

323 Canto V, 1123-24   Reference: Parodic
To be slain with pangs refined, / Or thrown to lions, or
made baits for fish.
Daniel 6:16
Then the king commanded, and they brought Daniel, and
cast him into the den of lions.

324 Canto VI, 20-21   Reference: Parodic
Beloved in her own way, and rather whisk / The stars from
out the sky, than not be free.
Daniel 8:10
And it waxed great, even to the host of heaven; and it cast
down some of the host and of the stars to the ground, and
stamped upon them.

325 Canto VI, 51-52   Reference: Parodic
For gentlemen must sometimes risk their skin / For that
sad tempter, a forbidden woman.
Genesis 3:1-24
Rf. Eve and the temptation by the serpent.

326 Canto VI, 82-83   Quote: Exact
The heathen also, though with lesser latitude, / Are apt to
carry things 'with a high hand. '
Exodus 14:8
And the children of Israel went out 'with an high hand. '

327 Canto VI, 253-55   Quote: Parodic
A slight example, just to cast a shade / Along the rest,
contrived to keep this 'den / Of beauties' cool as an Italian
convent.

Daniel 6:7
Whosoever shall ask a petition of any God or man for thirty days, save of thee, O king, he shall be cast into the 'den of lions. '

328 Canto VI, 541   Reference: Parodic
Or Lot's wife done in salt,--or what you will.
Genesis 19:26
But his wife looked back from behind him, and she became a pillar of salt.

329 Canto VI, 556-57   Quote: Exact
But ere 'the middle watch' was hardly over, / when the fading lamps waned dim.
Judges 7:19
So Gideon ... came unto the outside of the camp in the beginning of 'the middle watch. '

330 Canto VI, 593-94   Quote: Exact
At length she said, that in a slumber sound / She 'dream'd a dream, ' of walking in a wood.
Genesis 37:5
And Joseph 'dreamed a dream, ' and he told it his brethren.

331 Canto VI, 593-616   Reference: Subject
At length she said, that in a slumber sound / She dream'd a dream, of walking in a wood-- / ... And that this wood was full of pleasant fruits, / And trees of goodly growth and spreading roots; / And in the midst a golden apple grew,.. / A most prodigious pippin ... / when she least had hope, / It fell down of its own accord before / Her feet ... / just as her young lip began to open / Upon the golden fruit the vision bore, / A bee flew out and stung her to the heart.
Genesis 3:1-24
Rf. temptation of Eve.

332 Canto VI, 617-24   Reference: Parodic
All this she told with some confusion and / Dismay, the usual consequence of dreams / Of the unpleasant kind, with none at hand / To expound their vain and visionary gleams. / I've known some odd ones which seem'd really plann'd / Prophetically, or that which one deems / A 'strange coincidence, to use a phrase / By which such things are settled now-a-days.
Daniel 2, 4
Rf. the interpretation of dreams by Daniel.

333 Canto VII, 41-43   Quote: Exact
Ecclesiastes said, "that 'all is vanity' "-- / Most modern preachers say the same, or show it / By their examples of true Christianity.

Ecclesiastes 1:2
> Vanity of vanities, saith the Preacher, vanity of vanities;
> 'all is vanity.'

334   Canto VII, 197-200   Reference: Parodic
> One of the valorous "Smiths" whom we shall miss / ... But
> 't is a name so spread o'er "Sir" and "Madam," / That one
> would think the first who bore it "Adam."

Genesis 2:7-8, 19
> Rf. Adam, the first man.

335   Canto VII, 211-13   Quote: Parodic
> Or some contractor's personal cupidity, / 'Saving his soul'
> by cheating in the ware / Of homicide.

Ezekiel 18:27
> Again, when the wicked man turneth away from his wicked-
> ness ... he shall 'save his soul' alive.

336   Canto VII, 321-22   Quote: Exact
> ' "Let there be light!" said God, and there was light!' /
> "let there be blood!" says man, and there's a sea!

Genesis 1:3
> 'And God said, Let there be light: and there was light.'

337   Canto VII, 326-28   Reference: Parodic
> Summers could renovate, though they should be / Lovely as
> those which ripen'd Eden's fruit.

Genesis 1-3
> Rf. garden of Eden.

338   Canto VII, 326-28   Reference: Subject
> Summers could renovate, though they should be / Lovely as
> those which ripen'd Eden's fruit; / For war cuts up not
> only 'branch,' but 'root.'

Daniel 11:7
> But out of a 'branch' of her 'roots' shall one stand up in
> his estate, which shall come with an army, and shall enter
> into the fortress of the king.

339   Canto VII, 328   Reference: Subject
> For war cuts up not only branch, but root.

Malachi 4:1
> And the day that cometh shall burn them up, saith the Lord
> of hosts, that it shall leave them neither root nor branch.

340   Canto VII, 381-84   Quote: Parodic
> 'As a little dog will lead the blind,' / Or a bell-wether
> form the flock's connection / By tinkling sounds, when they
> go forth to victual; / Such is the sway of your great men
> o'er little.

Isaiah 11:6
> The wolf also shall dwell with the lamb, ... and 'a little
> child shall lead them.'

341 Canto VII, 415-16   Reference: Parodic
     He show'd them how to mount a ladder (which / Was not
     like Jacob's) or to cross a ditch.
     Genesis 28:10-15
     And Jacob ... dreamed, and behold a ladder set up on the
     earth, and the top of it reached to heaven: and behold the
     angels of God ascending and descending on it.

342 Canto VII, 501-502   Reference: Subject
     I have vow'd / To several saints, that shortly plough or
     harrow / Shall pass o'er what was Ismail.
     Jeremiah 26:18
     Thus saith the Lord of hosts; Zion shall be plowed like a
     field, and Jerusalem shall become heaps.

343 Canto VII, 509-10   Reference: Parodic
     A preacher had held forth (who nobly spurn'd / All earthly
     goods save tithes).
     Leviticus 27:30-32; Numbers 18:26
     Rf. Hebrew tithe offerings.

344 Canto VII, 560   Allusion
     Save wed a year, I hate recruits with wives.
     Deuteronomy 24:5
     When a man hath taken a new wife, he shall not go out to
     war, ... but he shall be free at home one year.

345 Canto VII, 613-15   Reference: Subject
     And cared as little for his army's loss / (So that their ef-
     forts should at length prevail) / As wife and friends did for
     the boils of Job.
     Job 2:7, 9
     Satan ... smote Job with sore boils. ... Then said his wife
     unto him, ... curse God, and die.

346 Canto VII, 687-88   Allusion
     How soon the smoke / Of Hell shall pall them in a deeper
     cloak!
     Deuteronomy 32:22
     For a fire is kindled in mine anger, and shall burn unto the
     lowest hell, and shall consume the earth with her increase,
     and set on fire the foundations of the mountains.

347 Canto VIII, 80   Parallelism
     " 'Ashes to Ashes' "--why not lead to lead?
     Genesis 3:19
     For 'dust' thou art, and 'unto dust' shalt thou return.

348 Canto VIII, 140-41   Reference: Subject
     In ditches, fields, or whereso'er they felt / Their clay for
     the last time their souls encumber.
     Genesis 3:19
     For dust thou art, and unto dust shalt thou return.

349 Canto VIII, 157-60   Reference: Parodic
     Repulsed by the close fire, / Which really pour'd as if all
     hell were raining / Instead of heaven, they stumbled back-
     wards o'er / A wounded comrade, sprawling in his gore.
     Genesis 19:24
     Then the Lord rained upon Sodom and upon Gomorrah brim-
     stone and fire from the Lord out of heaven.

350 Canto VIII, 209-10   Quote: Parodic
     Juan, by some strange chance, which oft 'divides / Warrior
     from warrior' in their grim career.
     Genesis 1:14, 18
     And God said, Let there be lights in the firmament of the
     heaven to 'divide the day from the night ... and to divide
     the light' from the darkness.

351 Canto VIII, 262-64   Parallelism
     And the loud cannon peal'd his hoarsest strains, / He rush'd,
     while 'earth' and air were sadly 'shaken' / By thy humane
     discovery, Friar Bacon!
     Isaiah 2:19
     He ariseth to 'shake' terribly the 'earth. '

352 Canto VIII, 287-88   Quote: Parodic
     Johnson retired a little, just to rally / Those who catch
     cold in " 'shadows of Death's valley. ' "
     Psalm 23:4
     Yea, though I walk through 'the valley of the shadow of
     death, ' I will fear no evil.

353 Canto VIII, 393-94   Quote: Parodic
     But never mind;--" 'God save the king' " and kings! / For
     if he don't, I doubt if men will longer.
     I Samuel 10:24
     And all the people shouted, and said, 'God save the king. '

354 Canto VIII, 395-96   Reference: Subject
     I think I hear 'a little bird, ' who sings / The people by and
     by will be the stronger.
     Ecclesiastes 10:20
     And curse not the rich in thy bedchamber: for 'a bird of
     the air' shall carry thy voice, and that which hath wings
     shall tell the matter.

355 Canto VIII, 399-400   Reference: Parodic
     And the mob / At last fall sick of imitating Job.
     Job 1:22
     In all this Job sinned not, nor charged God foolishly.

356 Canto VIII, 473-74   Reference: Subject
     The town was enter'd. Oh eternity!-- / "God made the
     country and man made the town. "

Genesis 1:1
In the beginning God created the heaven and the earth.

357   Canto VIII, 476-78   Reference: Subject
And I begin to be / Of his opinion, when I see cast down /
Rome, Babylon, Tyre, Carthage, 'Nineveh,' / All walls
men know, and many never known.
Jonah 3:4
And Jonah ... said, Yet forty days, and 'Nineveh' shall be
overthrown.

358   Canto VIII, 524   Allusion
The green woods were their portions.
Genesis 14:24
Save only that which the young men have eaten, and the por-
tion of the men which went with me, ... let them take their
portion.

359   Canto VIII, 659-61   Reference: Parodic
The serpent's head / Whose fangs Eve taught her human
seed to feel: / In vain he kick'd, and swore, and writhed,
and bled.
Genesis 3:14-15
And the Lord God said unto the serpent. ... And I will put
enmity between thee and the woman, and between thy seed
and her seed; it shall bruise thy head, and thou shalt bruise
his heel.

360   Canto VIII, 915-16   Reference: Subject
He shouted "Allah!" and saw Paradise / With all its veil of
mystery drawn apart.
Exodus 26:31-33
Rf. the veil of the Hebrew temple.

361   Canto VIII, 923-24   Quote: Exact
Or aught except his florid race / Who 'grew like cedars'
round him gloriously.
Psalm 92:12
The righteous shall flourish like the palm tree: he shall
'grow like a cedar' in Lebanon

362   Canto VIII, 1065-71   Reference: Parodic
Methinks these are the most tremendous words / Since
"Menè, Menè, Tekel," and "Upharsin," / Which hands or
pens have ever traced of swords. / Heaven help me! I'm
but little of a parson: / What Daniel read was short-hand
of the Lord's / Severe, sublime; the prophet wrote no farce
on / The fate of nations.
Daniel 5:25-30
Rf. the handwriting on the wall before Belshazzar.

363   Canto IX, 38-40   Reference: Parodic
      May like being praised for every lucky blunder, / Call'd
      "Saviour of the Nations"--not yet saved, / And "Europe's
      Liberator"--still enslaved.
      II Samuel 22:3
      He is my shield, and the horn of my salvation, my high
      tower, and my refuge, my saviour.

364   Canto IX, 102-103   Reference: Parodic
      Like bubbles on an ocean much less ample / Than the
      eternal deluge.
      Genesis 6-9
      Rf. the flood from which Noah was saved.

365   Canto IX, 110-12   Quote: Exact
      Could I dash on / Through fifty victories to shame or
      fame-- / Without a stomach what were 'a good name'?
      Proverbs 22:1
      'A good name' is rather to be chosen than great riches.

366   Canto IX, 146-48   Reference: Parodic
      We have / Souls to save, since Eve's slip and Adam's
      fall, / Which tumbled all mankind into the grave.
      Genesis 3:6
      And when the woman saw that the tree was good for food,
      and that it was pleasant ... she took of the fruit thereof,
      and did eat, and gave also unto her husband with her;
      and he did eat.

367   Canto IX, 151-52   Reference: Parodic
      Probably it [the fallen sparrow] perch'd / Upon the tree
      which Eve so fondly search'd.
      Genesis 3:6
      And when the woman saw that the tree was good for food,
      and that it was pleasant to the eyes, and a tree to be de-
      sired to make one wise, she took of the fruit thereof.

368   Canto IX, 161-63   Reference: Parodic
      But I, the mildest, meekest of mankind, / Like Moses,
      or Melancthon, who have ne'er / Done anything exceed-
      ingly unkind.
      Numbers 12:3
      Now the man Moses was very meek, above all the men
      which were upon the face of the earth.

369   Canto IX, 189   Quote: Exact
      'I know not' who may conquer.
      Genesis 4:9
      Where is Abel thy brother? And he said, 'I know not.'

370   Canto IX, 197-98   Quote: Parodic
      Whether 'they may sow scepticism to reap hell,' / As
      is the Christian dogma rather rough.

Hosea 8:7
For 'they have sown the wind, ' and 'they shall reap the whirlwind. '

371 Canto IX, 225-27   Reference: Parodic
Don Juan, who had shone in the late slaughter, / Was left upon his way with the despatch, / Where blood was talk'd of as we would of water.
Exodus 4:9
Thou shalt take of the water of the river, and pour it upon the dry land: and the water which thou takest out of the river shall become blood upon the dry land.

372 Canto IX, 246-48   Reference: Parodic
[Nature] nor admits a barge / On her canals, where God takes sea and land, / Fishery and farm, both 'unto his own hand. '
Psalm 95:4
'In his hand' are the deep places of the earth: the strength of the hills is his also.

373 Canto IX, 295-96   Allusion
First out of, and then back again to chaos, / The super-stratum which will overlay us.
Genesis 1:2
Rf. the creation from chaos.

374 Canto IX, 313-20   Reference: Subject
How will--to these young people, just thrust out / From some fresh Paradise, and set to plough, / And dig, and sweat, and turn themselves about, / And plant, and reap, and spin, and grind, and sow, / Till all the arts at length are brought about, / Especially of war and taxing,--how, I say, will these great relics, when they see 'em, / Look the monsters of a new museum?
Genesis 3:1-24
Rf. expulsion of Adam and Eve from Eden and their punishment.

375 Canto IX, 345-48   Reference: Parodic
Suppose him sword by side, and hat in hand, / Made up by youth, fame, and an army tailor-- / That great enchanter, at whose rod's command / Beauty springs forth.
Numbers 20:11
And Moses lifted up his hand, and with his rod he smote the rock twice: and the water came out abundantly.

376 Canto IX, 433-34   Quote: Approximate
Oh thou "teterrima causa" of all "belli"-- / Thou 'gate of' life and 'death'--thou nondescript!
Job 38:17
Have the 'gates of death' been opened unto thee? Or hast thou seen the doors of the shadow of death?

377   Canto IX, 437-40   Reference: Parodic
      How man fell I / Know not, since knowledge saw her branch-
      es stript / Of her first fruit; but how he falls and rises /
      Since, thou hast settled beyond all surmises.
      Genesis 3:1-24
      Rf. the tree of knowledge and man's fall.

378   Canto IX, 438-39   Reference: Parodic
      Since knowledge saw her branches stript / Of her first
      fruit.
      Genesis 3:1-7
      Rf. the eating of the forbidden fruit of the tree of knowledge
      by Adam and Eve.

379   Canto IX, 438-39   Quote: Approximate
      Since knowledge saw her branches stript / Of her 'first
      fruit. '
      Exodus 22:29
      Thou shalt not delay to offer the 'first of thy ripe fruits'
      and of thy liquors.

380   Canto IX, 441-43   Allusion
      Some call thee [the teterrima causa,* or God] "the worst
      cause of war," but I / Maintain thou art the best: for af-
      ter all / 'From thee we come, to thee we go. '
      Ecclesiastes 12:7
      Then shall the dust return to the earth as it was: and the
      spirit shall return unto God who gave it.

381   Canto IX, 510-12   Allusion: Parodic
      Whatever she [woman] has said / Or done, is light to what
      she'll say or do;-- / The oldest thing on record, and yet
      new!
      Genesis 3:1-24
      Rf. the sin of Eve.

382   Canto IX, 527-28   Allusion
      And by God's blessing / With youth and health all kisses
      are "heaven-kissing. "
      Exodus 32:29
      Consecrate yourselves to day to the Lord, even every man
      upon his son, ... that he may bestow upon you a blessing
      this day.

383   Canto IX, 545-48   Reference: Parodic
      Besides, he was of that delighted age / Which makes all
      female ages equal--when / We don't much care with whom
      we may engage, / As bold as Daniel in the lion's den.

*Teterrima causa (from adj. , taeter, L.)--foul, noissome, hateful,
hideous, disgraceful, abominable.

Daniel 6:16
Then the king commanded, and they brought Daniel, and
cast him into the den of lions.

384 Canto IX, 599-600   Reference: Subject
What a curious way / The whole thing is of clothing souls
in clay!
Genesis 2:7
And the Lord God formed man of the dust of the ground.

385 Canto X, 1-8   Reference: Parodic
When Newton saw an apple fall, he found / In that slight
startle from his contemplation--'Tis 'said' (for I'll not an-
swer above ground / For any sage's creed or calculation)-- /
A mode of proving that the earth turn'd round / In a most
natural whirl, called "gravitation"; / And this is the sole
mortal who could grapple, / Since Adam, with a fall or
with an apple.
Genesis 3:1-24
Rf. the fatal fruit and Adam's fall.

386 Canto X, 7-10   Reference: Parodic
And this is the sole mortal who could grapple, / Since Adam,
with a fall or with an apple, / Man fell with apples, and
with apples rose, / If this be true.
Genesis 3:1-24
Rf. eating of the forbidden fruit and consequent fall of
Adam.

387 Canto X, 39-42   Quote: Parodic
Of youth, and vigour, beauty, and those things / Which for
an instant clip enjoyment's wings. / But soon they grow a-
gain and leave their nest. / " 'Oh!' " saith the Psalmist,
" 'that I had a dove's / Pinions to flee away, and be at
rest!' "
Psalm 55:6
And I said, 'Oh that I had wings like a dove! for then
would I fly away, and be at rest.'

388 Canto X, 168   Allusion
[Revelry] made ice seem paradise, and winter sunny.
Genesis 2-3
Rf. the garden of Eden.

389 Canto X, 273-78   Reference: Subject
She was no hypocrite at least, poor soul, / But went to
heaven in as sincere a way / As any body on the 'elected'
roll, / Which portions out upon the judgment day. / Heav-
en's freeholds, in a sort of doomsday scroll.
Isaiah 42:1
Behold my servant, whom I uphold; mine 'elect,' in whom
my soul delighteth.

390 Canto X, 298-99   Reference: Subject
    The cankerworm / Will feed upon the fairest, freshest
    cheek.
    Joel 1:4
    That which the locust hath left hath the cankerworm eaten;
    and that which the cankerworm hath left hath the caterpiller
    eaten.

391 Canto X, 349-50   Quote: Approximate
    But when she saw his dazzling 'eye wax dim,' / And droop-
    ing like an eagle's with clipt pinion.
    I Samuel 3:2
    When Eli was laid down in his place, and his 'eyes began to
    wax dim,' that he could not see.

392 Canto X, 457-58   Quote: Exact
    They journey'd on through Poland and through Warsaw, / Fa-
    mous for mines of salt and 'yokes of iron.'
    Deuteronomy 28:48
    And he shall put a 'yoke of iron' upon thy neck, until he
    have destroyed thee.

393 Canto X, 486-87   Allusion
    Make my 'soul' pass the equinoctial line / Between the pre-
    sent and past worlds.
    Genesis 12:13
    And my 'soul' shall live because of thee.

394 Canto X, 627-28   Quote: Exact
    As Machiavel shows those in 'purple raiment,' / Such is
    the shortest way to general curses.
    Judges 8:26
    Beside ornaments, and collars, and 'purple raiment' that
    was on the kings of Midian.

395 Canto X, 641-42   Quote: Approximate
    The sun went down, 'the smoke rose up, as' from / A
    half-unquench'd volcano, o'er a space.
    Genesis 19:28
    And he looked toward Sodom and Gomorrah ... and, lo, 'the
    smoke' of the country 'went up as' the smoke of a furnace.

396 Canto XI, 24-31   Reference: Subject
    The world, which at the worst's a glorious blunder-- / If
    it be chance; or if it be according / To the old test, still
    better:--lest it should / Turn out so, we'll say nothing
    'gainst the wording, / As several people think such hazards
    rude. / They're right; our days are too brief for afford-
    ing / Space to dispute what 'no one' ever could / Decide.
    Genesis 1-2
    Rf. the creation

397 Canto XI, 51-54   Allusion: Parodic
    Who has sail'd where picturesque Constantinople is, / Or

seen Timbuctoo, or hath taken tea / In small-eyed China's crockery-ware metropolis, / Or sat amidst the bricks of Nineveh.

Jonah 3:1-2
And the word of the Lord came unto Jonah the second time, saying, Arise, go unto Nineveh, that great city, and preach unto it.

398   Canto XI, 89-90   Reference: Parodic
Juan, who did not understand a word / Of English, save their shibboleth, "God damn!"

Judges 12:6
Then said they unto him, Say now Shibboleth: and he said Sibboleth: for he could not frame to pronounce it right.

399   Canto XI, 154-55   Allusion: Parodic
Heroes must die; and by 'God's blessing' 'tis / Not long before the most of them go home.

Psalm 129:8
The 'blessing of the Lord' be upon you: we bless you in the name of the Lord.

400   Canto XI, 167-68   Reference: Parodic
Through "Rows" most modestly call'd "Paradise," which Eve might quit without much sacrifice.

Genesis 3:1-24
Rf. expulsion of Eve from Eden.

401   Canto XI, 177-78   Reference: Parodic
Through this, and much, and more, is the approach / Of travellers to mighty Babylon [i.e. London].

II Kings 24:10
At that time the servants of Nebuchadnezzar king of Babylon came up against Jerusalem, and the city was besieged.

402   Canto XI, 366   Reference: Parodic
A rib's a thorn in a wed gallant's side.

Genesis 2:21-24
And the Lord God caused a deep sleep to fall upon Adam, and he slept: and he took one of his ribs, and closed up the flesh instead thereof; And the rib, which the Lord God had taken from man, made he a woman, and brought her unto the man.

403   Canto XI, 442   Allusion
My Leipsic, and my Mount Saint Jean seems Cain.

Genesis 4:1-15
Rf. Cain's murder of Abel.

404   Canto XI, 451-52   Reference: Parodic
The Muses upon Sion's hill must ramble / With poets almost clergymen, or wholly.

Psalm 2:6
Yet have I set my King upon my holy hill of Zion.

405 Canto XI, 537-41   Reference: Parodic
     Thrice happy he who, after a survey / Of the good company,
     can win a corner, / A door that's in or boudoir out of the
     way / Where he may fix himself like small "Jack Horner," /
     And let the Babel round run as it may.
     Genesis 11:9
     Therefore is the name of it called Babel; because the Lord
     did there confound the language of all the earth: and from
     thence did the Lord scatter them abroad upon the face of
     all the earth.

406 Canto XI, 600   Quote: Parodic
     And dandies, all are gone 'on the wind's wings.'
     Psalm 18:10
     And he rode upon a cherub, and did fly: yea, he did fly
     'upon the wings of the wind.'

407 Canto XI, 639-41   Allusion
     There's little strange in this, but something strange is /
     The unusual quickness of these common changes. / Talk
     not of 'seventy years as age.'
     Psalm 90:10
     'The days of our years are threescore years and ten.'

408 Canto XI, 657-72   Parallelism
     'I have seen' the Landholders ... 'I have seen' Joanna South-
     cote--'I have seen'-- / The House of Commons ... 'I have
     seen' that sad affair ... 'I have seen' crowns worn ... 'I
     have seen' a Congress ... 'I have seen' some nations ...
     'I have seen' small poets ... 'I have seen' the funds ... 'I
     have seen' the funds ... 'I have seen' the people ... 'I have
     seen' malt liquors ... 'I have seen' John.
     Ecclesiastes 1:14; 3:10; 5:18; 8:9; 9:11; 10:5-7
     'I have seen' all the works that are done ... 'I have seen'
     the travail ... Behold that which 'I have seen' ... All this
     'have I seen ... I returned, and saw ... There is an evil
     which 'I have seen' ... 'I have seen' servants upon horses.

409 Canto XII, 121-23   Quote Approximate
     Now if the "court," and "camp," and "grove," be not / Re-
     cruited all with constant married men, / Who 'never cov-
     eted their neighbour's' lot.
     Exodus 20:17
     Thou shalt 'not covet thy neighbour's house, thou shalt not
     covet thy neighbour's wife, ... nor any thing that is thy
     neighbour's.

410 Canto XII, 137-42   Reference: Subject
     Some persons plead / In an appeal to the unborn, whom
     they, / In the faith of their procreative creed, / Baptize
     posterity, or future clay,-- / To me seems but a dubious
     kind of reed / To lean on for support in any way.

II Kings 18:21

> Now, behold thou trustest upon the staff of this bruised reed, even upon Egypt, on which if a man lean, it will go into his hand, and pierce it.

411 Canto XII, 205-206   Reference: Parodic

> And then men stare, as if a new ass spake / To Balaam.

Numbers 22:28

> And the Lord opened the mouth of the ass, and she said unto Balaam, What have I done unto thee?

412 Canto XII, 241-42   Reference: Subject

> And one or two sad, separate wives, without / A fruit to bloom upon their withering bough.

Ezekiel 17:9

> Shall he not ... cut off the fruit thereof, that it wither?

413 Canto XII, 302   Reference: Parodic

> Those became one who soon were to be two.

Genesis 2:24

> Therefore shall a man leave his father and his mother, and shall cleave unto his wife; and they shall be one flesh.

414 Canto XII, 463   Allusion: Parodic

> The single ladies wishing to be double.

Genesis 2:24

> Therefore shall a man leave his father and his mother, and shall cleave unto his wife; and they shall be one flesh.

415 Canto XII, 546-48   Allusion: Parodic

> They were fairer far / Than the more glowing dames whose 'lot is cast' / Beneath the influence of the eastern star.

Leviticus 16:8

> And Aaron shall 'cast lots' upon the two goats; one lot for the Lord, and the other lot for the scapegoat.

416 Canto XII, 589-90   Allusion

> And rather calmly into the heart glides, / Than storms it as a foe would take a city.

Proverbs 16:32

> He that ruleth his spirit [is better] than he that taketh a city.

417 Canto XIII, 15-16   Quote: Approximate

> In Britain--which of course true patriots find / 'The goodliest soil' of body and of mind.

Ezekiel 17:8

> It was planted in 'a good soil' by great waters.

418 Canto XIII, 75-76   Allusion

> Opposing singly the united strong, / From foreign yoke to free the helpless native.

Isaiah 9:4
   For thou hast broken the yoke of his burden, and the staff
of his shoulder, the rod of his oppressor, as in the day of
Midian.

419 Canto XIII, 131-32   Quote: Approximate
   His prepossessions, like 'the laws of Persians / And Medes,'
would ne'er revoke what went before.
Esther 1:19
   And let it be written among 'the laws of the Persians and
the Medes,' that it be not altered.

420 Canto XIII, 225-28   Quote: Parodic
   And since " 'there's safety in a multitude / Of counsellors,' "
as Solomon has said, / Or some one for him, in some sage,
grave mood.
Proverbs 11:14
   Where no counsel is, the people fall: but 'in the multitude
of counsellors there is safety.'

421 Canto XIII, 303-304   Quote: Approximate
   And your cold people are 'beyond all price,' / When once
you have broken their confounded ice.
Jeremiah 15:13
   Thy substance and thy treasures will I give to the 'spoil
without price,' and that for all thy sins.

422 Canto XIII, 396   Reference: Parodic
   The Gothic Babel [Lord Henry's Norman Abbey] of a thou-
sand years.
Genesis 11:4, 9
   And they said, Go to, let us build us a city and a tower ...
called Babel.

423 Canto XIII, 485   Quote: Parodic
   She made the earth below seem 'holy ground.'
Exodus 3:5
   Put off thy shoes from off thy feet, for the place whereon
thou standest is 'holy ground.'

424 Canto XIII, 558   Reference: Parodic
   Nimrods [horseback guests at the Norman Abbey] whose can-
vass scarce contain'd the steed.
Genesis 10:8-10
   Nimrod ... He was a mighty hunter before the Lord.

425 Canto XIII, 621-22   Quote: Parodic
   Even Nimrod's self might leave 'the plains of Dura,' / And
wear the Melton jacket for a space.
Daniel 3:1
   Nebuchadnezzar the king made an image ... he set it up in
'the plain of Dura.'

426   Canto XIII, 651-52   Quote: Exact
       I've seen 'a virtuous woman' put down quite / By the mere
       combination of a coterie.
       Proverbs 31:10
       Who can find 'a virtuous woman'? for her price is far a-
       bove rubies.

427   Canto XIII, 738-40   Reference: Parodic
       But Longbow wild as an Aeolian harp, / With which the
       'winds of heaven' can claim accord, / And make a music,
       whether flat or sharp.
       Daniel 7:2
       Daniel spake and said, I saw in my vision by night, and,
       behold, the four 'winds of the heaven' strove upon the great
       sea.

428   Canto XIII, 763-64   Reference: Parodic
       And, gentle reader! when you gather meaning, / You may
       be Boaz, and I--modest Ruth.
       Ruth 2:15
       And when she was risen up to glean, Boaz commanded his
       young men, saying, Let her glean even among the sheaves
       and reproach her not.

429   Canto XIII, 790-92   Reference: Parodic
       Albeit all human history attests / That happiness for man--
       the hungry sinner!-- / Since Eve ate apples, much depends
       on dinner.
       Genesis 3:6
       And when the woman saw that the tree was good for food,
       and that it was pleasant to the eyes, and a tree to be de-
       sired to make one wise, she took of the fruit thereof, and
       did eat, and gave also unto her husband with her; and he
       did eat.

430   Canto XIII, 793-94   Quote: Exact
       Witness 'the lands which "flow'd with milk and honey," ' /
       Held out into the hungry Israelites.
       Leviticus 20:24
       I will give it unto you to possess it, 'a land that floweth
       with milk and honey. '

431   Canto XIV, 25-26   Allusion
       A sleep without dreams, after a rough day / Of toil, is
       what we covet most.
       Ecclesiastes 5:12
       The sleep of a labouring man is sweet, whether he eat
       little or much: but the abundance of the rich will not suf-
       fer him to sleep.

432   Canto XIV, 25-27   Reference: Subject
       A sleep without dreams, after a rough day / Of toil, is
       what we covet most; and yet / How clay shrinks back from
       more quiescent clay !

Genesis 3:19
For dust thou art, and unto dust shalt thou return.

433   Canto XIV, 87-88
                                               Quote: Parodic
And what I write 'I cast upon the stream,' / To swim or
sing--I have had at least my dream.
Ecclesiastes 11:1
'Cast thy bread upon the waters': for thou shalt find it af-
ter many days.

434   Canto XIV, 177-83
                                               Reference: Parodic
And woman, since she fell'd / The world ... Condemn'd to
child-bed.
Genesis 3:16
Unto the woman he said, I will greatly multiply thy sorrow
and thy conception; in sorrow thou shalt bring forth children;
and thy desire shall be to thy husband, and he shall rule
over thee.

435   Canto XIV, 177-84
                                               Reference: Parodic
Alas! worlds fall--and woman, since she fell'd / The world
(as, since that history less polite / Than true, hath been a
creed so strictly held) / Has not yet given up the practice
quite / ... Condemn'd to child-bed.
Genesis 3:1-24
Rf. Eve's temptation of Adam and God's judgment on Eve.

436   Canto XIV, 239-40
                                               Parallelism
And work away like 'spirit upon matter,' / Embarrass'd
somewhat both with fire and water.
Genesis 1:2
And the earth was without form, and void; and darkness was
upon the face of the deep. And the 'Spirit' of God moved
'upon' the face of the 'waters.'

437   Canto XIV, 261-62
                                               Quote: Approximate
He broke, 'tis true, some 'statutes of the laws' / Of hunt-
ing--for the sagest youth is frail.
Exodus 18:16
And I do make them know the 'statutes of God, and his laws.'

438   Canto XIV, 261-62
                                               Reference: Parodic
He broke, 'tis true, some statutes of the laws / Of hunting.
Psalm 89:31
They break my statutes, and keep not my commandments.

439   Canto XIV, 377-78
                                               Reference: Parodic
O Job! you had two friends: one's quite enough, / Es-
pecially when we are ill at ease.
Job 2:11
Now when Job's three friends heard of all this evil that was
come upon him, they came every one from his own place.

440   Canto XIV, 395-98   Allusion: Parodic
       "I told you so," / Utter'd by friends, those prophets of the
       past, / Who, 'stead of saying what you now should do, /
       Own they foresaw that you would fall at last.
       Isaiah (and all prophetic books)
            Rf. the prophets.

441   Canto XIV, 439-40   Reference: Parodic
       She had consented to create again / That Adam, call'd "The
       happiest of men."
       Genesis 1:26-2:25
            Rf. creation of Adam.

442   Canto XIV, 465-68   Reference: Subject
       'Tis sad to hack into the roots of things, / They are so
       much intertwisted with the earth; / So that the branch a
       goodly verdure flings, / I reck not if an acorn gave it
       birth.
       Job 8:16-17
            He is green before the sun, and his branch shooteth forth
            in his garden. His roots are wrapped about the heap, and
            seeth the place of stones.

443   Canto XIV, 573-76   Allusion
       The Greek Eve, Helen, from the Spartan's bed; / Though
       on the whole, no doubt, the Dardan boy / Was much infer-
       ior to King Menelaus:-- / But thus it is some women will
       betray us.
       Genesis 3:1-24
            Rf. Eve's temptation of Adam.

444   Canto XIV, 617   Reference: Parodic
       Adam exchanged his Paradise for ploughing.
       Genesis 3:23
            Therefore the Lord God sent him [Adam] forth from the gar-
            den, to till the ground.

445   Canto XIV, 618   Reference: Parodic
       Eve made up millinery with fig leaves.
       Genesis 3:7
            And the eyes of them both were opened, and they knew that
            they were naked; and they sewed fig leaves together, and
            made themselves aprons.

446   Canto XIV, 618-20   Reference: Parodic
       Eve [gained] ... / The earliest knowledge from the tree so
       knowing, / As far as I know, that the church receives.
       Genesis 3:6
            And when the woman saw that the tree was good for food, ...
            and a tree to be desired to make one wise, she took of the
            fruit thereof, and did eat.

447 Canto XIV, 755-56   Reference: Parodic
     Had lovers not some reason to regret / The passion which
     made Solomon a zany.
     I Kings 11:4
     For it came to pass, when Solomon was old, that his wives
     turned away his heart after other gods.

448 Canto XIV, 791-92   Allusion: Parodic
     It is not clear that Adeline and Juan / Will fall; but if they
     do, 't will be their ruin.
     Genesis 3: 1-24
     Rf. fall of Adam and Eve.

449 Canton XV, 141-42   Allusion: Parodic
     Redeeming 'worlds' to be by bigots 'shaken,' / How was
     thy toil rewarded?
     Isaiah 24:18
     For the windows from on high are open, and the foundations
     of the 'earth' do 'shake. '

450 Canto XV, 223-24   Quote: Parodic
     As women hate half measures, on the whole, / She 'gan to
     ponder how to 'save his soul. '
     Ezekiel 18:27
     When the wicked man turneth away from his wickedness ...
     he shall 'save his soul' alive.

451 Canto XV, 297-99   Reference: Parodic
     Had Adeline read Malthus? I can't tell; / I wish she had:
     his book's the eleventh commandment, / Which says, "Thou
     shalt not marry," unless 'well. '
     Exodus 20:1-17; Deuteronomy 5:6-21
     Rf. the Ten Commandments.

452 Canto XV, 316   Allusion: Parodic
     Miss Raw, Miss Flaw, Miss Showman, and Miss 'Know-
     man. '
     Genesis 4:1, 17, 25
     And Adam 'knew Eve ... And Cain 'knew' his wife ... And
     Adam 'knew' his wife again.

453 Canto XV, 359-60   Reference: Subject
     She look'd as if she sat by Eden's door, / And grieved for
     those who could return no more.
     Genesis 3:23-24
     Therefore the Lord God sent him forth from the garden of
     Eden ... So he drove out the man.

454 Canto XV, 483-84   Reference: Parodic
     Adeline and Don Juan rather blended / Some acids with the
     sweets--for she was heady.
     Proverbs 27:7
     But to the hungry soul every bitter thing is sweet.

455   Canto XV, 549-50   Reference: Parodic
Who would suppose, from Adam's simple ration, / That
cookery could have call'd forth such resources [as the feast
at Lord Henry's]?

Genesis 3:6
And when the woman saw that the tree was good for food,
... she took of the fruit thereof, and did eat, and gave al-
so unto her husband.

456   Canto XV, 717-18   Reference: Parodic
'Tis time that some new prophet should appear, / Or old
indulge man with a second sight.

I Kings 13
Rf. the old prophet and the young prophet.

457   Canto XVI, 29-30   Quote: Parodic
Have you explored the limits of the coast, / Where all the
'dwellers of the earth' must dwell?

Isaiah 18:3
All ye inhabitants of the world, and 'dwellers on the earth,'
see ye.

458   Canto XVI, 198-200   Reference: Parodic
He was, he did surmise, / Waking already, and return'd
at length / Back to his chamber, shorn of half his strength.

Judges 16:19
And she [Delilah] made him [Samson] sleep upon her knees;
and she called for a man, and she caused him to shave off
the seven locks of his head; and she began to afflict him,
and his strength went from him.

459   Canto XVI, 334   Allusion: Parodic
And he did not seem form'd of clay, / For he's seen in
the porch, and he's seen in the church.

Genesis 2:7
And the Lord God formed man of the dust of the ground,
and breathed into his nostrils the breath of life; and man
became a living soul.

460   Canto XVI, 363-64   Quote: Parodic
He sweeps along in his dusky pall, / 'As o'er the grass the
dew. '

Proverbs 19:12
The king's wrath is as the roaring of a lion; but his favour
is 'as dew upon the grass. '

461   Canto XVI, 409-10   Reference: Parodic
In 'Babylon's' bravuras--as the home / Heart-ballads of
Green Erin or Gray Highlands.

II Kings 24:10
At that time the servants of Nebuchadnezzar King of 'Baby-
lon' came up against Jerusalem, and the city was besieged.

462 <u>Canto XVI, 505-506</u>   Reference: Parodic
     There was a modern Goth, I mean a Gothic / Bricklayer of
     Babel, call'd an architect.
     <u>Genesis 11:1-9</u>
     And they said one to another, Go to, let us make brick, and
     burn them throughly. And they had brick for stone, and
     slime had they for mortar ... Therefore is the name of it
     called Babel.

463 <u>Canto XVI, 687-88</u>   Reference: Parodic
     And makers of good matches, / And several who sung few-
     er psalms than catches.
     <u>Psalms</u>
     Rf. Hebrew psalms.

464 <u>Canto XVI, 949-50</u>   Quote: Approximate
     Again through shadows of the night sublime, / When 'deep
     sleep fell on' men.
     <u>Genesis 2:21</u>
     And the Lord God caused a 'deep sleep to fall upon' Adam,
     and he slept.

465 <u>Canto XVI, 953-54</u>   Quote: Approximate
     A noise like to wet fingers drawn on glass, / Which 'sets
     the teeth on edge. '
     <u>Jeremiah 31:29</u>
     The fathers have eaten a sour grape, and the children's
     'teeth are set on edge. '

ENGLISH BARDS AND SCOTCH REVIEWERS

---

466 <u>Lines 129-30</u>   Quote: Approximate
     'Thus saith the preacher: "Nought beneath the sun / Is
     new;" ' yet still from change to change we run.
     <u>Ecclesiastes 1:1, 9</u>
     'The words of the Preacher, ... there is no new thing un-
     der the sun. '

467 <u>Line 138</u>   Quote: Parodic
     Each country book-club 'bows the knee to Baal. '
     <u>I Kings 19:18</u>
     Yet I have left me seven thousand in Israel, all the 'knees
     which have not bowed unto Baal. '

468 <u>Line 195</u>   Quote: Approximate
     Empires have moulder'd from 'the face of earth. '
     <u>Genesis 1:29</u>
     And God said, Behold, I have given you every herb bearing

seed, which is upon 'the face of all the earth. '

469   Lines 320-31   Reference: Parodic
      Lo! the Sabbath bard, / Sepulchral Grahame, pours his
      notes sublime.
      Exodus 20:8
      Remember the sabbath day, to keep it holy.

470   Lines 325-26   Reference: Parodic
      And, undisturb'd by conscientious qualms, / Perverts the
      Prophets, and purloins the Psalms.
      Isaiah (et al.)
      Rf. the prophetic books of the Old Testament.

471   Lines 385-86   Quote: Exact
      Another epic! Who inflicts again / More books of blank
      upon 'the sons of men'?
      Ecclesiastes 3:10
      I have seen the travail, which God hath given to 'the sons
      of men' to be exercised in it.

472   Lines 420-21   Quote: Approximate
      Though fair they rose, and might have bloom'd at last, / His
      'hopes have perish'd' by the northern blast.
      Job 8:13
      And the hypocrite's 'hope shall perish. '

473   Line 421   Quote: Approximate
      His [Alcaeus] 'hopes have perish'd' by the northern blast.
      Job 8:13
      The hypocrite's 'hope shall perish. '

474   Lines 452-53   Reference: Subject
      His scribbling toils some recompense may meet, / And
      raise this Daniel to the judgment-seat.
      Daniel 2:48
      Then the king made Daniel a great man, ... and made him
      ruler over the whole province of Babylon.

475   Lines 470-71   Quote: Parodic
      Dark roll'd the sympathetic waves of Forth, / Low groan'd
      the startled 'whirlwinds of the north. '
      Isaiah 21:1
      As 'whirlwinds in the south' pass through; so it cometh
      from the desert.

476   Lines 504-506   Quote: Parodic
      So long shall last thine unmolested reign, / Nor any dare
      to 'take thy name in vain. '
      Exodus 20:7
      Thou shalt not 'take the name of the Lord thy God in vain';
      for the Lord will not hold him guiltless that 'taketh his
      name in vain. '

477   Lines 530-31   Quote: Exact
    Whatever blessing waits a genuine Scot, / In 'double por-
tion' swells thy glorious lot.
Deuteronomy 21:17
    But he shall acknowledge the son of the hated for the first-
born, by giving him a 'double portion' of all that he hath.

478   Lines 636-37   Reference: Parodic
    And beer undrawn, and beards unmown, display / Your holy
reverence for the Sabbath-day.
Exodus 20:8
    Remember the sabbath day, to keep it holy.

479   Lines 650-51   Reference: Parodic
    Comus all allows; / Champaign, dice, music, or your
neighbour's spouse.
Exodus 20:17
    Thou shalt not covet thy neighbour's house, thou shalt not
covet thy neighbour's wife.

480   Line 838   Reference: Subject
    She sow'd the seeds, but death has reap'd the fruit.
Micah 6:15
    Thou shalt sow, but thou shalt not reap.

481   Lines 957-58   Allusion
    When fame's loud trump hath blown its noblest blast, /
Though long the sound, the echo sleeps at last.
Exodus 19:16
    And the voice of the trumpet exceeding loud; so that all the
people that was in the camp trembled.

482   Lines 992-93   Quote: Approximate
    My country, what her sons should know too well, / 'Zeal
for her honour' bade me here.
II Kings 10:16
    And he said, Come with me, and see my 'zeal for the Lord.'
So they made him ride in his chariot.

483   Lines 1004-1005   Reference: Subject
    And Tyre's proud piers lie shatter'd in the main; / Like
these, thy strength may sink, in ruin hurl'd.
Ezekiel 26:3
    Therefore thus saith the Lord God; Behold, I am against
thee, O Tyrus, and will cause many nations to come up
against thee, as the sea causeth his waves to come up.

484   Lines 1059-60   Reference: Parodic
    [I have] learn'd to deride the critic's starch decree, / And
break him on the wheel he meant for me.
Isaiah 28:28
    Bread corn is bruised; because he will not ever be thresh-
ing it, nor break it with the wheel of his cart, nor bruise
it with his horsemen.

EPHEMERAL VERSES

"Impromptu"

485   Lines 1-6   Reference: Subject
       Beneath Blessington's eyes / The reclaim'd Paradise /
       Should be free as the former from evil; / But if the new
       Eve / For an Apple should grieve, / What mortal would
       not play the Devil?
       Genesis 3
       Rf. Eve's forbidden fruit and the serpent.

"To Penelope, January 2, 1821"

486   Lines 3-4   Reference: Parodic
       'Tis just six years since we were one, and five since we
       were two.
       Genesis 2:23-24
       Therefore shall a man leave his father and his mother, and
       shall cleave unto his wife: and they shall be one flesh.

THE GIAOUR

487   Lines 8-10   Quote: Exact
       Those blessed isles, / Which, seen from far Colonna's
       height, / 'Make glad the heart' that hails the sight.
       Psalm 104:15
       And wine that 'maketh glad the heart' of man, and oil to
       make his face to shine.

488   Lines 13-15   Reference: Subject
       Reflects the tints of many a peak / Caught by the Laughing
       tides that lave / These Edens of the eastern wave.
       Genesis 2-3
       Rf. garden of Eden.

489   Lines 62-65   Reference: Subject
       It is as though the fiends prevail'd / Against the seraphs
       they assail'd, / And, fix'd on heavenly thrones, should
       dwell / The freed inheritors of hell.
       Isaiah 14:12
       How art thou fallen from heaven, O Lucifer, son of the
       morning!

490   Lines 196-97   Quote: Exact
       Though bent on earth thine 'evil eye,' / As meteor-like thou
       glidest by.

Proverbs 23:6
Eat thou not the bread of him that hath an 'evil eye. '

491   Lines 480-82   Reference: Subject
Yea, Soul, and should our prophet say / That form was
nought but breathing clay, / By Alla! I would answer nay.
Genesis 2:7
And the Lord God formed man of the dust of the ground,
and breathed into his nostrils the breath of life; and man
became a living soul.

492   Lines 487-89   Allusion
Oh! who young Leila's glance could read / And keep that
portion of his creed, / Which saith that woman is but dust.
Genesis 2:7
And the Lord God formed man of the dust of the ground.

493   Lines 982-83   Reference: Subject
My 'days, ' though 'few, ' have pass'd below / In much of
joy, but more of woe.
Job 14:1
Man that is born of a woman is of 'few days, ' and full of
trouble.

494   Line 1026   Quote: Approximate
Then let Life 'go to him who gave. '
Ecclesiastes 12:7
Then shall the dust return to the earth as it was: and the
spirit shall 'return unto God who gave' it.

495   Lines 1056-59   Reference: Subject
She died--I dare not tell thee how; / But look--'tis written
on my brow! / There read of Cain the curse and crime, /
In characters unworn by time.
Genesis 4:15
And the Lord set a mark upon Cain, lest any finding him
should kill him.

496   Lines 1269-70   Allusion
I would not, if I might, be blest; / I want no paradise, but
rest.
Genesis 2-3
Rf. the garden of Eden.

HEAVEN AND EARTH

---

497   Part I, i, 1-3   Reference: Subject
It is the hour when they / Who love us are accustom'd to
descend.

Genesis 6:1-4
> The Sons of God saw the daughters of men that they were
> fair; and they took them wives of all which they chose.

498   Part I. i. 3   Allusion
> The deep clouds o'er rocky Ararat.
Genesis 8:4
> And the ark rested ... upon the mountains of Ararat.

499   Part I. i. 10   Reference: Subject
> And where is the impiety of loving / Celestial natures?
Genesis 6:1-4
> The sons of God saw the daughters of men that they were
> fair; and they took them wives of all which they chose.

500   Part I. i. 12   Reference: Subject
> I love our God less since his angel loved me.
Genesis 6:1-4
> The sons of God saw the daughters of men that they were
> fair; and they took them wives of all which they chose.

501   Part I. i. 18   Quote: Parodic
> Marry, and 'bring forth dust'!
Genesis 3:16
> Unto the woman he said, I will greatly multiply thy sorrow
> and thy conception; in sorrow thou shalt 'bring forth chil-
> dren. '

502   Part I. i. 28-30   Quote: Approximate
> Rather say, / That he will single forth some other 'daugh-
> ter / Of Earth. '
Genesis 6:1-4
> The sons of God saw the 'daughters of men' that they were
> fair; and they took them wives.

503   Part I. i. 31-32   Quote: Approximate
> And 'if it should be so, ' and she loved him, / Better thus
> than that he should weep for me.
Genesis 25:22
> And the children struggled together within her; and she said,
> 'If it be so, ' why am I thus?

504   Part I. i. 52-55   Allusion
> With me thou canst not sympathise, / Except in love, and
> there thou must / Acknowledge that more loving dust / Ne'er
> wept beneath the skies.
Genesis 2:7
> And the Lord God formed man of the dust of the ground.

505   Part I. i. 58-59   Reference: Subject
> As he hath made me of the least / Of those cast out from
> Eden's gate.

Genesis 3:23-24
> Therefore the Lord God sent him forth from the garden of Eden ... So he drove out the man.

506   Part I. i. 69-70   Allusion
> To an Adamite / Forgive, my Seraph! that such thoughts appear.

Genesis 1-3
> Rf. the descendants of Adam.

507   Part I. i. 70-74   Reference: Subject
> That such thoughts appear, For sorrow is our element; / Delight / An Eden kept afar from sight / Though sometimes with our visions blent.

Genesis 3:23-24
> Therefore the Lord God sent him forth from the garden of Eden, ... So he drove out the man.

508   Part I. i. 84-86   Allusion
> Warring with the spirits who may dare / Dispute with him / Who made all empires, empire.

Isaiah 14:12
> How art thou fallen from heaven, O Lucifer, son of the morning!

509   Part I. i. 95-96   Reference: Subject
> Descend and share my lot! / Though I be form'd of clay.

Genesis 2:7
> And the Lord God formed man of the dust of the ground.

510   Part I. i. 106-107   Reference: Subject
> Death and decay / Our mother Eve bequeath'd us.

Genesis 2:16-17; 3:1-24
> Rf. punishment of Eve.

511   Part I. i. 114   Quote: Exact
> Into my ears this truth--"Thou 'liv'st for ever'!"

Genesis 3:22
> And the Lord God said, Behold, the man is become as one of us, to know good and evil: and now, lest he put forth his hand, and take also of the tree of life, and eat, and 'live for ever. '

512   Part I. i. 126   Quote: Exact
> No! though the serpent's sting should 'pierce me through. '

Numbers 24:8
> He shall ... 'pierce them through' with his arrows.

513   Part I. i. 149-50   Reference: Subject
> On Ararat's late secret crest / A mild and many-colour'd bow.

Genesis 8:4, 8:13
> And the ark rested ... upon the mountains of Ararat.... I

do set my bow in the cloud, and it shall be for a token of a covenant between me and the earth.

514   Part I. ii. 190-91   Reference: Subject
      If weighed / Against the metal of the sons of Cain.
      Genesis 4:16-24
      Rf. descendants of Cain.

515   Part I. ii. 209   Quote: Exact
      'I feel no evil' thought, and 'fear no evil.'
      Psalm 23:4
      Yea, though I walk through the valley of the shadow of death,
      'I will fear no evil.'

516   Part I. ii. 243   Quote: Approximate
      'Where is thy brother Japhet?'
      Genesis 4:9
      And the Lord said unto Cain, 'Where is Abel thy brother?'

517   Part I. ii. 252-53   Quote: Approximate
      He / Still loves this 'daughter of a fated race.'
      Genesis 6:2
      The sons of God saw the 'daughters of men' that they were
      fair.

518   Part I. iii. 271-72   Reference: Subject
      When the Redeemer cometh; first in pain, / And then in
      glory.
      Isaiah 19:20
      For they shall cry unto the Lord because of the oppressors,
      and he shall send them a saviour.

519   Part I. iii. 273-75   Reference: Subject
      Yet, in a few days, / Perhaps even hours, ye will be
      changed, rent, hurl'd / Before the mass of waters.
      Genesis 6-9
      Rf. the flood.

520   Part I. iii. 277-78   Allusion
      Its depths search'd by the sweeping wave, / And dolphins
      gambol in the lion's den!
      Daniel 6:16
      Then the king commanded, and they brought Daniel, and
      cast him into the den of lions.

521   Part I. iii. 278   Quote: Approximate
      And dolphins gambol in 'the lion's den'!
      Daniel 6:12
      Hast thou not signed a decree, that every man that shall
      ask a petition of any God or man within thirty days, save
      of thee, O king, shall be cast into 'the den of lions'?

522   Part I. iii. 320-21   Quote: Approximate
      In 'the name / Of the Most High,' what art thou?

Psalm 7:17
> I will praise the Lord according to his righteousness: and
> will sing praise to 'the name of the Lord most high. '

523   Part I. iii. 323-26   Reference: Subject
> By the approaching deluge! by the earth / Which will be
> strangled by the ocean! by / The deep which will lay open
> all her fountains! / The heaven which will convert her
> clouds to seas.

Genesis 6-9 (esp. 7:11)
> The same day were all the fountains of the great deep brok-
> en up, and the windows of heaven were opened.

524   Part I. iii. 330-31   Quote: Exact
> Spirit: 'Why weep'st thou'?   Japhet: For earth and all her
> children.

I Samuel 1:8
> Then said Elkanah her husband to her, Hannah, 'why weep-
> est thou'?

525   Part I. iii. 332-34   Reference: Subject
> How the fiend mocks the tortures of a world, / The com-
> ing desolation of an orb, / On which the sun shall rise
> and warm no life!

Genesis 6-9
> Rf. the flood.

526   Part I. iii. 340-46   Reference: Subject
> Rejoice! / The abhorred race / Which could not keep in
> Eden their high place, / But listen'd to the voice / Of
> knowledge without power, / Are nigh the hour of death!

Genesis 3:1-24
> Rf. man's fall in Eden.

527   Part I. iii. 369-70   Allusion
> All merged within the universal fountain, / Man, earth, and
> fire, shall die.

Genesis 7:11
> In the six hundredth year of Noah's life ... were the fount-
> ains of the great deep broken up.

528   Part I. iii. 385   Quote: Exact
> Shall search you in your 'secret place. '

Deuteronomy 27:15
> Cursed be the man that maketh any graven or molten im-
> age ... and putteth it in a 'secret place. '

529   Part I. iii. 394-98   Quote: Approximate
> Thy new world and new race shall be of woe-- / Less good-
> ly in their aspect, in their years / Less than the glorious
> 'giants, who / Yet walk the world' in pride, / The 'Sons
> of Heaven' by many a mortal bride.

Genesis 6:1-4
There were 'giants in the earth' in those days; and also after that, when the 'sons of God' came in unto the daughters of men.

530   Part I. iii. 394   Reference: Subject
The new world and new race shall be of woe.
Isaiah 65:17
For, behold, I create new heavens and a new earth: and the former shall not be remembered.

531   Part I. iii. 400-402   Quote: Exact
And art thou not ashamed / Thus to survive, / And 'eat, and drink, ' and wive?
Isaiah 22:13
Let us 'eat and drink': for to morrow we shall die.

532   Part I. iii. 406   Reference: Subject
Bid thee await the world-dissolving wave.
Genesis 7:23-24
And every living substance was destroyed which was upon the face of the ground, ... And the waters prevailed upon the earth an hundred and fifty days.

533   Part I. iii. 415-16   Quote: Approximate
There is not one who hath not left a throne / Vacant in heaven to 'dwell in darkness' here.
I Kings 8:12
Then spake Solomon, The Lord said that he would 'dwell in the thick darkness. '

534   Part I. iii. 420-23   Reference: Subject
And when the annihilating waters roar / Above what they have done, / Envy the giant patriarchs then no more, / And scorn thy sire as the surviving one!
Genesis 6-9
Rf. giants in the earth; the flood.

535   Part I. iii. 433-34   Reference: Subject
To whom the omission of a sacrifice / Is vice.
Genesis 4:3-5
Cain brought of the fruit of the ground an offering unto the Lord ... But unto Cain and to his offering he [God] had not respect.

536   Part I. iii. 442-45   Reference: Subject
Even the brutes, in their despair, / Shall cease to prey on man and on each other, / And the striped tiger shall lie down to die / Beside the lamb, as though he were his brother.
Isaiah 11:6-7
The wolf also shall dwell with the lamb, and the leopard shall lie down with the kid; and the calf and the young lion

and the fatling together ... Their young ones shall lie down
together.

537   Part I. iii. 450-53   Reference: Subject
      The little remnant of the past creation, / To generate new
      nations for his use: / This remnant, floating o'er the un-
      dulation / Of the subsiding deluge.
      Genesis 6-9
      Rf. the flood.

538   Part I. iii. 459-62   Quote: Approximate
      The eternal will / Shall deign to expound this dream / Of
      good and evil; and 'redeem / Unto himself' all times, all
      things.
      II Samuel 7:23
      Like Israel, whom God went to 'redeem for a people to
      himself. '

539   Part I. iii. 464-69   Reference: Subject
      And to the expiated Earth / Restore the beauty of her
      birth, / Her Eden in an endless paradise, / Where man
      no more can fall as once he fell, / And even the very de-
      mons shall do well!
      Genesis 3:1-24
      Rf. the fall of Adam and Eve.

540   Part I. iii. 481   Allusion
      But the same moral storms / Shall oversweep the future,
      as the waves / In a few hours the glorious 'giants'' graves.
      Genesis 6:1-4
      Rf. the flood's obliteration of the race of giants.

541   Part I. iii. 490-91   Quote: Exact
      'The fountains of the great deep' shall be broken, / And
      heaven set wide her windows.
      Genesis 7:11
      The same day were all 'the fountains of the great deep'
      broken up, and the windows of heaven were opened.

542   Part I. iii. 491-93   Quote: Exact
      While mankind / View, unacknowledged, each tremendous
      token-- / Still, as they were 'from the beginning, ' blind.
      Psalm 119:160
      Thy word is true 'from the beginning. '

543   Part I. iii. 493   Quote: Approximate
      They were 'from the beginning, ' blind.
      Genesis 1:1
      'In the beginning' God created the heaven and the earth.

544   Part I. iii. 500-501   Reference: Subject
      Oh Earth! / Thy death is nearer than thy recent birth.

Genesis 1:6-9
 Rf. creation and the destruction of the world by flood.

545   Part I. iii. 510-13   Reference: Subject
 While man shall long in vain for his broad wings, / The
 wings which could not save:-- / Where could he rest them,
 while the whole space brings / Nought to his eye beyond
 the deep, his grave?

Genesis 8:9
 But the dove found no rest for the sole of her foot, and
 she returned unto him into the ark, for the waters were on
 the face of the whole earth.

546   Part I. iii. 516-21   Reference: Subject
 All die, / Save the slight remnant o Seth's seed--The seed
 of Seth, / Exempt for future sorrow's sake from death.
 But of the sons of Cain / None shall remain.

Genesis 4:25-5:8
 Rf. Seth and his descendants.

547   Part I. iii. 534-37   Reference: Subject
 We fell! / They fall! / So perish all / These petty foes
 of Heaven who shrink from hell!

Isaiah 14:12
 How art thou fallen from heaven, O Lucifer, son of the
 morning!

548   Part I. iii. 551-55   Reference: Subject
 The sun will rise upon the earth's last day / As on the
 fourth day of creation, when / God said unto him, "Shine!"
 and he broke forth / Into the dawn, which lighted not the
 yet / Unform'd forefather of mankind.

Genesis 1
 Rf. the creation.

549   Part I. iii. 557-59   Quote: Exact
 The birds, / Which 'in the open firmament of heaven' /
 Have wings like angels.

Genesis 1:20
 And fowl that may fly above the earth 'in the open firma-
 ment of heaven. '

550   Part I. iii. 559-60   Allusion
 And like them salute / Heaven first each day before the
 Adamites.

Genesis 1-5
 Rf. the race of Adam.

551   Part I. iii. 566-67   Reference: Subject
 Ay, day will rise; but upon what?--a chaos / Which was
 ere day.

Genesis 1:2
 And the earth was without form, and void.

552   Part I, iii. 568-70
                                                    Reference: Subject
        Without life, what are the hours? / No more to dust than
        is eternity / Unto Jehovah, who created both.
        Genesis 2:7
        And the Lord God formed man of the dust of the ground.

553   Part I, iii. 571-72
                                                    Allusion
        Without him, even eternity would be / A void.
        Genesis 1:2
        And the earth was without form, and void.

554   Part I, iii. 572-74
                                                    Reference: Subject
        Time, as made for man, / Dies with man, and is swallow'd
        in that deep / Which has no fountain.
        Genesis 7:11
        In the same day were all the fountains of the great deep
        broken up.

555   Part I, iii. 583-84   Allusion
        They shall be / Welcome as Eden.
        Genesis 2-3
        Rf. the garden of Eden.

556   Part I, iii. 587-88
                                                    Reference: Subject
        Lo, / A son of Adam.
        Genesis 5
        Rf. descendants of Adam.

557   Part I, iii. 602   Allusion
        Back to thy tents, insulting son of Noah!
        Genesis 10
        Rf. Japhet and Noah.

558   Part I, iii. 606-607
                                                    Reference: Subject
        Son of the patriarch, who hath ever been / Upright before
        his God.
        Genesis 6:9
        Noah was a just man and perfect in his generations, and
        Noah walked with God.

559   Part I, iii. 615-17
                                                    Reference: Subject
        Hast thou the power / To save this beautiful--these beau-
        tiful / Children of Cain?
        Genesis 4:16-26
        Rf. descendants of Cain.

560   Part I, iii. 621-22   Allusion
        I ne'er thought till now / To hear an Adamite speak riddles
        to me.
        Genesis 1-4
        Rf. the descendants of Adam.

561   Part I, iii. 623
                                                    Quote: Exact
        And hath not 'the Most High' expounded them?

Numbers 24:16
> He hath said, which heard the words of God, and knew the knowledge of 'the most High. '

562   Part I, iii. 637-38   Reference: Subject
> We are sent / Upon the earth to toil and die.

Genesis 3:19
> In the sweat of thy face shalt thou eat bread, till thou return unto the ground; for out of it wast thou taken: for dust thou art, and unto dust shalt thou return.

563   Part I, iii. 652   Allusion
> The last and loveliest of Cain's race.

Genesis 4
> Rf. descendants of Cain.

564   Part I, iii. 653-54   Reference: Subject
> The ark which shall receive a remnant of / The seed of Seth.

Genesis 4:25-6:18
> Rf. Seth's descendants and the ark.

565   Part I, iii. 654-58   Reference: Subject
> And dost thou think that we, / With Cain's, the eldest born of Adam's, blood / Warm in our veins, --strong Cain! who was begotten / In Paradise, --would mingle with Seth's children? / Seth, the last offspring of old Adam's dotage?

Genesis 4:1-5:8
> Rf. Cain and Seth.

566   Part I, iii. 663-65   Reference: Subject
> Too much of the forefather whom thou vauntest / Has come down in that haughty blood which springs / From him who shed the first, and that a brother's!

Genesis 4:1-15
> Rf. Cain and Abel.

567   Part I, iii. 669-72   Reference: Subject
> Thou who dost rather make me dream that Abel / Had left a daughter, whose pure pious race / Survived in thee, so much unlike thou art / The rest of the stern Cainites, save in beauty.

Genesis 4:1-26
> Rf. Cain and Abel.

568   Part I, iii. 675-76   Reference: Subject
> If 'I' partook thy thought, / And dream'd that aught of 'Abel' was in 'her'!

Genesis 4:1-8
> Rf. Cain and Abel.

569   Part I, iii. 677   Allusion
> Get thee hence, son of Noah; thou makest strife.

Genesis 6-9
    Rf. Japhet and Noah.

570   Part I. iii. 677   Quote: Exact
      'Get thee hence, ' son of Noah; thou makest strife.
   I Kings 17:3
      'Get thee hence, ' and turn thee eastward.

571   Part I. iii. 678-79   Reference: Subject
      Japh. Offspring of Cain, thy father did so! Aho. But /
      He slew not Seth.
   Genesis 4:1-26
      Rf. Cain, Abel, and Seth.

572   Part I. iii. 682-83   Quote: Approximate
      I had not named his deed, but that thyself / Didst seem to
      'glory in him. '
   Isaiah 41:16
      And thou shalt rejoice in the Lord, and shalt 'glory in the
      Holy One of Israel. '

573   Part I. iii.684-87   Reference: Subject
      He was our father's father; / The eldest born of man, the
      strongest, bravest, / And most enduring.--Shall I blush
      for him / From whom we had our being?
   Genesis 4
      Rf. Cain, son of Adam.

574   Part I. iii. 693-94   Allusion
      Whate'er our God decrees, / The God of Seth as [of] Cain,
      I must obey.
   Genesis 4:25
      And Adam knew his wife again; and she bare a son, and
      called his name Seth: For God, said she, hath appointed
      me another seed instead of Abel, whom Cain slew.

575   Part I. iii. 696-97   Reference: Subject
      But could I dare to pray in his dread hour / Of universal
      vengeance.
   Genesis 6-9
      Rf. God's destruction of the world through the flood.

576   Part I. iii. 702-703   Reference: Subject
      All the life, and all / The things which sprang up with me,
      like the stars.
   Genesis 1
      Rf. the creation.

577   Part I. iii. 708   Quote: Approximate
      What, hath 'this dreamer, ' with his father's ark.
   Genesis 37:19
      Behold, 'this dreamer' cometh.

578   Part I, iii. 711-12   Reference: Subject
        Must we / Cling to a son of Noah for our lives?
      Genesis 6:10
        And Noah begat three sons, Shem, Ham and Japheth.

579   Part I, iii. 720-22   Reference: Subject
        Japhet: He whose one produced them. Aholibamah: Who
        heard that word? Japhet: The universe, which leap'd / To
        life before it. Ah! smilest thou still in scorn?
      Genesis 1
        Rf. the creation.

580   Part I, iii. 725   Reference: Subject
        I have ever hail'd our 'Maker,' Samiasa.
      Job 4:17
        Shall a man be more pure than his 'maker'?

581   Part I, iii. 728-29   Reference: Subject
        He who made earth in love had soon to grieve / Above its
        first and best inhabitants.
      Genesis 6-9
        Rf. those destroyed in the flood.

582   Part I, iii. 736-38   Reference: Subject
        These are they, then, / Who leave the throne of God, to
        take them wives / From out the race of Cain.
      Genesis 6:1-4
        The sons of God saw the daughters of men that they were
        fair; and they took them wives of all which they chose.

583   Part I, iii. 743   Quote: Approximate
        Was not 'man made in' high 'Jehovah's image'?
      Genesis 1:26
        And God said, Let us 'make man in our image,' after our
        likeness.

584   Part I, iii. 762-63   Reference: Subject
        They soon shall cease to be; / While thou shalt be the sire
        of a new world.
      Isaiah 65:17
        For, behold, I create new heavens and a new earth: and
        the former shall not be remembered.

585   Part I, iii. 768-70   Reference: Subject
        Ask him who made thee greater than myself / And mine,
        but not less subject to his own / Almightiness.
      Genesis 1-2
        Rf. God's creation of man.

586   Part I, iii. 786-89   Reference: Subject
        Earth! which saw / Jehovah's footsteps not disdain her
        sod! / The world he loved, and made / For love.

Genesis 1-2; 3:8
   Rf. the creation.

587   Part I. iii. 820-21
                                          Quote: Approximate
      I came to call ye back to your fit sphere, / 'In the great
      name' and at the word 'of God. '
      Psalm 20:5
      We will rejoice in thy salvation, and 'in the name of our
      God' we will set up our banners.

588   Part I. iii. 825-30
                                          Reference: Subject
      True, earth must die! / Her race, return'd into her womb,
      must wither, / And much which she inherits: but oh! why
      / Cannot this earth be made, or be destroy'd / Without
      involving ever some vast void / In the immortal ranks?
      Genesis 6-9
      Rf. those destroyed by the flood.

589   Part I. iii. 840-50
                                          Reference: Subject
      Long must I war / With him who deem'd it hard / To be
      created, and to acknowledge him / Who midst the cheru-
      bim / Made him as suns to a dependent star, / Leaving
      the archangels at his right hand dim. / I loved him--beau-
      tiful he was: oh heaven! / Save his who made, what beau-
      ty and what power / Was ever like to Satan's!
      Isaiah 14:12
      How art thou fallen from heaven, O Lucifer, son of the
      morning!

590   Part I. iii. 845-46
                                          Reference: Subject
      Leaving the archangels at his right hand dim. / I love
      him--beautiful he was.
      Isaiah 14:12
      How art thou fallen from heaven, O Lucifer, son of the
      morning!

591   Part I. iii. 855-58
                                          Reference: Subject
      But man hath listen'd to his voice, / And ye to woman's--
      beautiful she is, / The serpent's voice less subtle than her
      kiss-- / The snake but vanquish'd dust.
      Genesis 3:1-7
      Rf. the serpent's temptation of Eve.

592   Part I. iii. 884-85
                                          Reference: Subject
      The race of Cain / Must lift their eyes to Adam's God in
      vain.
      Genesis 4
      Rf. the curse on Cain.

593   Part I. iii. 896
                                          Quote: Exact
      Weep for the myriads who can 'weep no more. '
      Isaiah 30:19
      For the people shall dwell in Zion at Jerusalem: thou shalt
      'weep no more. '

594   Part I, iii. 906-908   Reference: Subject
       Nor see ye lose a portion of his grace, / For all the mer-
       cy which Seth's race / Find still.
       Genesis 4:25-26
       Rf. Seth, brother of Cain and Abel.

595   Part I, iii. 928-29   Reference: Subject
       Too much already hast thou deign'd / To one of Adam's
       race!
       Genesis 1-3
       Rf. the descendants of Adam.

596   Part I, iii. 933-35   Reference: Subject
       The first who taught us knowledge hath been hurl'd / From
       his once archangelic throne / Into some unknown world.
       Genesis 3:1-24
       Rf. the fall of man and the tree of knowledge of good and
       evil.

597   Part I, iii. 960-61   Reference: Subject
       Be a man! / Amd bear what Adam's race must bear, and
       can.
       Genesis 2:16-17; 3:1-24
       Rf. punishment of Adam and Eve.

598   Part I, iii. 963-65   Reference: Subject
       And we are alone, / Floating upon the azure desert, and
       / The depth beneath us hides our own dear land.
       Genesis 6-9
       Rf. the ark in the flood.

599   Part I, iii. 972-77   Reference: Subject
       Renew not Adam's fall: / Mankind were then but twain, /
       But they are numerous now as are the waves / And the
       tremendous rain, / Whose drops shall be less thick than
       would their graves, / Were graves permitted to the seed
       of Cain.
       Genesis 3:1-24
       Rf. fall of Adam and Eve.

600   Part I, iii. 1015-16   Reference: Subject
       Hence to where our all-hallow'd ark uprears / Its safe and
       wreckless sides!
       Genesis 6-9
       Rf. Noah's ark.

601   Part I, iii. 1034   Reference: Subject
       Nor perish like heaven's children with man's daughters.
       Genesis 6:1-4
       The sons of God saw the daughters of men that they were
       fair; and they took them wives of all which they chose.

602   Part I, iii. 1035-38   Reference: Subject
       The tempest cometh; heaven and earth unite / For the

annihilation of all life. / Unequal is the strife / Between
our strength and the Eternal Might!
Genesis 6-9
  Rf. the flood.

603   Part I. iii. 1050-52   Reference: Subject
      The flaming sword, / Which chased the first-born out of
      Paradise, / Still flashes in the angelic hands.
      Genesis 3:24
        So he drove out the man; and he placed at the east of the
        garden of Eden Cherubims, and a flaming sword which turn-
        ed every way, to keep the way of the tree of life.

604   Part I. iii. 1060   Reference: Subject
      The heavens and earth are mingling.
      Genesis 2:1, 4
        Rf. Heaven and earth as opposites at creation.

605   Part I. iii. 1066-68   Quote: Approximate
      Yet, yet, Jehovah! yet withdraw thy 'rod / Of wrath,' and
      pity thine own world's despair! / Hear not man only but
      all nature plead!
      Lamentations 3:1
        I am the man that hath seen affliction by the 'rod of his
        wrath.'

606   Part I. iii. 1078-80   Allusion
      Quit this chaos-founded prison, / To which the elements
      again repair, / To turn it into what it was.
      Genesis 1:2
        And the earth was without form, and void.

607   Part I. iii. 1080-81   Quote: Approximate
      'Beneath / The shelter of these wings' thou shalt be safe.
      Psalm 17:8
        Keep me as the apple of the eye, hide me 'under the sha-
        dow of thy wings.'

608   Part I. iii. 1095-96   Allusion
      While safe amidst the elemental strife, / Thou sitt'st with-
      in thy guarded ark?
      Genesis 6-9
        Rf. the flood, Noah, and his ark.

609   Part I. iii. 1110-11   Reference: Subject
      With him who made / Thee and thy race, for which we
      are betray'd!
      Genesis 1-2
        Rf. God's creation of man.

610   Part I. iii. 1120-21   Reference: Subject
      Accursed / Be he who made thee and thy sire!

Genesis 1-2
Rf. God's creation of man.

611   Part I. iii. 1127-28   Reference: Subject
If he hath made earth, let it be his shame, / To make a
world for torture.
Genesis 1-2
Rf. God's creation of the world.

612   Part I. iii. 1132-34   Reference: Subject
When Paradise upsprung, / Ere Eve gave Adam knowledge
for her dower, / Or Adam his first hymn of slavery sung.
Genesis 3:1-24
Rf. the fall of Adam and Eve, and the tree of knowledge.

613   Part I. iii. 1142-43   Allusion
Fly, son of Noah, fly! and take thine ease / In thine allot-
ted ocean-tent.
Genesis 6-9
Rf. Noah's ark.

614   Part I. iii. 1146-47   Quote: Exact
Then to Jehovah raise / Thy 'song of praise'!
Nehemiah 12:46
There were chief of the singers, and 'songs of praise' and
thanksgiving unto God.

615   Part I. iii. 1151-54   Reference: Subject
Yet, as 'his word, / Be the decree adored! / He gave me
life--he taketh but / The breath which is his own.
Genesis 2:7
And the Lord God ... breathed into his nostrils the breath
of life.

616   Part I. iii. 1153-54   Reference: Subject
He gave me life--he taketh but / The breath which is his
own.
Job 1:21
The Lord gave, and the Lord hath taken away.

617   Part I. iii. 1170-71   Quote: Approximate
Where shall we 'fly'? / Not 'to the mountains' high.
Psalm 11:1
How say ye to my soul, 'Flee as a bird to your mountain'?

618   Part I. iii. 1187-88   Quote: Exact
And not a leaf appear'd about to fall;-- / And now 'they
are not'!
Jeremiah 10:20
My children are gone forth of me, and 'they are not.'

HEBREW MELODIES

"All Is Vanity, Saith the Preacher"

619   Title   Quote: Approximate
      Ecclesiastes 1:2
          Vanity of vanities, saith the Preacher, vanity of vanities;
          all is vanity.

620   Entire poem   Reference: Subject
      Ecclesiastes 1:2
          Vanity of vanities, saith the Preacher, vanity of vanities;
          all is vanity.

621   Lines 9-10   Quote: Approximate
          I strive 'to number o'er what days' / Remembrance can
          discover.
      Psalm 90:12
          So teach us 'to number our days,' that we may apply our
          hearts unto wisdom.

622   Lines 17-20   Quote: Exact
          The 'serpent of the field,' by art / and spells, is won from
          harming; / But that which coils around the heart, / Oh!
          who hath power of charming?
      Genesis 3:1
          Now 'the serpent' was more subtil than any beast 'of the
          field' which the Lord God had made. And he said unto the
          woman, Yea, hath God said, Ye shall not eat of every tree
          of the garden?

"By the Rivers of Babylon We Sat Down and Wept"

623   Entire poem   Reference: Subject
      Psalm 137
          Rf. the captivity of Israel.

624   Lines 1-2   Quote: Approximate
          'We sate down and wept by the waters / Of Babel,' and
          thought of the day.
      Psalm 137:1
          'By the rivers of Babylon, there we sat down,' yea, we
          'wept,' when we remembered Zion.

625   Lines 3-4   Allusion
          When our foe, in the hue of his slaughters, / Made 'Sa-
          lem's' high places his prey.
      Genesis 14:18
          And ... king of 'Salem' brought forth bread and wine.

626   Lines 17-18   Quote: Approximate
     And ne'er shall its soft tones be blended / With the voice
     of 'the spoiler' by me!
    Isaiah 16:4
     Be thou a covert to them from the face of 'the spoiler': for
     the extortioner is at an end, 'the spoiler' ceaseth.

"The Destruction of Sennacherib"

627   Entire poem   Reference: Subject
    Isaiah 36:1
     Sennacherib king of Assyria came up against all the defenced
     cities of Judah.

"The Harp the Monarch Minstrel Swept"

628   Entire poem   Reference: Subject
    Psalms
     Rf. David's composition of the psalms.

629   Lines 1-2   Reference: Subject
     The harp the monarch minstrel swept, / The King of men,
     the loved of Heaven.
    I Samuel 16:23
     David took an harp, and played with his hand.

630   Lines 2-4   Reference: Subject
     The king of men, the loved of Heaven, / Which Music hal-
     low'd while she wept / O'er tones her heart of hearts had
     given.
    I Samuel 13:14
     The Lord hath sought him a man [David] after his own
     heart.

631   Lines 6-7   Reference: Subject
     It soften'd men of iron mould, / It gave them virtues not
     their own.
    I Samuel 16:16-23
     Rf. David's playing to quiet Saul's madness.

632   Lines 12-13   Reference: Subject
     It wafted glory to our God; / It made our gladden'd valleys
     ring.
    Psalm 65:13
     The valleys also are covered over with corn; they shout for
     joy, they also sing.

"Jephtha's Daughter"

633   Entire poem   Reference: Subject
    Judges 11:29-40
     Jephtha's rash vow and the consequences to his daughter.

"My Soul Is Dark"

634   Entire poem   Reference: Subject
      I Samuel 16:14-23
          Rf. Saul's madness.

"Oh! Weep for Those"

635   Entire poem   Reference: Subject
      Psalm 137
          Rf. Israel in Babylonian captivity.

636   Line 1   Quote: Approximate
          Oh! weep for those that wept 'by Babel's stream. '
      Psalm 137:1
          'By the rivers of Babylon, ' there we sat down, yea, we
          wept, when we remembered Zion.

637   Line 4   Reference: Subject
          Mourn--where their God hath dwelt, the godless dwell!
      Exodus 25:8
          And let them make me a sanctuary; that I may dwell among
          them [God to Moses].

638   Line 6   Reference: Subject
          And when shall Zion's songs again seem sweet?
      Psalm 137:3
          And they that wasted us required of us mirth, saying, Sing
          us one of the songs of Zion.

639   Line 9   Reference: Subject
          Tribes of the wandering foot and weary breast [Israel].
      Numbers 14:33
          And your children shall wander in the wilderness forty
          years.

640   Lines 9-10   Quote: Approximate
          Tribes of the wandering foot and weary breast, / How shall
          ye 'flee away and be at rest'!
      Psalm 55:6
          Oh that I had wings like a dove! for then would I 'fly away,
          and be at rest. '

"On Jordan's Banks"

641   Line 1   Reference: Subject
          On Jordan's banks the Arab's camels stray.
      Numbers 34:12
          And the border shall go down to Jordan.

642   Line 2   Allusion
          On Sion's hill the False One's votaries pray.
      Psalm 2:6
          Yet have I set my king upon my holy hill of Zion.

643   Line 3   Reference: Subject
        The Baal-adorer bows on Sinai's steep.
        I Kings 19:18
        Yet I have left ... all the knees which have not bowed unto
        Baal.

644   Line 5   Reference: Subject
        There--where thy finger scorch'd the tablet stone!
        Exodus 32:15-16
        And Moses turned, and went down from the mount, and the
        two tables of the testimony were in his hand: the tables
        were written on both their sides; on the one side and on the
        other were they written.   And the tables were the work of
        God, and the writing was the writing of God, graven upon
        the tables.

645   Lines 6-7   Reference: Subject
        Where thy shadow to thy people shone, / Thy glory shroud-
        ed in its garb of fire.
        Exodus 34:29-35
        Rf. God's appearing to Moses on Mount Sinai.

646   Line 8   Reference: Subject
        Thyself--none living see and not expire!
        Exodus 33:20
        And he said, Thou canst not see my face: for there shall
        no man see me, and live.

"On the Day of the Destruction of Jerusalem by Titus"

647   Lines 1-2   Reference: Subject
        From the last 'hill' that looks on thy once holy dome / I
        beheld thee, oh 'Sion'! when render'd to Rome.
        Psalm 2:6
        Yet have I set my king upon my holy hill of Zion.

648   Lines 17-18   Reference: Subject
        But the Gods of the Pagan shall never profane / The shrine
        where Jehovah disdain'd not to reign.
        II Chronicles 7:19-22
        Rf. the forsaking of the temple by God.

649   Lines 19-20   Reference: Subject
        And scatter'd and scorn'd as thy people may be, / Our wor-
        ship, oh Father, is only for thee.
        I Kings 14:15
        And he shall root up Israel out of this good land, which he
        gave to their fathers, and shall scatter them beyond the
        river.

"Saul"

650   The entire poem   Reference: Subject

I Samuel 28
Rf. Samuel raised from the dead.

651 Lines 27-28   Reference: Subject
And the falchion by thy side / To thy heart thy hand shall
guide.
I Samuel 31:4
Then said Saul unto his armourbearer, Draw thy sword, and
thrust me through therewith ... But his armourbearer
would not; for he was sore afraid. Therefore Saul took a
sword, and fell upon it.

"Song of Saul Before His Last Battle"

652 Entire poem   Reference: Subject
I Samuel 31
Rf. the death of Saul.

653 Line 2   Quote: Approximate
Pierce me in leading the 'host of the Lord.'
Genesis 32:2
And when Jacob saw them, he said, This is 'God's host.'

654 Lines 9-10   Reference: Subject
Farewell to others, but never we part, / Heir to my roy-
alty, son of my heart!
II Samuel 1:12
And they mourned, and wept, and fasted until even, for
Saul, and for Jonathan his son, ... because they were fall-
en by the sword.

"A Spirit Pass'd Before Me"

655 Entire poem   Reference: Subject
Job 40:1-2
Moreover the Lord answered Job, and said, Shall he that
contendeth with the Almighty instruct him? he that reprov-
eth God, let him answer it.

656 Line 9   Reference: Subject
Creatures of clay--vain dwellers in the dust!
Genesis 2:7
And the Lord God formed man of the dust of the ground.

"Vision of Belshazzar"

657 Entire poem   Reference: Subject
Daniel 4:19-37
Rf. Nebuchadnezzar's punishment, acting as a beast.

658 Lines 5-8   Reference: Subject
A thousand cups of gold, / In Judah deem'd divine-- / Je-
hovah's vessels hold / The godless Heathen's wine!

II Kings 16
>Rf. the spoiling of the temple and its furnishings by Assyrians.

"Were My Bosom As False As Thou Deem'st It To Be"

659   Entire poem   Reference: Subject
II Kings 24-25
>Rf. the Babylonian captivity of Israel.

660   Line 5   Quote: Exact
>If the bad never triumph, then 'God is with thee'!
Genesis 21:22
>The chief captain of his host spake unto Abraham, saying, 'God is with thee' in all that thou doest.

"When Coldness Wraps This Suffering Clay"

661   Lines 1-4   Reference: Subject
>When coldness wraps this suffering clay, / Ah! whither strays the immortal mind? / It cannot die, it cannot stay, / But leaves its darken'd dust behind.
Ecclesiastes 12:7
>Then shall the dust return to the earth as it was: and the spirit shall return unto God who gave it.

662   Lines 17   Allusion
>Its [the mind's] eye shall roll through chaos back.
Genesis 1:2
>And the earth was without form, and void.

"The Wild Gazelle"

663   Lines 1-3   Quote: Approximate
>The wild gazelle on Judah's hills / Exulting yet may bound, / And drink from all the 'living rills. '
Song of Solomon 4:15
>A fountain of gardens, a well of 'living waters, ' and streams from Lebanon.

664   Lines 3-4   Quote: Exact
>And drink from all the living rills / That gush on 'holy ground. '
Exodus 3:5
>Put off thy shoes from off thy feet, for the place whereon thou standest is 'holy ground. '

665   Lines 7-8   Allusion
>A step as fleet, an eye more bright, / Hath Judah witness'd there.
Genesis 29:35
>And she said, Now will I praise the Lord: therefore she called his name Judah

666 <u>Lines 11-12</u>   <u>Reference: Subject</u>
    The 'cedars' wave 'on Lebanon, ' / But Judah's statelier
    maids are gone!
    <u>Judges 9:15</u>
        Let fire come out of the bramble, and devour the 'cedars
        of Lebanon. '

667 <u>Lines 13-14</u>   <u>Reference: Subject</u>
    More blest each palm that shades those plains / Than Is-
    rael's scatter'd race.
    <u>I Kings 14:15</u>
        For the Lord shall smite Israel, ... and shall scatter them
        beyond the river.

668 <u>Lines 15-16</u>   <u>Allusion</u>
    For, taking root, it [palm tree, contrasted with Israel]
    there remains / In solitary grace.
    <u>II Kings 19:30</u>
        And the remnant that is escaped or the house of Judah shall
        yet again take root downward, and bear fruit upward.

669 <u>Lines 19-20</u>   <u>Reference: Subject</u>
    But we must wander witheringly, / In other lands to die.
    <u>II Kings 17:23</u>
        So was Israel carried away out of their own land to Assyria
        unto this day.

670 <u>Lines 21-22</u>   <u>Reference: Subject</u>
    And where our fathers' ashes be, / Our own may never lie.
    <u>I Kings 13:22</u>
        Thy carcase shall not come unto the sepulchre of thy fathers.

671 <u>Lines 23-24</u>   <u>Quote: Parodic</u>
    Our temple hath not left a stone, / And 'Mockery sits on
    Salem's throne. '
    <u>Jeremiah 13:13</u>
        I will fill all the inhabitants of this land, even the 'kings
        that sit upon David's throne. '

HINTS FROM HORACE

---

672 <u>Lines 79-80</u>   <u>Quote: Parodic</u>
    New words find credit in 'these latter days, ' / If neatly
    grafted on a Gallic phrase.
    <u>Job 19:25</u>
        For I know that my redeemer liveth, and that he shall
        stand at 'the latter day' upon the earth.

673 Lines 105-106   Reference: Subject
‾‾‾‾‾ The immortal wars which gods and angels wage, / Are
they not shown in Milton's sacred page?
Isaiah 14:12
‾‾‾‾‾ How art thou fallen from heaven, O Lucifer, son of the
morning!

674 Lines 201-204   Reference: Subject
‾‾‾‾‾ Soft as the gentler breathing of the lute, / "Of man's first
disobedience and the fruit" / He speaks, but, as his sub-
ject swells along, / Earth, heaven, and Hades echo with
the song.
Genesis 2-3
‾‾‾‾‾ Rf. the forbidden fruit and the fall of Adam and Eve.

675 Line 210   Allusion
‾‾‾‾ Not smoke from brightness, but from darkness-light.
Genesis 1:3-4
‾‾‾‾‾ And God said, Let there be light: and there was light. And
God saw the light, that it was good: and God divided the
light from the darkness.

676 Line 320   Reference: Subject
‾‾‾‾ What harm, if David danced before the ark?
I Chronicles 15:28-29
‾‾‾‾‾ Thus all Israel brought up the ark of the covenant of the
Lord with shouting, ... king David dancing and playing.

677 Lines 379-80   Reference: Parodic
‾‾‾‾‾ E'en now the 'songs of Solyma' begin; / Faith cants, per-
plex'd apologist of sin!
Song of Solomon
‾‾‾‾‾ Rf. the entire book.

678 Lines 539-40   Reference: Parodic
‾‾‾‾‾ Expect no credit for too wondrous tales, / Since Jonas only
springs alive from whales!
Jonah 2:10
‾‾‾‾ And the Lord spake unto the fish, and it vomited out Jonah
upon the dry land.

679 Lines 599-601   Reference: Subject
‾‾‾‾‾ Arise, my Jeffrey! or my inkless pen / Shall never blunt
its edge on meaner men; / Till thee or thine mine 'evil
eye' discerns.
Deuteronomy 28:54
‾‾‾‾‾ The man that is tender among you, and very delicate, his
'eye' shall be 'evil' toward his brother.

680 Lines 771-72   Allusion: Parodic
‾‾‾‾‾ Then spouts and foams, and foams, and cries at every line
/ (The Lord forgive him!), "Bravo! grand! divine!"

HOURS OF IDLENESS

"Answer to Some Elegant Verses Sent by a Friend to the Author,
Complaining That One of His Descriptions Was Rather Too Warmly
Drawn"

681   Lines 37-39
                                              Allusion
      For me, I fain would please the chosen few, / Whose
      souls, to felling and to nature true, / Will spare the child-
      ish verse.
      Deuteronomy 4:37
      And because he loved thy fathers, therefore he chose their
      seed after them.

"Childish Recollections"

682   Lines 393-94
                                              Allusion
      Say, can ambition's fever'd dream bestow / So sweet a
      balm to soothe your hours of woe?
      Jeremiah 8:22
      Is there no balm in Gilead?

"The Death of Calmar and Orla"

683   Paragraph 1
                                        Quote: Exact
      But their fame rises on the harp; their souls 'ride on the
      wings of the wind. '
      Psalm 18:10
      And he rode upon a cherub, and did fly: yea, he did 'fly
      upon the wings of the wind. '

684   Paragraph 9
                                        Reference: Subject
      Who would share the spoils of the battle with Calmar?
      I Chronicles 26:27
      Out of the spoils won in battles did they dedicate.

"Elegy on Newstead Abbey"

685   Line 48
                                        Quote: Approximate
      No friend, no home, no 'refuge, ' but 'their God. '
      Deuteronomy 33:27
      The eternal 'God is thy refuge, ' and underneath are the
      everlasting arms.

"The First Kiss of Love"

686   Lines 21-24
                                        Reference: Parodic
      Oh! cease to affirm that man, since his birth, / From
      Adam till now, has with wretchedness strove; / Some por-
      tion of paradise still is on earth, / And Eden revives in
      the first kiss of love.

Genesis 2-3
>Rf. Adam and Eve in Eden.

687 Line 26   Quote: Approximate
For years fleet away with the 'wings of the dove.'
Psalm 55:6
And I said, Oh that I had 'wings like a dove'!

"A Fragment" ("When, to their airy hall")

688 Line 6   Parallelism
To mark the spot where 'earth to earth returns'!
Genesis 3:19
Till thou return unto the ground; for out of it wast thou ta-
ken: for dust thou art, and 'unto dust shalt thou return.'

"From the Prometheus Vinctus of Aeschylus"

689 Lines 7-8   Allusion
My voice shall raise no impious strain / 'Gainst him who
rules the sky and azure main.
Isaiah 14:12
How art thou fallen from heaven, O Lucifer, son of the
morning!

"Granta--A Medley"

690 Lines 67-68   Quote: Exact
A numerous crowd, 'arrayed in white,' / Across the green
in numbers fly.
II Chronicles 5:12
Also the Levites ... being 'arrayed in white' linen.

691 Lines 81-84   Reference: Subject
If David, when his toils were ended, / Had heard these
blockheads sing before him, / To us his psalms had ne'er
descended, -- / In furious mood he would have tore 'em.
Psalms
Rf. David's composition of psalms.

692 Lines 85-92   Reference: Subject
The luckless Israelites, when taken / By some inhuman
tyrant's order, / Were ask'd to sing, by joy forsaken, / On
Babylonian river's border.
Psalm 137:1-3
By the rivers of Babylon, there we sat down, yea, we wept,
... and they that wasted us required of us mirth, saying,
Sing us one of the songs of Zion.

"Lachin Y Gair"

693 Lines 19-20   Quote: Approximate
Surely the soul of the hero rejoices, / And 'rides on the
wind,' o'er his own Highland vale.

Job 30:22
    Thou liftest me up to 'the wind'; thou causest me 'to ride
upon it, ' and dissolvest my substance.

"Lines: Addressed to the Rev. J. T. Becher. ... "

694 Line 36   Quote: Approximate
    Why waste upon folly 'the days of my youth'?
Ecclesiastes 12:7
    Remember now thy Creator in 'the days of thy youth. '

"On the Death of a Young Lady"

695 Lines 7-8   Quote: Exact
    'The King of Terrors' seized her as his prey, / Not worth,
nor beauty, have her life redeem'd.
Job 18:14
    His confidence shall be rooted out of his tabernacle, and it
shall bring him to 'the king of terrors. '

696 Lines 17-20   Allusion
    And shall presumptuous mortals Heaven arraign, / And,
madly, godlike Providence accuse? / Ah! no far fly from
me attempts so vain;-- / I'll ne'er submission to my God
refuse.
Isaiah 14:12
    How art thou fallen from heaven, O Lucifer, son of the
morning!

"Oscar of Alva"

697 Lines 129-30   Quote: Approximate
    'Oscar! my son'!--thou God of Heaven; / Restore the prop
of sinking age!
II Samuel 18:33; 19:4
    And the king ... said, O my son Absalom, my son, my son
Absalom! would God I had died for thee, O 'Absalom, my
son, ' my son!

698 Lines 129-30   Quote: Exact
    Thou 'God of Heaven'; / Restore the prop of sinking age!
II Chronicles 36:23
    All the kingdoms of the earth hath the Lord 'God of heaven'
given me.

"The Prayer of Nature"

699 Lines 31-32   Allusion
    Shall reptiles, grovelling on the ground, / Their great
Creator's purpose know?
Genesis 3:14
    And the Lord God said unto the serpent, Because thou hast
done this, ... upon thy belly shalt thou go, and dust shalt
thou eat all the days of thy life.

"To Caroline: Oh when shall the grave hide"

700   Line 6   Reference: Subject
       I blast not the fiends who have hurl'd me from bliss.
       Isaiah 14:12
       Rf. Lucifer's expulsion from heaven.

"To Edward Noel Long, Esq. "

701   Lines 8-10   Reference: Subject
       I hail the sky's celestial bow / Which spreads the sign of
       future peace / And bids the war of tempests cease.
       Genesis 9:13-16
       Rf. the rainbow sent after the flood.

"Translation from Catullus: Ad Lesbiam"

702   Lines 13-14   Quote: Approximate
       Whilst trembling with a thousand fears, / 'Parch'd to the
       throat my tongue adheres. '
       Psalm 137:6
       If I do not remember thee, let 'my tongue cleave to the
       roof of my mouth. '

703   Lines 13-14   Reference: Subject
       Whilst trembling with a thousand fears, / Parch'd to the
       throat my tongue adheres.
       Ezekiel 3:26
       And I will make thy tongue cleave to the roof of thy mouth.

THE ISLAND

---

704   Canto I, 111-12   Quote: Approximate
       Could these have charms for rudest seaboys, driven / Be-
       fore the mast by every 'wind of heaven'?
       Daniel 7:2
       Daniel spake and said, I saw in my vision by night, and,
       behold, the 'four winds of the heaven' strove upon the great
       sea.

705   Canto I, 120-21   Quote: Exact
       Then aught we know beyond our little day. / Yet still there
       whispers the 'small voice' within.
       I Kings 19:12
       But the Lord was not in the fire: and after the fire a still
       'small voice. '

706   Canto I, 124   Quote: Exact
       Man's conscience is 'the oracle of God. '

II Samuel 16:23
And the counsel of Ahithophel ... was as if a man had en-
quired at 'the oracle of God. '

707 Canto I, 233-34   Reference: Parodic
And yet they seek to 'nestle with the dove, ' / And tame
their fiery spirits down to love.
Isaiah 11:6
The wolf also shall 'dwell with' the lamb, and the leopard
shall 'lie down with' the kid; and the calf and the young lion
and the fatling together.

708 Canto II, 45-46   Quote: Approximate
Strike up the dance! the cava bowl fill high! / Drain every
drop!--'to-morrow we may die. '
Isaiah 22:13
Let us eat and drink; for 'to morrow we shall die. '

709 Canto II, 69-70   Allusion
The sordor of civilisation, mix'd / With all the savage
which man's fall hath fix'd.
Genesis 3:1-24
Rf. fall of Adam and Eve.

710 Canto II, 155-57   Quote: Exact
Root up the spring, and trample on the wave, / And crush
'the living waters' to a mass.
Zechariah 14:8
And it shall be in that day that 'living waters' shall go out
from Jerusalem.

711 Canto II, 161-62   Quote: Parodic
And they who fall but fall as worlds will 'fall, / To rise, '
if just, a spirit o'er them all.
Isaiah 24:20
And the transgression thereof shall be heavy upon it; and it
shall 'fall, and not rise again. '

712 Canto II, 179-82   Reference: Subject
Placed in the Arab's clime, he would have been / As bold
a rover as the sands have seen, / And graved their thirst
with as enduring lip / As Ishmael, wafted on his desert
ship.
Genesis 16; 21:9-21
Rf. expulsion of Ishmael and Hagar.

713 Canto II, 373   Allusion
His soul is gone before his dust to heaven.
Genesis 3:19
For dust thou art, and unto dust shalt thou return.

714 Canto II, 390-91   Reference: Subject
Dissolve this clog and clod of clay before / Its hour, and
merge our soul in the great shore.

Ecclesiastes 12:7
Then shall the dust return to the earth as it was: and the
spirit shall return unto God who gave it.

715 Canto II, 480-83   Reference: Parodic
And, 'stead of trousers (ah! too early torn! / For even
the mildest woods will have their thorn) / A curious sort
of somewhat scanty mat / Now served for inexpressibles
and hat.
Genesis 3:1-24
Rf. fig leaf clothing of Adam and Eve.

716 Canto III, 25-26   Quote: Approximate
But now at rest, 'a little remnant' drew / Together
Isaiah 1:9
Except the Lord of hosts had left unto us 'a very small
remnant.'

717 Canto III, 56-58   Quote: Approximate
Even Greece can boast but one Thermophlae, / Till now,
when she has forged her broken chain / Back to a sword,
and 'dies and lives again'!
Job 14:14
If a man 'die,' shall he 'live again?

THE LAMENT OF TASSO

---

718 Lines 21-23   Allusion
For I have battled with mine agony, / And made me wings
wherewith to overfly / The narrow circus of my dungeon
wall.
Psalm 18:29
And by my God I leaped over a wall.

719 Lines 26-27   Quote: Exact
And 'pour'd my spirit' over Palestine, / In honour of the
sacred war for Him.
Isaiah 44:3
I will 'pour my spirit' upon thy seed, and my blessing upon
thine offspring.

720 Lines 31-32   Reference: Subject
I have employ'd my penance to record / How Salem's
shrine was won, and how adored.
Genesis 14:18
Rf. Salem (i. e. Jerusalem).

721 Lines 40-42   Reference: Subject
Thou too art gone--and so is my delight: / And therefore

do I weep and inly bleed / With this last bruise upon a
broken reed.
II Kings 18:21
Now, behold, thou trustest upon the staff of this bruised
reed.

722 Lines 87-88   Reference: Subject
And each is tortured in his separate hell-- / For we are
crowded in our solitudes.
II Samuel 22:6
The sorrows of hell compassed me about; the snares of
death prevented me.

723 Lines 138-39   Reference: Subject
I know not how--thy genius master'd mine-- / My 'star
stood still' before thee.
Joshua 10:12-13
Then spake Joshua ... Sun, stand thou still upon Gibeon;
and thou, Moon, in the valley of Ajalon. And the 'sun
stood still,' and the moon stayed.

724 Lines 166-67   Allusion
And with my years my soul began to pant / With feelings
of strange tumult and soft pain.
Psalm 42:1
As the hart panteth after the water brooks, so panteth my
soul after thee, O God.

725 Lines 198-99   Quote: Exact
I thought 'mine enemies' had been but Man, / But Spirits
may be leagued with them.
Psalm 23:5
Thou preparest a table before me in the presence of 'mine
enemies.'

726 Lines 200-202   Quote: Exact
Heaven forgets me; in the dearth / Of such defence 'the
Powers of Evil' can / It may be, tempt me further.
Habakkuk 2:9
Woe to him that coveteth an evil covetousness ... that he
may be delivered from 'the power of evil'!

727 Lines 204-205   Allusion
Why in this furnace is my spirit proved / Like steel in
tempering fire? because I loved?
Daniel 3:23
And these three men, Shadrach, Meshach, and Abednego,
fell down bound into the midst of the burning fiery furnace.

728 Lines 209-10   Quote: Approximate
My scars are callous, or I should have 'dash'd / My brain
against these bars.'

Psalm 91:12
They shall bear thee up in their hands, lest thou 'dash thy
foot against a stone. '

LARA

---

729   Canto I, 314-16   Reference: Subject
As if the worst had fall'n which could befall, / He stood a
stranger in this breathing world, / An erring spirit from
another hurl'd.
Isaiah 14:12
How art thou fallen from heaven, O Lucifer, son of the
morning!

730   Canto II, 17-18   Quote: Approximate
But 'creeping things' shall revel in their spoil, / And fit
thy clay to fertilise the soil.
Genesis 1:26
And God said, Let us make man in our image, after our
likeness: and let them have dominion ... over every 'creep-
ing thing' that creepeth upon the earth.

731   Canto II, 161-62   Quote: Approximate
Long war without and frequent broil within / Had made a
path for blood and 'giant sin. '
Genesis 20:9
And what have I offended thee, that thou hast brought on
me and on my kingdom a 'great sin'?

732   Canto II, 506-507   Parallelism
He saw the head his breast would still sustain, / Roll down
like 'earth to earth' upon the plain.
Genesis 3:19
For 'dust' thou art, and 'unto dust' shalt thou return.

MANFRED

---

733   Act I. i. 9-10   Reference: Subject
But grief should be the instructor of the wise; / 'Sorrow is
knowledge. '
Ecclesiastes 1:18
For in much wisdom is much grief: and he that increaseth
'knowledge increaseth sorrow. '

734   Act I, i, 10-12   Reference: Subject
          Sorrow is knowledge: they who know the most / Must
          mourn the deepest o'er the fatal truth, / The Tree of Know-
          ledge is not that of Life.
      Genesis 2:9, 17; 3:1-6
          Rf. fall of Adam and Eve after eating of the tree of know-
          ledge.

735   Act I, i, 41   Quote: Exact
          'If it be so. '
      Genesis 25:22
          And she said, 'If it be so, ' why am I thus?

736   Act I, i, 75   Quote: Approximate
          And 'what with me wouldst Thou'?
      Joshua 15:18
          And she lighted off her ass; and Caleb said unto her, 'What
          wouldest thou'?

737   Act I, i, 100-101   Reference: Subject
          I am the Rider of the wind, / The Stirrer of the storm.
      Job 30:22
          Thou liftest me up to the wind; thou causest me to ride up-
          on it.

738   Act I, i, 169   Quote: Exact
          Accursed! 'what have I to do with' days?
      II Samuel 16:10
          And the king said, 'What have I to do with' you?

739   Act I, i, 174-75   Quote: Exact
          One moment, ere we part-- / I would behold ye 'face to
          face. '
      Exodus 33:11
          And the Lord spake unto Moses 'face to face. '

740   Act I, i, 249-50   Reference: Subject
          And by thy brotherhood of Cain, / I call upon thee!
      Genesis 4:1-17
          Rf. the curse on Cain.

741   Act I, ii, 300-301   Reference: Subject
          We / half dust, half deity, alike unfit / To sink or soar,
          with our mix'd essence make / A conflict of its elements.
      Genesis 2:7
          And the Lord God formed man of the dust of the ground,
          and breathed into his nostrils the breath of life; and man
          became a living soul.

742   Act I, ii, 303-304   Quote: Parodic
          'Breathe / The breath of degradation' and of pride.
      Genesis 2:7
          And the Lord God formed man of the dust of the ground, and
          'breathed' into his nostrils 'the breath of life. '

743   Act I. ii, 362-63   Allusion
          For the love / Of him who made you, stand not on that
          brink!
       Genesis 2:7
          And the Lord God formed man of the dust of the ground,
          and breathed into his nostrils the breath of life.

744   Act II. i. 11-12   Quote: Exact
          My 'way of life' leads me but rarely down / To bask by
          the huge hearths of those old halls.
       Proverbs 10:17
          He is in the 'way of life' that keepeth instruction.

745   Act II. i. 21-22   Allusion
          There's blood upon the brim! / Will it then never--never
          sink in the earth?
       Genesis 4:10
          And he said, What hast thou done? the voice of thy brother's
          blood crieth unto me from the ground.

746   Act II. ii. 144-45   Quote: Exact
          'From my youth' upwards / My spirit walk'd not with the
          souls of men.
       I Kings 18:12
          I thy servant fear the Lord 'from my youth. '

747   Act II. ii. 150-53   Allusion
          Though I wore the form, / I had no sympathy with breaking
          flesh, / Nor midst the creatures of clay that girded me /
          Was there but one who--but of her anon.
       Genesis 2:7
          And the Lord God formed man of the dust of the ground,
          and breathed into his nostrils the breath of life.

748   Act II. ii. 156-58   Reference: Subject
          My joy was in the Wilderness, to breathe / The difficult
          air of the iced mountain's top, / Where the birds dare not
          build.
       Jeremiah 48:40; 49:16, 22
          Rf. the eagle's nest on high.

749   Act II. ii. 172-73   Allusion
          I felt myself degraded back to them, / And was all clay
          again.
       Genesis 2:7
          And the Lord God formed man of the dust of the ground,
          and breathed into his nostrils the breath of life.

750   Act II. ii. 242-43   Quote: Exact
          I dwell in my despair-- / And live--and 'live for ever. '
       Daniel 4:34
          And I blessed and honoured him that 'liveth for ever, ' whose
          dominion is an everlasting dominion.

751   Act II. ii. 260-61   Quote: Exact
      Dreading still to die. / In 'all the days of' this detested
      yoke.
      II Kings 23:22
      Surely there was not holden such a passover ... in 'all the
      days of' the kings of Israel.

752   Act II. ii. 266-69   Allusion
      We can number / How few, how less than few, wherein the
      soul / Forbears to 'pant for death,' and yet draws back /
      As from a stream in winter.
      Psalm 42:1-2
      As the 'hart panteth' after the water brooks, so panteth my
      soul after thee, O God. My soul thirsteth for God.

753   Act II. ii. 275-76   Reference: Subject
      The buried Prophet answered to the Hag / of Endor.
      I Samuel 28:1-25
      Rf. Samuel and the witch of Endor.

754   Act II. iii. 314-17   Reference: Subject
      The Captive Usurper, / Hurl'd down from the throne, / Lay
      buried in torpor, / Forgotten and lone.
      Isaiah 14:12
      How art thou fallen from heaven, O Lucifer, son of the
      morning!

755   Act II. iii. 354-55   Reference: Parodic
      We only give to take again / The spirits of our slaves!
      Job 1:21
      The Lord gave, and the Lord hath taken away.

756   Act II. iii. 360-62   Quote: Parodic
      I was detain'd repairing shatter'd thrones, / Marrying fools,
      restoring dynasties, / 'Avenging men upon their enemies.'
      Isaiah 1:24
      Therefore saith the Lord, ... I will ease me of mine ad-
      versaries, and 'avenge me of mine enemies.'

757   Act II. iii. 367-78   Quote: Exact
      And mortals dared to ponder for themselves, / To 'weigh
      kings in the balance,' and to speak.
      Daniel 5:27
      Thou art 'weighed in the balances,' and art found wanting.

758   Act II. iii. 369   Reference: Subject
      Of freedom, the forbidden fruit.
      Genesis 2:19-27; 3:1-7
      Rf. the fruit of the tree of knowledge of good and evil.

759   Act II. iv. 459-60   Quote: Approximate
      Of the mould of thy clay / Which 'return'd to the earth.'

Ecclesiastes 12:7
Then shall the dust 'return to the earth' as it was.

760 Act III. i. 37-38   Quote: Approximate
The many evil and unheavenly spirits / Which walk 'the
valley of the shade of death.'
Psalm 23:4
Yea though I walk through 'the valley of the shadow of death,'
I will fear no evil.

761 Act III. i. 39-40   Allusion
Mankind, / Thy fellows in creation.
Genesis 2:7
And the Lord God formed man of the dust of the ground,
and breathed into his nostrils the breath of life.

762 Act III. i. 63-65   Quote: Approximate
" 'Vengeance is mine alone!' " / So saith the Lord, and
with all humbleness / His servant echoes back the awful
word.
Deuteronomy 32:35
'To me belongeth vengeance,' and recompence; their foot
shall slide in due time.

763 Act III. i. 82-85   Reference: Subject
Which all who seek may win, whatever be / Their earthly
errors, so they be atoned: / And the commencement of
atonement is / The sense of its necessity.
Exodus 29:33-37
Rf. the annual day of atonement for sins.

764 Act III. i. 151-52   Quote: Approximate
Then wonder not that 'I / Am what I am,' but that I ever
was.
Exodus 3:14
And God said unto Moses, 'I am That I Am.'

765 Act III. i. 160-67   Reference: Subject
He / Hath all the energy which would have made / A good-
ly frame of glorious elements, / Had they been wisely min-
gled; as it is, / It is an awful chaos--light and darkness, /
And mind and dust, and passions and pure thoughts, / Mix'd,
and contending without end or order, / All dormant or de-
structive.
Genesis 1-2
Rf. the creation.

766 Act III. i. 164-67   Reference: Subject
It is an awful chaos--light and darkness, / And mind and
dust, and passions and pure thoughts, / Mix'd, and con-
tending without end or order, / All dormant or destructive.
Genesis 1-2
Rf. the creation.

767   Act III. i. 165-66   Quote: Exact
      And mind and dust, and passions and pure thoughts, / Mix'd,
      and contending 'without end' or order.
      Isaiah 45:17
      Ye shall not be ashamed nor confounded world 'without end. '

768   Act III. i. 168-69   Reference: Subject
      I will try once more, / For such are worth redemption.
      Leviticus 25:51
      He shall give again the price of his redemption out of the
      money.

769   Act III. ii. 175-77   Reference: Subject
      The vigorous race / Of undiseased mankind, the giant sons
      / Of the embrace of angels.
      Genesis 6:1-4 (esp. v. 4)
      There were giants in the earth in those days; and also af-
      ter that, when the sons of God came in unto the daughters
      of men, and they bare children to them, the same became
      mighty men which were of old, men of renown.

770   Act III. ii. 180-82   Allusion
      Most glorious orb! that wert a worship, ere / The mystery
      of thy making was reveal'd! / Thou earliest minister of
      the Almighty.
      Genesis 1:16
      And God made two great lights; the greater light to rule the
      day, and the lesser light to rule the night: he made the
      stars also.

771   Act III. iv. 314   Quote: Approximate
      'My days are number'd, ' and my deeds recorded.
      Psalm 90:12
      So teach us to 'number our days, ' that we may apply our
      hearts unto wisdom.

772   Act III. iv. 333-34   Quote: Approximate
      Alas! lost mortal! 'what' with guests like these / 'Hast
      thou to do'? I tremble for thy sake.
      I Kings 17:18
      And she said unto Elijah, 'What have I to do with thee, ' O
      thou man of God?

773   Act III. iv. 353-54   Quote: Exact
      Ye have no power where piety hath power, / And I do charge
      ye 'in the name. '
      Ezra 5:1
      Then the prophets ... prophesied unto the Jews ... 'in the
      name of' the God of Israel.

774   Act III. iv. 362-63   Allusion
      Earthly strength / To wrestle, though with spirits.
      Genesis 32:24-32
      Rf. Jacob's wrestling with an angel.

775 Act III. iv. 377-79   Reference: Subject
    When the earth / Saw men and spirits walking side by side /
    And gave ye no supremacy.
    Genesis 6:1-4
    Rf. giants in the earth.

MARINO FALIERO, DOGE OF VENICE

---

776 Act I. ii. 150-51   Quote: Exact
    The blood and sweat of almost eighty years, / Were
    'weigh'd i' the balance,' 'gainst the foulest strain.
    Daniel 5:27
    Thou art 'weighed in the balances,' and art found wanting.

777 Act I. ii. 258-60   Reference: Subject
    In th' olden time / Some sacrifices ask'd a single victim,
    / Great expiations had a hecatomb.
    Leviticus 1-7
    Rf. the Mosaic sacrifices for various trespasses.

778 Act II. i. 56-58   Reference: Subject
    Marianna: Some sacrifice is due to slander'd virtue.
    Angiolina: Why, what is virtue if it needs a victim?   Or
    if it must depend upon men's words?
    Leviticus 1-10
    Rf. sacrifices of animals.

779 Act II. i. 111   Quote: Exact
    And then he has been rash 'from his youth' upwards.
    Genesis 8:21
    And the Lord said ... for the imagination of man's heart
    is evil 'from his youth.'

780 Act II. i. 207-10   Reference: Subject
    Yes--the same sin that overthrew the angels, / And of all
    sins most easily bests / Mortals the nearest to the angelic
    nature: / The vile are only vain; the great are proud.
    Isaiah 14:12
    How art thou fallen from heaven, O Lucifer, son of the
    morning!

781 Act II. i. 244, 248   Parallelism
    Does not the law of Heaven say 'blood for blood'?... / Do
    not the laws of man say 'blood for honour'?
    Exodus 21:24
    'Eye for eye,' tooth for tooth, hand for hand, foot for foot.

782 Act II. i. 395   Reference: Subject
    The once fall'n woman must for ever fall.

Genesis 3:1-24
   Rf. the fall of Eve.

783   Act II. i. 500-503   Quote: Approximate
   My gentle child, forgive me; thou wert made / For better
   fortunes than to share in mine, / Now darkling in their
   close toward 'the deep vale / Where Death sits robed in
   his' all-sweeping 'shadow. '
Psalm 23:4
   Yea, though I walk through 'the valley of the shadow of
   death. '

784   Act II. ii. 617-19   Allusion
   A soul / Which multiplies itself throughout all time, / When
   wicked men wax mighty.
Genesis 1:28
   And God blessed them, and God said unto them, Be fruitful,
   and multiply, and replenish the earth.

785   Act II. ii. 630-31   Quote: Approximate
   These 'unmanly creeping things' / Command our swords,
   and rule us with a word.
Leviticus 5:2
   Or if a soul touch ... the carcase of 'unclean creeping
   things' ... he also shall be unclean, and guilty.

786   Act III. i. 14-15   Reference: Subject
   And I am tainted, and must wash away / The plague spots
   in the healing wave.
Leviticus 13:53, 58
   Rf. ritual of cleansing items in contact with disease.

787   Act III. ii. 360   Quote: Exact
   'With all my soul' and sword, I yield assent.
Deuteronomy 6:5
   And thou shalt love the Lord with all thine heart, and 'with
   all thy soul, ' and with all thy might.

788   Act III. ii. 482-83   Parallelism
   I had one only 'fount of quiet' left, / And 'that' they poi-
   son'd!
Psalm 36:9
   For with thee is the 'fountain of life': in thy light shall
   we see light.

789   Act III. ii. 488-90   Quote: Approximate
   It hurt me, but I bore it-- / Till this last 'running over of
   the cup' / Of bitterness.
Psalm 23:5
   Thou anointest my head with oil; 'my cup runneth over. '

790   Act III. ii. 541-44   Reference: Subject
   Revenge, / Which, like the sheeted fire from heaven, must
   blast / Without distinction, as it fell of yore / Where the

Dead Sea hath quench'd two cities' ashes.
Genesis 19
Rf. the destruction of Sodom and Gomorrah.

791 Act III. ii. 578-79   Allusion
They smote you, and oppress'd you, and despised you; / So
they have me: but you ne'er spake with them.
Isaiah 53:3
He is despised and rejected of men; a man of sorrows and
acquainted with grief: ... he was despised, and we esteemed
him not.

792 Act III. ii. 614-15   Reference: Parodic
And hew the highest genealogic trees / Down to the earth,
strew'd with their bleeding fruit.
Daniel 4:14
He cried aloud, and said thus, Hew down the tree, and cut
off his branches, shake off his leaves, and scatter his fruit.

793 Act IV. i. 156-57
Since Time / Has changed his slow scythe for the 'two-
edged sword. '
Psalm 149:6
Let the high praises of God be in their mouth, and a 'two-
edged sword' in their hand.

794 Act IV. i. 249-50   Quote: Exact
'The only son' / Of him who was a friend unto thy father.
Genesis 22:16
By myself have I sworn, saith the Lord, for because thou
hast done this thing, and hast not withheld thy son, 'thine
only son. '

795 Act IV. ii. 376   Quote: Exact
Nor 'bow the knee' before a civic senate.
Genesis 41:43
And they cried before him, 'Bow the knee. '

796 Act IV. ii. 405-408   Reference: Subject
And the mere instinct of the first-born Cain, / Which ever
lurks somewhere in human hearts / Though circumstance
may keep it in abeyance, / Will urge the rest on like to
wolves.
Genesis 4:1-18
Rf. Cain and Abel.

797 Act IV. ii. 512-13   Reference: Subject
The blood of tyrants is not human; they, / Like to incar-
nate Molochs, feed on ours.
Amos 5:26
Your Moloch and Chiun your images, the star of your god,
which ye made to yourselves.

798   Act IV. ii. 517-18   Reference: Subject
          That we must work by crime to punish crime? / And slay
       as if Death had but this one gate.
       Job 38:17
          Have the gates of death been opened unto thee?

799   Act IV. ii. 572-73   Reference: Subject
          Our fate is trembling in the balance, and / Woe to the
       vanquish'd!
       Daniel 5:27
          Thou art weighed in the balances, and art found wanting.

800   Act IV. ii. 621-22   Quote: Approximate
          It is in vain to war with Fortune; / 'The Glory hath de-
       parted' from our house.
       Ezekiel 10:18
          Then 'the glory of the Lord departed' from off the threshold
       of the house.

801   Act V. i. 20   Quote: Exact
          So 'let them die the death. '
       Numbers 23:10
          'Let me die the death' of the righteous, and let my last
       end be like his!

802   Act V. i. 98   Quote: Exact
          And Heaven 'have mercy on' their souls!
       Psalm 4:1
          Hear me when I call, O God of my righteousness: thou
       hast enlarged me when I was in distress; 'have mercy upon'
       me, and hear my prayer.

803   Act V. i. 198-99   Quote: Exact
          Not even contented with a sceptre, till / They can convert
       it to 'a two-edged sword'!
       Psalm 149:6
          Let the high praises of God be in their mouth, and 'a two-
       edged sword' in their hand.

804   Act V. i. 246-47   Quote: Approximate
          A spark creates the flame--'tis the last drop / Which makes
       'the cup run o'er, ' and mine was full.
       Psalm 23:5
          Thou anointest my head with oil; 'my cup runneth over. '

805   Act V. i. 281-82   Reference: Subject
          But walls have ears--nay, more, they have tongues; and
       if / There were no other way for truth to o'erleap them.
       Job 18:29
          For by thee I have run through a troop; and by my God
       have I leaped over a wall.

806   Act V. i. 394-96   Reference: Subject
          Thy suing to these men were but the bleating / Of the lamb
          to the butcher, or the cry of seamen to the surge.
      Isaiah 53:7
          He is brought as a lamb to the slaughter, and as a sheep
          before her shearers is dumb, so he openeth not his mouth.

807   Act V. i. 521-22   Quote: Exact
          Thy head shall be struck off; and Heaven 'have mercy / Up-
          on' thy soul!
      Psalm 4:1
          Hear me when I call, O God of my righteousness: thou
          hast enlarged me when I was in distress; 'have mercy upon'
          me, and hear my prayer.

808   Act V. i. 524-25   Quote: Exact
          'Make thy peace with God': / Within an hour thou must be
          in His presence.
      Isaiah 27:5
          Or let him take hold of my strength, that he may 'make
          peace with me'; and he shall 'make peace with me. '

809   Act V. i. 526-27   Reference: Subject
          My blood will rise / To Heaven before the souls of those
          who shed it.
      Genesis 4:10
          And he said, What hast thou done? the voice of thy bro-
          ther's blood crieth unto me from the ground.

810   Act V. i. 543-44   Allusion
          From henceforth, know / I am devoted unto God alone.
      Leviticus 27:28
          No devoted thing, that a man shall devote unto the Lord of
          all he hath, ... Shall be sold or redeemed: every devoted
          thing is most holy unto the Lord.

811   Act V. ii. 630-33   Reference: Subject
          On my return from Rome, a mist of such / Unwonted den-
          sity went on before / The Becentaur, like the columnar
          cloud / Which usher'd Israel out of Egypt.
      Exodus 13:21
          And the Lord went before them by day in a pillar of a
          cloud, to lead them the way.

812   Act V. ii. 654-55   Quote: Exact
          I am at peace: the peace of certainty / That a sure hour
          will come, when 'their sons' sons. '
      Deuteronomy 4:9
          But teach them thy sons, and 'thy sons' sons. '

813   Act V. ii. 656-59   Quote: Exact
          And these azure waters, / And all which makes them em-
          inent and bright, / Shall be 'a desolation and a curse,' / A

hissing and a scoff unto the nations, / A Carthage, and a
Tyre, an Ocean Babel!
II Kings 22:19
    I spake against the inhabitants thereof, that they should be-
come 'a desolation and a curse. '

814   <u>Act V. ii. 657-60</u>   Reference: Subject
    And all which makes them eminent and bright, / Shall be
    a 'desolation' and a curse, / A 'hissing' and a scoff unto
    the nations, / A Carthage, and a Tyre, an Ocean Babel!
    <u>Micah 6:16</u>
        I should make thee a 'desolation, ' and the inhabitants there-
        of 'an hissing': therefore ye shall bear the reproach of my
        people.

815   <u>Act V. ii. 659-60</u>   Allusion
    A hissing and a scoff unto the nations, / A Carthage, and
    a Tyre, an Ocean Babel!
    <u>Genesis 11:4-9</u>
        And they said, Go to, let us build us a city and a tower,
        whose top may reach unto heaven, ... the name of it called
        Babel.

816   <u>Act V. ii. 660</u>   Allusion
    A Carthage, and a Tyre, an Ocean Babel!
    <u>Genesis 10:10; 11:1-9</u>
        Rf. the tower of Babel.

817   <u>Act V. iii. 794-95</u>   Quote: Approximate
    Thou den of 'drunkards with the blood' of princes! / Ge-
    henna of the waters! thou sea Sodom!
    <u>Jeremiah 45:10</u>
        And the sword shall devour, and it shall be satiate and
        made 'drunk with their blood. '

818   <u>Act V. iii. 795</u>   Reference: Subject
    Gehenna of the waters! thou sea Sodom!
    <u>Genesis 13:13</u>
        But the men of Sodom were wicked and sinners before the
        Lord exceedingly.

819   <u>Act V. iii. 795</u>   Allusion
    Thou sea Sodom!
    <u>Genesis 18:20; 19:24</u>
        And the Lord said, Because the cry of Sodom and Gomorrah
        is great, and because their sin is very grievous ... Then
        the Lord rained upon Sodom and upon Gomorrah brimstone
        and fire.

820   <u>Act V. iii. 765-67</u>   Reference: Subject
    Proud of some name they have disgraced, or sprung / From
    an adulteress boastful of her guilt / With some large gon-
    dolier or foreign soldier.

Proverbs 30:20
> Such is the way of an adulterous woman; she eateth, and
> wipeth her mouth, and saith, I have done no wickedness.

MAZEPPA

---

821   Lines 147-48   Reference: Parodic
> He was the Polish Solomon,-- / So sung his poets, all but
> one.

I Kings 10:7
> Howbeit I believed not the words, until I came, ... and,
> behold, the half was not told me: thy [Solomon's] wisdom
> and prosperity exceedeth the fame which I heard.

822   Lines 158-59   Reference: Parodic
> And he was proud, ye may divine, / As if from heaven he
> had been sent.

Psalm 110:2
> The Lord shall send the rod of thy strength out of Zion:
> rule thou in the midst of thine enemies.

823   Lines 183-86   Quote: Approximate
> There were few, or boys or men, / Who, 'in my dawning
> time of day,' / Of vassal or of knight's degree, / Could
> vie in vanities with me.

Judges 19:26
> Then came the woman 'in the dawning of the day,' and fell
> down at the door.

824   Lines 423-24   Quote: Approximate
> Away, away, my steed and I, / 'Upon the pinions of the
> wind.'

Psalm 18:10
> And he rode upon a cherub, and did fly: yea, he did fly
> 'upon the wings of the wind.'

825   Lines 752-54   Reference: Subject
> The tree of his new Paradise, / To-morrow would have
> given him all.

Genesis 2-3
> Rf. the tree of knowledge of good and evil.

MISCELLANEOUS POEMS

"Address, Spoken at the Opening of Drury-Lane Theatre, Saturday,
October 10, 1812"

826   Lines 1-2   Reference: Subject
         In one dread night our city saw, and sigh'd, / Bow'd to
         the dust the Drama's tower of pride.
      Genesis 11:1-9
         And they said, Go to, let us build us a city and a tower,
         whose top may reach unto heaven, ... the name of it called
         Babel.

827   Lines 5-8   Reference: Parodic
         Ye who beheld (oh! sight admired and mourn'd, / Whose
         radiance mock'd the ruin it adorn'd!), / Through clouds of
         fire the massy fragments riven, / Like Israel's pillar,
         chase the night from heaven.
      Exodus 13:21
         And the Lord went before them by day in a pillar of a
         cloud, to lead them the way; and by night in a pillar of
         fire, to give them light.

"The Adieu"

828   Line 106   Reference: Subject
         Bow down beneath the Almighty's Throne.
      Genesis 17:1
         The Lord appeared to Abram, and said unto him, I am the
         Almighty God.

"And Wilt Thou Weep When I Am Low?"

829   Lines 7-8   Quote: Exact
         And when I perish, thou alone / Wilt sigh above my 'place
         of rest. '
      Isaiah 34:14
         The screech owl also shall rest there, and find for herself
         a 'place of rest. '

"Away, Away, Ye Notes of Woe"

830   Lines 13-14   Quote: Exact
         Yes, Thyrza! yes, they breathe of thee, / Beloved dust!
         since 'dust thou art. '
      Genesis 3:19
         Till thou return unto the ground; for out of it wast thou ta-
         ken: for 'dust thou art, ' and unto dust shalt thou return.

"Bright Be the Place of Thy Soul"

831   Line 8   Quote: Exact
         When we know that thy 'God is with thee. '
      Genesis 21:22
         The chief captain of his host spake unto Abraham, saying,
         'God is with thee' in all that thou doest.

"Churchill's Grave"

832 <u>Lines 19-22</u>   Reference: <u>Subject</u>
       As I said, / The Architect of all on which we tread, / For
       Earth is but a tomb-stone, did essay / To extricate re-
       membrance from the clay.
     <u>Genesis 2:7</u>
       And the Lord God formed man of the dust of the ground.

"Darkness"

833 <u>Line 69</u>   Quote: <u>Approximate</u>
       'The world was void. '
     <u>Genesis 1:2</u>
       And 'the earth was' without form, and 'void. '

"The Devil's Drive"

834 <u>Line 11</u>   Reference: <u>Subject</u>
       "And what shall I ride in?" quoth Lucifer then.
     <u>Isaiah 14:12</u>
       How art thou fallen from heaven, O Lucifer, son of the
       morning!

835 <u>Line 153</u>   Reference: <u>Parodic</u>
       I shall hint to friend Moloch to call him to order.
     <u>Amos 5:26</u>
       By ye have borne the tabernacle of your Moloch and Chiun
       your images.

"Fill the Goblet"

836 <u>Lines 9-10</u>   Quote: <u>Exact</u>
       'In the days of my youth, ' when the heart's in its spring, /
       And dreams that affection can never take wing.
     <u>Job 29:4</u>
       As I was 'in the days of my youth, ' when the secret of God
       was upon my tabernacle.

"Impromptu"

837 <u>Lines 1-3</u>   Reference: <u>Parodic</u>
       Beneath Blessington's eyes / The reclaim'd Paradise /
       Should be free as the former from evil.
     <u>Genesis 3:1-24</u>
       Rf. the garden of Eden.

838 <u>Lines 4-6</u>   Reference: <u>Parodic</u>
       But if the new Eve / For an Apple should grieve, / What
       mortal would not play the Devil?
     <u>Genesis 3:1-24</u>
       Rf. Eve's temptation with the forbidden fruit.

"The Irish Avatar"

839   Lines 58-60   Reference: Parodic
    If the idol of brass find his feet are of clay, / Must what
terror or policy wring forth be class'd / With what monarch
ne'er give?
Daniel 2:31-35
    Thou, O king, sawest, and behold a great image ... his
feet part of iron and part of clay.

840   Lines 73-74   Reference: Subject
    Ay! 'Build him a dwelling!' let each give his mite! / Till,
like Babel, the new royal dome [a palace] hath arisen!
Genesis 11:1-9
    And they said, Go to, let us build us a city and a tower,
whose top may reach unto heaven; and let us make us a
name, lest we be scattered abroad ... the name of it called
Babel.

841   Line 86   Quote: Parodic
    'On his right hand' behold a Sejanus appears!
I Kings 2:19
    And the king ... caused a seat to be set for the king's
mother; and she sat 'on his right hand.'

"Monody on the Death of the Right Hon. R. B. Sheridan"

842   Lines 41-44   Reference: Subject
    When the loud cry of trampled Hindostan / Arose to Hea-
ven in her appeal from man, / His was the thunder, his
the avenging 'rod,' / The wrath, the delegated voice 'of
God.'
Job 9:34
    Let him take 'his rod' away from me, and let not his fear
terrify me.

"Ode from the French"

843   Lines 11-12   Parallelism
    A crimson cloud it spreads and glows, / But 'shall return
to whence it rose.'
Ecclesiastes 12:7
    Then 'shall' the dust 'return to the earth as it was': and
the spirit 'shall return unto God' who gave it.

844   Lines 83-84   Reference: Subject
    Freedom, such as God hath given / Unto all beneath his
heaven, / With their breath.
Genesis 2:7
    And the Lord God formed man of the dust of the ground,
and breathed into his nostrils the breath of life; and man
became a living soul.

"Ode to Napoleon Buonaparte"

845   Lines 8-9   Reference: Subject
        Since he, miscall'd the Morning Star, / Nor man nor fiend
        hath fallen so far.
        Isaiah 14:12
        How art thou fallen from heaven, O Lucifer, son of the
        morning!

846   Lines 26-27   Reference: Subject
        These Pagod things of sabre sway, / With fronts of brass
        and feet of clay.
        Daniel 2:31-45
        Thou, O king, sawest, and behold a great image ... His
        breast and his arms of silver, his belly and his thighs of
        brass, his legs of iron, his feet part of iron and part of
        clay.

847   Lines 30-31   Quote: Exact
        The earthquake voice of Victory, / To thee 'the breath of
        life. '
        Genesis 2:7
        And the Lord God formed man of the dust of the ground,
        and breathed into his nostrils 'the breath of life'; and man
        became a living soul.

848   Lines 80-81   Reference: Subject
        To think that God's fair 'world' hath been / The 'footstool'
        of a thing so mean.
        Isaiah 66:1
        Thus saith the Lord, ... the 'earth' is my 'footstool. '

849   Lines 131-32   Reference: Subject
        Unless, like he of Babylon, / All sense is with thy sceptre
        gone.
        Daniel 4:19-37
        Rf. Nebuchadnezzar's punishment, acting as a beast.

850   Lines 140-44   Reference: Subject
        Foredoom'd by God--by man accurst, / And that last act,
        though not thy worst, / The very Fiend's arch mock; / He
        in his fall preserved his pride, / And, if a mortal, had as
        proudly died!
        Isaiah 14:12
        How art thou fallen from heaven, O Lucifer, son of the
        morning!

"Prometheus"

851   Lines 19-22   Allusion: Parodic
        And the deaf tyranny of Fate, / The ruling principle of
        Hate, / Which for its pleasure doth create / The things it
        may annihilate.

Genesis 3:19
> In the sweat of thy face shalt thou eat bread, till thou re-
> turn unto the ground; for out of it wast thou taken: for
> dust thou art, and unto dust shalt thou return.

852   Lines 47-48   Reference: Subject
> Like thee, Man is in part divine, / A troubled stream from
> a pure source.

Genesis 1:27
> So God created man in his own image, in the image of God
> created he him.

"Stanzas for Music: There Be None of Beauty's Daughters"

853   Lines 3-4   Quote: Approximate
> And like 'music on the waters' / Is thy sweet voice to me.

Ecclesiastes 11:1
> Cast thy 'bread upon the waters': for thou shalt find it af-
> ter many days.

"Stanzas to the Po"

854   Line 51   Quote: Approximate
> 'To dust if I return,' from dust I sprung.

Genesis 3:19
> For dust thou art, and 'unto dust shalt thou return.'

"To a Lady (When Man, Expelled)"

855   Lines 1-4   Reference: Subject
> When Man, expell'd from Eden's bowers, / A moment ling-
> er'd near the gate, / Each scene recall'd the vanish'd
> hours, / And bade him curse his future fate.

Genesis 3:1-24
> Rf. expulsion from Eden.

856   Lines 15-16   Reference: Parodic
> I cannot view my paradise / Without the wish of dwelling
> there.

Genesis 3:1-24
> Rf. expulsion of Adam and Eve from Eden.

"To Belshazzar"

857   Entire poem   Reference: Subject
Daniel 5:25-31
> Rf. Belshazzar weighed and found wanting before God.

"Translation of the Romaic Song"

858   Lines 19-20   Quote: Exact
> But when drunk to escape from thy malice, / The draught
> shall be 'sweet to my soul.'

Job 16:24
Pleasant words are as an honeycomb, 'sweet to the soul,'
and health to the bones.

THE MORGANTE MAGGIORE

---

859 Canto I, 91-92   Allusion
Here are we, counts, kings, dukes, to own thy sway, /
Hamo, and Otho, Ogier, Solomon.
I Kings 1-9
Rf. Solomon, king of Israel.

860 Canto I, 109   Quote: Exact
Best 'speak the truth' when there's a reason why.
Psalm 15:2
He that walketh uprightly, and worketh righteousness, and
'speaketh the truth' in his heart.   ⁕

861 Canto I, 193-200   Reference: Subject
Our ancient fathers living the desert in, / For just and
holy works were duly fed; / Think not they lived on locusts
sole, 'tis certain / That manna was rain'd down from hea-
ven instead; / But here 'tis fit we keep on the alert in /
Our bounds, or taste the stones shower'd down for bread /
From off yon mountain daily raining faster, / And flung by
Passamont and Alabaster.
Exodus 14-21
Rf. the manna fed to the Israelites.

862 Canto I, 281-82   Allusion
Saying, "What grace to me thou'st this day given! / And
I to thee, oh Lord! am ever bound.
Genesis 49:18
I have waited for thy salvation, O Lord.

863 Canto I, 289   Quote: Exact
And having said this much, he 'went his way.'
Genesis 18:33
And the Lord 'went his way,' as soon as he had left com-
muning with Abraham.

864 Canto I, 290-92   Quote: Approximate
And Alabaster he found out below, / Doing the very best
that in him lay / 'To root from out' a bank a rock or two.
Job 31:12
For it is a fire that consumeth to destruction, and would
'root out' all mine increase.

865   Canto I, 388   Quote: Approximate
        And, since it is 'God's pleasure,' pardon me.
      Ezra 10:11
        Now therefore make confession unto the Lord 'God' of your
        fathers, and do 'his pleasure.'

866   Canto I, 390-92   Reference: Subject
        And our true Scripture soundeth openly, / Good is reward-
        ed, and chastised the ill, / Which the Lord never faileth to
        fulfil.
      Proverbs 11:12
        The wicked worketh a deceitful work: but to him that sow-
        eth righteousness shall be a sure reward.

867   Canto I, 403   Reference: Subject
        That in their thoughts who praise in heaven the Lord.
      Psalm 148:1
        Praise ye the Lord from the heavens.

868   Canto I, 415   Allusion
        What pleases God to them must joy inspire.
      Numbers 23:27
        Peradventure it will please God.

869   Canto I, 421-22   Parallelism
        Just as you tell me 'tis in heaven obey'd-- / 'Ashes to
        ashes,'--merry let us be!
      Genesis 3:19
        For out of it wast thou taken: for 'dust' thou art, and 'un-
        to dust' shalt thou return.

870   Canto I, 612-14   Reference: Subject
        Heaven reward you with all good / The God so true, the
        eternal Lord sublime, / Whose kingdom at the last hath
        open stood.
      Isaiah 22:20-22
        And it shall come to pass in that day, ... the key of the
        house of David will I lay upon his [Eliakim's] shoulder; so
        he shall open, and none shall shut; and he shall shut, and
        none shall open.

871   Canto I, 630-31   Quote: Approximate
        For thousand virtues which your bosom fosters, / That
        'whereso'er you go I too shall be,' / And, on the other
        part, you rest with me.
      Ruth 1:16
        And Ruth said, ... for 'whither thou goest, I will go.'

872   Canto I, 688   Quote: Approximate
        'From evil keep you' the high King of glory!
      I Chronicles 4:10
        And that thine hand might be with me and that thou wouldest
        'keep me from evil,' that it may not grieve me!

873 Canto I, 688   Quote: Exact
<u>From evil</u> keep you the high 'King of glory'!
Psalm 24:7
And be ye lift up, ye everlasting doors; and the 'King of
glory' shall come in.

ODE ON VENICE

---

874 Lines 58-60   Allusion
The flow and ebb of each recurring age, / The 'everlast-
ing' to be which hath been, / Hath taught us nought or
little.
Psalm 90:2
From 'everlasting' to 'everlasting,' thou art God.

875 Lines 58-60   Quote: Exact
The flow and ebb of each recurring age, / The everlasting
to be 'which hath been,' / Hath taught us nought or little.
Ecclesiastes 3:15
That 'which hath been' is now; and that which is to be hath
already been.

876 Lines 144-48   Allusion
She has taught / Her Esau-brethren that the haughty flag,
/ The floating fence of Albion's feebler crag, / May strike
to those whose red right hands have bought / Rights cheaply
earn'd with blood.
Genesis 25:33-34
And Jacob said, Swear to me this day; and he sware unto
him: and he sold his birthright unto Jacob. Then Jacob
gave Esau bread and pottage of lentils; and he did eat and
drink, and rose up, and went his way: thus Esau despised
his birthright.

PARISINA

---

877 Lines 65-66   Quote: Approximate
And Hugo is gone to his lonely bed, / 'To covet there
another's bride.'
Exodus 20:17
Thou shalt not covet thy neighbour's house, thou shalt not
'covet thy neighbour's wife.'

878   Line 118   Quote: Approximate
      While in his thought her 'days are number'd.'
      Psalm 90:12
      So teach us 'to number our days,' that we may apply our
      hearts unto wisdom.

879   Lines 134-35   Quote: Exact
      The chief of Este's ancient sway / Upon his 'throne of
      judgment' sate.
      Proverbs 20:8
      A king that sitteth in the 'throne of judgment' scattereth
      away all evil with his eyes.

880   Lines 203-204   Quote: Exact
      There breathes not one / Who would not 'do as I have done.'
      Ezekiel 24:22
      And ye shall 'do as I have done': ye shall not cover your
      lips, nor eat the bread of men.

881   Lines 241-42   Reference: Subject
      Thou gav'st, and may'st resume my breath, / A gift for
      which I thank thee not.
      Job 1:21
      The Lord gave, and the Lord hath taken away; blessed be
      the name of the Lord.

882   Lines 252-53   Parallelism
      'Tis true that I have done thee wrong, / But 'wrong for
      wrong.'
      Exodus 21:23-25
      Thou shalt give life for life, 'eye for eye, tooth for tooth,
      hand for hand, foot for foot, burning for burning, wound
      for wound, stripe for stripe.'

883   Line 256   Allusion
      Thou saw'st, and covetedst her charms.
      Exodus 20:17
      Thou shalt not covet thy ... neighbour's wife.

884   Lines 312-13   Reference: Subject
      'Begot in sin,' to die in shame, / My life begun and ends
      the same.
      Psalm 51:5
      Behold I was 'shapen in iniquity'; and 'in sin' did my mother
      conceive me.

885   Lines 373-74   Quote: Exact
      Could this be still 'the earth beneath, / The sky above,'
      and men around.
      Exodus 20:4
      Thou shalt not make unto thee any graven image, or any
      likeness of any thing that is in 'heaven above,' or that is
      'in the earth beneath,' or that is in the water under the
      earth.

THE PROPHECY OF DANTE

886   Canto I, 23-27   Reference: Subject
    And meeting thee in heaven was but to meet / That without
which my soul, like the arkless dove, / Had wander'd still
in search of, nor her feet / Relieved her wing till found.
Genesis 8:6-12
    Rf. the dove and Noah's ark.

887   Canto I, 44-46   Quote: Exact
    I am old in days, / And deeds, and contemplation, and
have met / Destruction face to face 'in all his ways.'
Psalm 145:17
    The Lord is righteous 'in all his ways,' and holy in all his
works.

888   Canto I, 45-46   Quote: Exact
    And have met / Destruction 'face to face' in all his ways.
Exodus 33:11
    And the Lord spake unto Moses 'face to face.'

889   Canto I, 64-65   Reference: Subject
    Beneath a parent pinion, hadst thou heard / My voice; but
as the adder, deaf and fierce.
Psalm 58:4
    They are like the deaf adder that stoppeth her ear.

890   Canto I, 77-80   Reference: Subject
    Let my dust / Lie where it falls; nor shall the soil which
gave / Me breath, but in her sudden fury thrust / Me forth
to breathe elsewhere.
Genesis 2:7
    And the Lord God formed man of the dust of the ground,
and breathed into his nostrils the breath of life; and man
became a living soul.

891   Canto I, 118-21   Reference: Subject
    Great God ... be my shield!
Genesis 15:1
    The word of the Lord came unto Abram ... saying, Fear
not, Abram: I am thy shield.

892   Canto I, 120-21   Allusion
    Thine almighty rod / Will fall on those who smote me,--be
my shield!
Psalm 2:8-9
    Ask of me, and I shall give thee the heathen for thine in-
heritance, ... Thou shalt break them with a rod of iron.

893   Canto I, 127-28   Quote: Approximate
    Even in that glorious vision, which to 'see / And live' was

never granted until now.
Exodus 33:20
Thou canst not see my face: for there shall no man 'see'
me, 'and live. '

894 Canto I, 139-40   Quote: Exact
On the lone rock of desolate Despair / 'To lift my eyes'
more to the passing sail.
Psalm 123:1
Unto thee 'lift I up mine eyes, ' O thou that dwellest in the
heavens.

895 Canto II, 1-2   Reference: Subject
The Spirit of the fervent days of Old, / When words were
things that came to pass.
Numbers 11:23
Thou shalt see now whether my word shall come to pass
unto thee or not.

896 Canto II, 1-2   Quote: Approximate
The Spirit of the fervent days of Old, / When 'words' were
things that 'came to pass. '
Jeremiah 28:9
The prophet which prophesieth of peace, when the 'word' of
the prophet shall 'come to pass, ' then shall the prophet be
known, that the Lord hath truly sent him.

897 Canto II, 8-9   Reference: Subject
What the great Seers of Israel wore within, / 'That spirit
was on them, ' and is on me.
Numbers 11:17
And I will take of 'the spirit which is upon thee, ' and will
put it upon them.

898 Canto II, 10-12   Quote: Approximate
If, Cassandra-like, amidst the din / Of conflict none will
hear, or hearing heed / This 'voice from out the Wilder-
ness. '
Isaiah 40:3
The 'voice of him that crieth in the wilderness, ' Prepare
ye the way of the Lord.

899 Canto II, 45   Quote: Parodic
" 'Let there be darkness!' " and thou grow'st a tomb!
Genesis 1:3
And God said, 'Let there be light': and there was light.

900 Canto II, 47-49   Reference: Subject
Thou, Italy! so fair that Paradise, / Revived in thee,
blooms forth to man restored; / Ah! must the sons of
Adam lose it twice?
Genesis 3:1-24
Rf. fall of Adam and Eve.

901   Canto II, 49-50   Quote: Exact
      Ah! must 'the sons of Adam' lose it twice? / Thou, Italy!
      Deuteronomy 32:8
      He separated 'the sons of Adam,' he set the bounds of the
      people according to the number of the children of Israel.

902   Canto II, 76-79   Allusion
      And the hue / Of human sacrifice and Roman slaughter /
      Troubles the clotted air, of late so blue, / And deepens
      into red the saffron water.
      Exodus 7:17
      Behold, I will smite with the rod that is in mine hand upon
      the waters which are in the river, and they shall be turned
      to blood.

903   Canto II, 109-11   Reference: Subject
      Her sandy ocean, and the sea waves' sway / Roll'd over
      Pharaoh and his thousands,--why, / Mountains and waters,
      do ye not as they?
      Exodus 14:27-28
      The Lord overthrew the Egyptians in the midst of the sea.
      And the waters returned, and covered the chariots, and the
      horsemen, and all the host of Pharaoh that came into the
      sea after them; there remained not so much as one of them.

904   Canto III, 8   Allusion
      Yes, all, though not by human pen, is graven.
      Exodus 24:12
      And the Lord said unto Moses, Come up to me into the
      mount, and be there: and I will give thee tables of stone,
      and a law, and commandments which I have written.

905   Canto III, 9-10   Quote: Exact
      There where the farthest suns and stars have birth, /
      Spread like a banner at 'the gate of heaven.'
      Genesis 28:17
      How dreadful is this place! this is none other but the house
      of God, and this is 'the gate of heaven.'

906   Canto III, 53-54   Reference: Subject
      And even yet he may be born-- / The mortal saviour who
      shall set thee free.
      Isaiah 9:6
      For unto us a child is born, unto us a son is given ... The
      Prince of Peace.

907   Canto III, 93-95   Reference: Subject
      He toils through all, still trembling to be wrong: / For
      fear some noble thoughts, like heavenly rebels, / Should
      rise up in high treason to his brain.
      Isaiah 14:12
      Rf. Lucifer's revolt from heaven.

908 Canto III, 112-13   Reference: Subject
       His 'fire,' / Like that 'of Heaven,' immortal.
    Genesis 19:24
       Then the Lord rained upon Sodom and upon Gomorrah
       brimstone and 'fire' from the Lord out 'of heaven.'

909 Canto III, 119-20   Quote: Approximate
       The second, of a tenderer, sadder mood, / Shall 'pour his
       soul out' o'er Jerusalem.
    Psalm 42:4
       When I remember these things, I 'pour out my soul' in me.

910 Canto III, 122-24   Quote: Approximate
       And his high 'harp' / Shall, 'by the willow' over Jordan's
       flood, / Revive 'a song of Sion.'
    Psalm 137:2-3
       We hanged our 'harps upon the willows' in the midst there-
       of. For there they that carried us away captive required
       of us a song ... , saying Sing us one of the 'songs of Zi-
       on.'

911 Canto III, 159-60   Quote: Approximate
       And is this the whole / Of such men's destiny 'beneath the
       sun'?
    Ecclesiastes 1:3
       What profit hath a man of all his labour which he taketh
       'under the sun'?

912 Canto IV, 31-32   Reference: Subject
       They who kneel to idols so divine / Break no commandment.
    Exodus 20:1-17
       Rf. the Ten Commandments.

913 Canto IV, 54-56   Reference: Subject
       Such sight hath been unfolded by a door / As this, 'to which
       all nations shall repair,' / And lay their sins at this huge
       gate of heaven.
    Psalm 86:9
       All 'nations' whom thou hast made 'shall come' and worship
       before thee, O Lord.

914 Canto IV, 61-62   Reference: Subject
       The Hebrew, at whose word / Israel left Egypt.
    Exodus 1-14
       Rf. Israel's deliverance from Egypt by Moses.

915 Canto IV, 95-100   Reference: Subject
       Oh, Power that rulest and inspirest! Is it that they on
       earth, whose earthly power / Is likest thine in heaven in
       outward show, / Least like to thee in attributes divine, /
       Tread on the universal necks that bow, / And then assure
       us that their rights are thine?
    Deuteronomy 3:24
       O Lord God, thou hast begun to shew thy servant thy

greatness, and thy mighty hand: for what God is there in heaven or in earth, that can do according to thy works, and according to thy might?

916 Canto IV, 150-51   Reference: Subject
The evil days to gifted souls foreshown, / Foretelling them to those who will not hear.
Jeremiah 17:23
Neither inclined their ear, ... that they might not hear.

SARDANAPALUS

---

917 Act I. i. 5-7   Allusion
I will not see / The blood of Nimrod and Semiramis [i. e. Sardanapalus as their descendant] / Sink in the earth.
Genesis 10:8-10
Nimrod ... He was a mighty hunter before the Lord.

918 Act I. ii. 111   Allusion
By the god Baal!
Judges 2:13
And they forsook the Lord, and served Baal and Ashtaroth.

919 Act I. ii. 133   Allusion
Respect for Nimrod's line [i. e. Sardanapalus as his descendant].
Genesis 10:8-10
Nimrod ... He was a mighty hunter before the Lord.

920 Act I. ii. 159   Allusion
O glorious Baal!
Judges 2:13
And they forsook the Lord, and served Baal and Ashtaroth.

921 Act I. ii. 206-207   Allusion
Bring me the golden goblet thick with gems, / Which bears the name of Nimrod's chalice.
Genesis 10:8-10
Nimrod ... He was a mighty hunter before the Lord.

922 Act I. ii. 277-79   Allusion
Nor decimated them with savage laws, / Nor sweated them to build up pyramids, / Or Babylonian walls.
Jeremiah 51:44
Yea, the wall of Babylon shall fall.

923 Act I. ii. 291-92   Allusion
By Baal, the cities, though well built, / Are not more goodly than the verse!

Judges 2:13
And they forsook the Lord, and served Baal and Ashtaroth.

924   Act I, ii. 305   Quote: Exact
'Fall down and worship, ' or get up and toil.
Daniel 3:5
At what time ye hear the sound of ... all kinds of musick,
ye 'fall down and worship' the golden image that Nebuchad-
nezzar the king hath set up.

925   Act I, ii. 326   Reference: Subject
The doom of Nineveh is seal'd. --Woe--woe.
Jonah 3:4
And Jonah began to enter into the city a day's journey, and
he cried, and said, Yet forty days, and Nineveh shall be
overthrown.

926   Act I, ii. 363-64   Allusion
And a bow / And javelin, which might furnish Nimrod forth.
Genesis 10:8-10
Nimrod ... He was a mighty hunter before the Lord.

927   Act I, ii. 371-72   Quote: Parodic
I'll use the 'sword' / Till they shall wish it turn'd 'into a
distaff. '
Isaiah 2:4
And they shall beat their 'swords into plowshares, ' and
their spears into pruninghooks.

928   Act I, ii. 419-20   Reference: Subject
Better / They had conjured up stern Nimrod from his ash-
es.
Genesis 10:8-10
Nimrod ... He was a mighty hunter before the Lord.

929   Act I, ii. 447   Allusion
I have loved, and lived, and multiplied my image.
Genesis 1:26-28
And God blessed them, and God said unto them, Be fruitful,
and multiply.

930   Act I, ii. 461-63   Quote: Approximate
Oh, men! ye must be ruled with scythes, not sceptres, /
And 'mow'd down like the grass, ' all we reap / Is rank
abundance.
Psalm 37:2
For they shall soon be 'cut down like the grass, ' and wither
as the green herb.

931   Act I, ii. 589-90   Quote: Exact
A king of feasts, and flowers, and wine, and revel, / And
love, and mirth, was never 'king of glory. '

Psalm 24:7
And be ye lift up, ye everlasting doors; and the 'King of glory' shall come in.

932   Act I. ii. 606-609   Reference: Subject
No, like sovereigns, / The shepherd kings of patriarchal times, / Who knew no brighter gems than summer wreaths, / And none but tearless triumphs.
I Samuel 16:11, 13
Rf. King David, the shepherd.

933   Act I. ii. 672-73   Allusion
With Baal, Nimrod, and Semiramis, / Sole in Assyria, or with them elsewhere.
Genesis 10:8-10
Nimrod ... He was a mighty hunter before the Lord.

934   Act I. ii. 672-73   Allusion
With Baal, Nimrod, and Semiramis, / Sole in Assyria, or with them elsewhere.
Judges 2:13
And they forsook the Lord, and served Baal and Ashtaroth.

935   Act I. ii. 681-82   Allusion
Ye slaves, deck / The hall of Nimrod [i.e. of Sardanapalus, descendant of Nimrod] for the evening revel.
Genesis 10:8-10
Nimrod ... He was a mighty hunter before the Lord.

936   Act II. i. 14-16   Quote: Approximate
Thou true sun! / The burning oracle of all that live, / As 'fountain of all life. '
Proverbs 13:14
The law of the wise is a 'fountain of life, ' to depart from the snares of death.

937   Act II. i. 52-53   Reference: Subject
The first cup which he drains will be the last / Quaff'd by the line of Nimrod.
Genesis 10:8-10
Nimrod ... He was a mighty hunter before the Lord.

938   Act II. i. 55-56   Reference: Subject
Its founder was a hunter-- / I am a soldier.
Genesis 10:8-10
Nimrod ... He was a mighty hunter before the Lord.

939   Act II. i. 76-78   Allusion
I own thee / As firm in fight as Babylonia's captain, / As skilful in Chaldea's worship.
Jeremiah 20:4
And I will give all Judah into the hand of the king of Babylon, and he shall carry them captive into Babylon, and shall slay them with the sword.

940 Act II. i. 115   Allusion
     It was: the place, the hall of Nimrod [i. e. of Sardanapa-
     lus, descendant of Nimrod].
     Genesis 10:8-10
     Nimrod ... He was a mighty hunter before the Lord.

941 Act II. i. 132   Allusion
     But in the hall of Nimrod [i. e. of Sardanapalus, descen-
     dant of Nimrod].
     Genesis 10:8-10
     Nimrod ... He was a mighty hunter before the Lord.

942 Act II. i. 236-38   Reference: Subject
     He blasphemes / The worship of the land, which 'bows the
     knee' / Before your fathers.
     I Kings 19:18
     Yet I have left me seven thousand in Israel, all the 'knees
     which have not bowed' unto Baal.

943 Act II. i. 250   Allusion
     Deafen'd with dead men and Baal.
     Judges 2:13
     And they forsook the Lord, and served Baal and Ashtaroth.

944 Act II. i. 352   Allusion
     Methought he look'd like Nimrod as he spoke.
     Genesis 10:8-10
     Nimrod ... He was a mighty hunter before the Lord.

945 Act II. i. 516-17   Quote: Exact
     'Get thee hence, ' then; / And, prithee, think more gently
     of thy brother.
     I Kings 17:3
     'Get thee hence, ' and turn thee eastward.

946 Act II. i. 530-31   Allusion
     Questions which mortal never dared to ask me, / Nor Baal.
     Judges 2:13
     And they forsook the Lord, and served Baal and Ashtaroth.

947 Act II. i. 549-50   Allusion
     Jove!--ay, your Baal-- / Ours also has a property in
     thunder.
     Judges 2:13
     And they forsook the Lord, and served Baal and Ashtaroth.

948 Act III. i. 5   Allusion
     Is not this better now than Nimrod's huntings?
     Genesis 10:8-10
     Nimrod ... He was a mighty hunter before the Lord.

949 Act III. i. 17-18   Reference: Subject
     All hearts are happy, and all voices bless / The king of
     peace, who holds a world in jubilee.

Leviticus 25:9-25
Rf. the Mosaic redemption of land at each fifty-year jubilee.

950　Act III. i. 17-18　　　　　　　　　　/　Quote: Approximate
All hearts are happy, and all voices bless / 'The king of
peace, ' who holds a world in jubilee.
Isaiah 9:6
And his name shall be called Wonderful, Counsellor, the
mighty God, The Everlasting Father, 'The Prince of Peace. '

951　Act III. i. 27-28　　　　　　　　　　Allusion
Mightier than / His father Baal, the god Sardanapalus!
Judges 2:13
And they forsook the Lord, and served Baal and Ashtaroth.

952　Act III. i. 254-55　　　　　　　　　Allusion
Farewell to all of Nimrod! Even the name / Is now no
more [i. e. Sardanapalus' death as the descendant of Nim-
rod].
Genesis 10:8-10
Nimrod ... He was a mighty hunter before the Lord.

953　Act III. i. 312-13　　　　　　　　　Allusion
Baal himself / Ne'er fought more fiercely to win empire.
Judges 2:13
And they forsook the Lord, and served Baal and Ashtaroth.

954　Act III. i. 315-19　　　　　　　Reference: Subject
And like / The close and sultry summer's day, which
bodes / A twilight tempest, bursts forth in such thunder /
As sweeps the air and deluges the earth.
Genesis 6-9
Rf. the flood.

955　Act IV. i. 27-28　　　　　　　　Reference: Subject
Hence--hence-- / Old hunter of the earliest brutes!
Genesis 10:8-10
Nimrod ... He was a mighty hunter before the Lord.

956　Act IV. i. 65　　　　　　　　　　Allusion
The dust we tread upon was once alive.
Genesis 2:7
And the Lord God formed man of the dust of the ground,
and breathed into his nostrils the breath of life; and man
became a living soul.

957　Act IV. i. 88-91　　　　　　　　Reference: Subject
His long locks curl'd down / On his vast bust, whence a
huge quiver rose / With shaft-heads feather'd from the
eagle's wing, / That peep'd up bristling through his serpent
hair. [Excerpt from Nimrod dream, 11. 78-101].
Genesis 10:9
[Nimrod] was a mighty hunter before the Lord.

958   Act IV. i. 179   Reference: Subject
      The hunter-founder of our race.
      Genesis 10:8-10
      Nimrod ... He was a mighty hunter before the Lord.

959   Act IV. i. 280-82   Reference: Subject
      They'll learn / Too soon the scorn of crowds for crown-
      less princes, / And find that all their father's sins are
      theirs.
      Numbers 14:18
      The Lord is longsuffering, ... visiting the iniquity of the
      fathers upon the children unto the third and fourth genera-
      tion.

960   Act IV. i. 293-94   Quote: Exact
      In his last hours did more for his own memory / Than
      many monarchs 'in a length of days. '
      Job 12:12
      With the ancient is wisdom; and 'in length of days' under-
      standing.

961   Act IV. i. 314-16   Allusion
      All monarchs in their mansions-- / Now swarm forth in
      rebellion, and demand / His death who made their lives a
      jubilee.
      Leviticus 25:10
      And ye shall hallow the fiftieth year, ... it shall be a ju-
      bile unto you.

962   Act IV. i. 377-78   Reference: Subject
      The extinction of / The line of Nimrod.
      Genesis 10:8-10
      Nimrod ... He was a mighty hunter before the Lord.

963   Act V. i. 189-94   Reference: Subject
      The wall which skirted near the river's brink / Is thrown
      down by the sudden inundation / Of the Euphrates, which
      now rolling, swoln / From the enormous mountains where
      it rises / By the late rains of the tempestuous region, /
      O'erfloods its banks, and hath destroy'd the bulwark.
      Isaiah 8:7
      Now, therefore, behold the Lord bringeth up upon them the
      waters of the river, strong and many, even the king of
      Assyria, and all his glory: and he shall come up over all
      his channels, and go over all his banks.

964   Act V. i. 208   Quote: Exact
      'My father's house' shall never be a cave.
      Genesis 24:7
      The Lord God of heaven, which took me from 'my father's
      house, ' and from the land of my kindred.

965 Act V. i. 329-30 Allusion
Would it then suit the last hours of a line / Such as is
that of Nimrod.
Genesis 10:8-10
Nimrod ... He was a mighty hunter before the Lord.

966 Act V. i. 420-21 Reference: Subject
The ever-burning lamp that burns without / Before Baal's
shrine in the adjoining hall?
Judges 2:13
And they forsook the Lord, and served Baal and Ashtaroth.

967 Act V. i. 436-39 Quote: Approximate
And the light of this / Most royal of funereal pyres shall
be / Not a mere 'pillar form'd of cloud and flame,' / A
beacon in the horizon for a day, / And then a mount of
ashes, but a light.
Exodus 13:21
And the Lord went before them by day in a 'pillar of a
cloud,' to lead them the way; and by night in a 'pillar of
fire,' to give them light.

THE SIEGE OF CORINTH

---

968 Lines 294-95 Reference: Subject
But within his soul / The thoughts like troubled waters
roll.
Psalm 46:3
The waters thereof roar and be troubled.

969 Lines 491-92 Quote: Exact
And see worms of the earth, and 'fowls of the air,' /
Beasts of the forest, all gathering there.
Genesis 7:3
Of 'fowls' also 'of the air' by sevens, the male and the fe-
male.

970 Lines 491-92 Quote: Exact
And see worms of the earth, and fowls of the air, / 'Beasts
of the forest,' all gathering there.
Psalm 104:20
Thou makest darkness, and it is night: wherein all the
'beasts of the forest' do creep forth.

971 Lines 499-500 Quote: Exact
It will leave no more / Of the 'things to come' than the
things before!

Isaiah 45:11
Thus saith the Lord, ... Ask me of 'things to come' concerning my sons.

972 Line 535   Quote: Approximate
'God of my fathers' what is here?
Deuteronomy 26:7
And when we cried unto the Lord 'God of our fathers,' the Lord heard.

973 Lines 735-37   Reference: Subject
Even as they fell, in files they lay; / Like the mower's grass at the close of day / When his work is done on the levell'd plain.
Psalm 129:6-7
Let them be as the grass upon the housetops ... Wherewith the mower filleth not his hand.

974 Lines 855-56   Allusion
In heaven; / From whence thy traitor soul is driven.
Isaiah 14:12
How art thou fallen from heaven, O Lucifer, son of the morning!

975 Lines 986-87   Quote: Approximate
The foe came on, and few remain / To strive, and those must 'strive in vain.'
Jeremiah 51:58
And the people shall 'labour in vain,' and the folk in the fire, and they shall be weary.

976 Line 1021   Quote: Approximate
The shatter'd town--'the walls thrown down.'
Jeremiah 50:15
She hath given her hand: her foundations are fallen, her 'walls are thrown down.'

977 Lines 1023-24   Reference: Subject
The hills that shake, although unrent, / As if an earth-quake pass'd.
Psalm 46:3
The mountains shake with the swelling thereof.

978 Line 1057   Quote: Approximate
'All the living things' that heard / That deadly earth-shock disappear'd.
Genesis 1:28
And God said unto them, ... have dominion over ... 'every living thing' that moveth upon the earth.

SONNET ON CHILLON

979   Lines 7-8   Quote: Approximate
    Their country conquers with their martyrdom, / And Free-
dom's fame finds 'wings on every wind. '
Psalm 18:10
    And he rode upon a cherub, and did fly: yea, he did fly
upon the 'wings of the wind. '

980   Line 9   Quote: Exact
    Chillon! thy prison is a 'holy place. '
Exodus 28:29
    When he goeth in unto the 'holy place, ' for a memorial be-
fore the Lord.

THE TWO FOSCARI

981   Act I. i. 218-19   Quote: Exact
    They are there within, or were at least / An hour since,
'face to face, ' as judge and culprit.
Genesis 32:30
    And Jacob called the name of the place Peniel: for I have
seen God 'face to face. '

982   Act I. i. 334-35   Quote: Exact
    A saint had done so, / Even with the 'crown of glory' in
his eye.
Proverbs 4:9
    She shall give to thine head an ornament of grace: a
'crown of glory' shall she deliver to thee.

983   Act I. ii. 361-63   Allusion
    He's 'silent' in his hate, as Foscari / Was 'in his suffer-
ing'; and the poor wretch moved me / More by his silence
than a thousand outcries / Could have effected.
Isaiah 53:7
    He was oppressed, and he was afflicted, yet he opened not
his mouth: ... as a sheep before her shearers is dumb, so
he openeth not his mouth.

984   Act II. i. 76-77   Quote: Approximate
    That they beheld them perish piecemeal not / 'Stretch'd
forth a hand' to save them?
Exodus 7:19
    Say unto Aaron, Take thy rod, and 'stretch out thine hand'
upon the waters of Egypt.

985   Act II. i. 117-18   Quote: Approximate
       Could it be else that / 'Men,' who have 'been of women
       born' and suckled.
       Job 14:1
       'Man that is born of a woman' is of few days, and full of
       trouble.

986   Act II. i. 132-34   Quote: Approximate
       Woman, this clamorous grief of thine, I tell thee, / Is no
       more 'in the balance weigh'd' with that / Which--but I pity
       thee, my poor Marina!
       Daniel 5:27
       Thou art 'weighed in the balances,' and art found wanting.

987   Act II. i. 332-33   Allusion
       All things are so to mortals; who can read them / Save he
       who made?
       Isaiah 55:8-9
       For my thoughts are not your thoughts, neither are your
       ways my ways, saith the Lord. For as the heavens are
       higher than the earth, so are my ways higher than your
       ways, and my thoughts than your thoughts.

988   Act II. i. 349-51   Reference: Subject
       And the original ordinance, that man / Must sweat for his
       poor pittance, keeps all passions / Aloof, save fear of
       famine!
       Genesis 3:17-19
       In the sweat of thy face shalt thou eat bread.

989   Act II. i. 367-68   Allusion
       And how then shall we judge each other, / Who are all
       earth.
       Genesis 2:7
       And the Lord God formed man of the dust of the ground.

990   Act III. i. 147-49   Reference: Subject
       This crowd of palaces and prisons is not / A paradise;
       its first inhabitants / Were wretched exiles.
       Genesis 2-3
       Rf. garden of Eden and expulsion of Adam and Eve.

991   Act III. i. 156-59   Reference: Subject
       Had I gone forth / From my own land, like the old patri-
       archs seeking / Another region with their flocks and herds.
       Genesis 12
       Rf. Abraham immigration to Canaan.

992   Act III. i. 186-87   Quote: Approximate
       Ay, there it is; 'tis like a mother's curse / Upon my soul--
       the 'mark is set upon' me.
       Genesis 4:15
       And the Lord 'set a mark upon' Cain, lest any finding him
       should kill him.

993   Act III. i. 189-90   Allusion
      Their 'hands upheld each other' by the way, / Their tents
      were pitch'd together.
      Isaiah 41:10
      I will help thee; yea, I 'will uphold thee with the right
      hand' of my righteousness.

994   Act III. i. 237-38   Allusion
      Floating on the free waves--away--away-- / Be it to the
      earth's end.
      Psalm 48:10
      According to thy name, O God, so is thy praise unto the
      ends of the earth.

995   Act III. i. 340   Quote: Exact
      Jacopo! 'my son, my son'!
      II Samuel 18:33
      He said, O 'my son' Absalom, 'my son, my son' Absalom!
      would God I had died for thee, O Absalom, 'my son, my
      son. '

996   Act III. i. 419-20   Quote: Approximate
      And I will find an hour to 'wipe away / Those tears, ' or
      add my own.
      Isaiah 25:8
      And the Lord God will 'wipe away tears' from off all faces.

997   Act IV. i. 22-23   Quote: Exact
      'Tis moderate--not even 'life for life, ' the rule / Denounced
      of retribution from all time.
      Exodus 21:23
      And if any mischief follow, then thou shalt give 'life for
      life. '

998   Act IV. i. 141-45   Reference: Subject
      Till the mariners, / Appall'd, turn their despairing eyes
      on me, / As the Phenicians did on Jonah, then / Cast me
      out from amongst them as an offering / To appease the
      waves.
      Jonah 1:5, 12
      Then the mariners were afraid, and cried every man unto
      his god ... And he said unto them, Take me up, and cast
      me forth into the sea; so shall the sea be calm.

999   Act IV. i. 174   Quote: Approximate
      May 'the worm which ne'er dieth' feed upon them!
      Isaiah 66:24
      For 'their worm shall not die, ' neither shall their fire be
      quenched.

1000 Act IV. i. 195-96   Quote: Exact
      'Hold thy peace, ' old man! / I am no daughter now--thou
      hast no son.

Judges 18:19
    And they said unto him, 'Hold thy peace,' lay thine hand
    upon thy mouth.

1001   Act IV. i. 218-21   Reference: Subject
    Ah! the devil come to insult the dead! Avaunt! / Incar-
    nate Lucifer! 'tis holy ground. / A martyr's ashes now
    lie there, which make it / A shrine.
    Isaiah 14:12
    Rf. Lucifer [only biblical mention of Lucifer].

1002   Act V. i. 215-20   Reference: Subject
    As old as I am, and I'm very old, / Have served you,
    so have I, and I and they / Could tell a tale; but I in-
    voke them not / To fall upon you! else they would, as
    erst / The pillars of stone Dagon's temple on / The Is-
    raelite and his Philistine foes.
    Judges 16
    Rf. Samson's pulling down of the temple of Dagon.

THE VISION OF JUDGMENT

1003   Lines 36-37   Reference: Parodic
    Each day too 'slew its thousands six or seven,' / Till at
    the crowning carnage, Waterloo, / They [angels and
    saints] threw their pens down in divine disgust.
    I Samuel 18:7
    And the women answered one another as they played, and
    said, Saul hath 'slain' his 'thousands,' and David his 'ten
    thousands.'

1004   Lines 47-48   Reference: Parodic
    Here Satan's sole good work deserves insertion-- / 'Tis,
    that he has both generals in reversion.
    I Chronicles 21:1
    And Satan stood up against Israel.

1005   Lines 81-82   Reference: Parodic
    So mix his [George I] body with the dust! It might / Re-
    turn to what it must far sooner.
    Genesis 3:19
    For dust thou art, and unto dust shalt thou return.

1006   Lines 81-84   Reference: Parodic
    So mix his body with the dust! It might / Return to what
    it 'must' far sooner, were / The natural compound left
    alone to fight / Its way back into the earth, fire and air.

Genesis 3:19
For dust thou art, and unto dust shalt thou return.

1007   Lines 97-98   Quote: Exact
" 'God save the king!' " It is a large economy / In God
to save the like.
I Samuel 10:24
And all the people shouted, and said, 'God save the king.'

1008   Line 136   Reference: Parodic
Is Lucifer come back with all this clatter?
Isaiah 14:12
How art thou fallen from heaven, O Lucifer, son of the
morning!

1009   Line 189   Allusion
His [the archangel Michael] brow was like the deep when
tempest-toss'd.
Isaiah 54:11
Oh thou afflicted, tossed with tempest, and not comforted.

1010   Lines 219-20   Reference: Subject
Like a banner streaming / Victorious from some world-
o'erthrowing fight.
Isaiah 14:12
How art thou fallen from heaven, O Lucifer.

1011   Lines 222-24   Reference: Parodic
The night / Of clay obscures our best conceptions, sav-
ing / Johanna Southcote or Bob Southey raving.
Isaiah 7:14
Behold, a virgin shall conceive, and bear a son, and shall
call his name Immanuel.

1012   Lines 227-28   Reference: Parodic
There's scarce a scribbler has not one [angel] to show, /
From the fiends' leader to the angels' prince.
Isaiah 14:12
How art thou fallen from heaven, O Lucifer, son of the
morning!

1013   Lines 251-52   Reference: Subject
Such was their power, that neither could forget / His for-
mer friend and future foe.
Isaiah 14:12
How art thou fallen from heaven, O Lucifer, son of the
morning!

1014   Lines 260-62   Quote: Parodic
And that " 'the sons of God,' " like those of clay, / Must
keep him company / and we might show / From the same
book.
Genesis 6:1-4
'The sons of God' saw the daughters of men that they were

fair; and they took them wives of all which they chose.

1015   Lines 263-64   Quote: Exact
       The dialogue is held between the Powers / 'Of Good and
       Evil'--but 't would take up hours.
       Genesis 2:17
       But of the tree of the knowledge 'of good and evil, ' thou
       shalt not eat of it.

1016   Lines 265-68   Reference: Parodic
       And this is not a theologic tract, / To prove with Hebrew
       and with Arabic / If Job be allegory or a fact.
       Job
       Rf. the entire book.

1017   Lines 273-74   Quote: Exact
       The spirits were in neutral space, before / 'The gates
       of heaven. '
       Genesis 28:17
       And he was afraid, and said, How dreadful is this place!
       this is none other but the house of God, and this is 'the
       gate of heaven. '

1018   Lines 286-87   Reference: Subject
       Satan met his ancient friend / With more hauteur, as
       might an old Castilian.
       I Chronicles 21:1
       And Satan stood up against Israel.

1019   Lines 297-98   Quote: Approximate
       What wouldst thou with this man, / Now dead, and 'brought
       before the Lord'?
       Numbers 16:17
       And take every man his censer, and put incense in them,
       and 'bring ye before the Lord' every man his censer.

1020   Lines 313-14   Allusion: Parodic
       Look to our earth, or rather mine; it was, / Once, more
       thy master's.
       Genesis 3:1-24
       Rf. expulsion of Adam and Eve from Eden.

1021   Lines 318-20   Allusion: Parodic
       In worship round him, he may have forgot / Yon weak
       creation of such paltry things: / I think few worth dam-
       nation save their kings.
       Genesis 1:26
       And God said, Let us make man in our image, after our
       likeness.

1022   Lines 324-26   Reference: Subject
       They are grown so bad, / That hell has nothing better
       left to do / Than leave them to themselves.

Psalm 18:5
The sorrows of hell compassed me about.

1023   Lines 497-98   Reference: Parodic
Why, my dear Lucifer, would you abuse / My call for
witnesses?
Isaiah 14:12
How art thou fallen from heaven, O Lucifer, son of the
morning!

1024   Lines 500-501   Allusion: Parodic
'Tis even superfluous, since two honest, clean, / True
testimonies are enough.
Deuteronomy 17:6
At the mouth of two witnesses, or three witnesses, shall
he that is worthy of death be put to death; but at the
mouth of one witness he shall not be put to death.

1025   Lines 524-25   Quote: Exact
For all the fashions 'of the flesh' stick long / By people
in the next world.
Ecclesiastes 12:12
Much study is a weariness 'of the flesh. '

1026   Lines 525-28   Reference: Parodic
Where unite / All the costumes since Adam's, right or
wrong, / From Eve's fig-leaf down to the petticoat, / Al-
most as scanty, or days less remote.
Genesis 3:7
And the eyes of them both were opened, and they knew
that they were naked; and they sewed fig leaves together,
and made themselves aprons.

1027   Lines 551-52   Quote: Approximate
And I, for one, / Have told them what I thought 'beneath
the sun. '
Ecclesiastes 1:3 (and throughout)
What profit hath a man of all his labour which he taketh
'under the sun'?

1028   Lines 579-81   Reference: Parodic
The spit / Where Belial, upon duty for the day, / With
Fox's lard was basting William Pitt.
Deuteronomy 13:13
Certain men, the children of Belial, are gone out from
among you, and have withdrawn the inhabitants of their
city, saying, Let us go and serve other gods, which ye
have not known.

1029   Lines 641-43   Reference: Parodic
I don't see wherefore letters should not be / Written with-
out hands, since we daily view / Them written without
heads.

Daniel 5:24
Then was the part of the hand sent from him [God]; and
this writing was written.

1030   Lines 665-66   Quote: Approximate
       What I have written, I have written: let / The rest 'be
       on his head' or mine!
       Joshua 2:19
       His blood shall 'be on our head, ' if any hand be upon him.

1031   Lines 709-10   Reference: Parodic
       Who knows to what his ribaldry may run, / When such an
       ass as this, like Balaam's, prates?
       Numbers 22:28
       And the Lord opened the mouth of the ass, and she said
       unto Balaam, What have I done unto thee?

1032   Lines 757-58   Quote: Parodic
       Few will twice / 'Lift up their lungs' when fairly over-
       crow'd.
       Isaiah 24:14
       They shall 'lift up their voice, ' they shall sing for the
       majesty of the Lord.

1033   Lines 823-24   Quote: Approximate
       Michael took refuge in his trump--but, lo! / His 'teeth
       were set on edge, ' he could not blow!
       Jeremiah 31:29
       The fathers have eaten a sour grape, and the 'children's
       teeth are set on edge. '

1034   Lines 847-48   Reference: Parodic
       And when the tumult dwindled to a calm, / I left him
       practising the hundredth psalm.
       Psalm 100
       Make a joyful noise unto the Lord, ... come before his
       presence with singing ... Enter into his gates with thanks-
       giving, and into his courts with praise ... His mercy is
       everlasting.

THE WALTZ

1035   Line 28   Allusion
       And give both Belial and his dance their due!
       Deuteronomy 13:13
       The children of Belial, are gone out from among you, ...
       saying, Let us go and serve other gods, which ye have
       not known.

1036   Lines 83-84   Reference: Subject
        Not decent David, when before the ark / His grand pas-
        seul excited some remark.
        II Samuel 6:16
        And as the ark of the Lord came into the city of David,
        Michal ... saw king David leaping and dancing before the
        Lord; and she despised him in her heart.

1037   Lines 136-37   Reference: Parodic
        Back to the ball-room speed your spectred host: / Fool's
        Paradise is dull to that you lost.
        Genesis 3:23
        Therefore the Lord God sent him [Adam] forth from the
        garden of Eden.

WERNER; OR, THE INHERITANCE

1038   Act I. i. 92-98   Reference: Subject
        Since his strange disappearance from my father's, / En-
        tailing, as it were, my sins upon / Himself, no tidings
        have reveal'd his course. / I parted with him to his grand-
        sire, on / The promise that his anger would stop short /
        Of the third generation; but Heaven seems / To claim her
        stern prerogative, and visit / Upon my boy his father's
        faults and follies.
        Exodus 20:5
        A jealous God, visiting the iniquity of the fathers upon the
        children unto the third and fourth generation.

1039   Act I. i. 139   Allusion
        Thou mightst have earn'd thy bread, as thousands earn it.
        Genesis 3:19
        In the sweat of thy face shalt thou eat bread.

1040   Act I. i. 352   Quote: Exact
        The spark which lights the matchlock, 'we are brethren. '
        Genesis 13:8
        For 'we be brethren. '

1041   Act I. i. 401   Reference: Subject
        He's poor as Job, and not so patient.
        Job 1-2
        Rf. the patience of Job.

1042   Act I. i. 618-19   Quote: Exact
        This cool, calculating fiend, who walks / Between me and
        'my father's house. '

Genesis 24:7
The Lord God of heaven, which took me from 'my father's house,' and from the land of my kindred.

1043   Act I. i. 640-41   Allusion
It will serve me as a 'den / Of secrecy' for some hours, at the worst.
Daniel 6:7
O king, he shall be cast into the 'den of lions.'

1044   Act I. i. 713-15   Quote: Exact
And every vine / Rain'd, as it were, the beverage which 'makes glad / The heart of man.'
Psalm 104:15
And wine that 'maketh glad the heart of man,' and oil to make his face to shine.

1045   Act I. i. 741   Quote: Exact
But 'whence comest thou'?
II Kings 5:25
And Elisha said unto him, 'Whence comest thou,' Gehazi!

1046   Act II. i. 136-38   Quote: Exact
I've heard that nothing can reclaim your Indian, / Or tame the tiger, though their infancy / Were fed on 'milk and honey.'
Exodus 3:8
And I am come down to deliver them ... unto a land flowing with 'milk and honey.'

1047   Act II. i. 317-20   Reference: Subject
Could you order / The Oder to divide, as Moses did / The Red Sea (scarcely redder than the flood of the swoln stream), and be obey'd.
Exodus 14:21
And Moses stretched out his hand over the sea; and the Lord caused the sea to go back by a strong wind.

1048   Act II. ii. 343-44   Reference: Subject
At such an hour, too, / He comes not only as a son, but saviour.
Isaiah 19:20
And he shall send them a saviour, and a great one, and he shall deliver them.

1049   Act II. ii. 367-69   Reference: Subject
Alas! I have had that upon my soul / Which makes me look on all men with an 'eye' / That only knows the 'evil' at first glance.
Deuteronomy 28:54
The man that is tender among you, and very delicate, his 'eye' shall be 'evil' toward his brother.

1050   Act II. ii. 494-95   Reference: Subject
        Condemn him not from his own mouth, but trust / to me.
        Job 15:6
        Thy own mouth condemneth thee.

1051   Act II. ii. 691   Quote: Exact
        " 'What have I to do with thee?' "
        II Samuel 16:10
        And the king said, 'What have I to do with you,' ye sons
        of Zeruiah?

1052   Act II. ii. 721-22   Reference: Subject
        This way-worn stranger--stands between you and / This
        Paradise?--(As Adam did between / The devil and his).
        Genesis 3:1-24
        Rf. the fall of Adam and Eve.

1053   Act III. i. 33-36   Quote: Approximate
        All the outspread gold / Of the New World the Spaniard
        boasts about / Could never tempt the man who knows its
        worth, / 'Weigh'd' at its proper value 'in the balance.'
        Daniel 5:27
        Thou art 'weighed in the balances,' and art found wanting.

1054   Act III. i. 49-50   Reference: Subject
        To-morrow I will try the waters as / The dove did,
        trusting that they have abated.
        Genesis 8:6-12
        Rf. the dove sent from the ark.

1055   Act III. iii. 415-17   Reference: Subject
        Were it the star of Lucifer himself, / Or he himself girt
        with its beams, I could / contain no longer.
        Isaiah 14:12
        How art thou fallen from heaven, O Lucifer, son of the
        morning!

1056   Act III. iv. 527-28   Allusion
        But this my sudden flight will give the Moloch / Suspicion
        two new victims.
        Amos 5:26
        Ye have borne the tabernacle of your Moloch and Chiun
        your images.

1057   Act III. iv. 597   Allusion
        To save a father is a child's chief honour.
        Exodus 20:12
        Honour thy father and thy mother.

1058   Act IV. i. 249-51   Quote: Exact
        Believe me, 'twould be mark'd in any house, / But most
        in ours, that one should be 'found wanting' / at such a
        time and place.

Daniel 5:27
  Thou art weighed in the balances, and art 'found wanting. '

1059   Act IV. i. 340-42   Quote: Exact
  At once / To wean thee from the perils of thy youth /
  And 'haughty spirit. '
Proverbs 16:18
  Pride goeth before destruction, and an 'haughty spirit' be-
  fore a fall.

1060   Act IV. i. 457-60   Quote: Approximate
  Siegendorf: The schismatic Swede, Gustavus, is / Gone
  home. Prior: To the 'endless home' of unbelievers, /
  Where there is everlasting wail and woe.
Ecclesiastes 12:5
  Desire shall fail: because man goeth to his 'long home, '
  and the mourners go about the streets.

1061   Act IV. i. 510-11   Quote: Parodic
  Ay!--you may look upon me! / 'I am not the man. '
II Samuel 12:7
  And Nathan said to David, 'Thou art the man. '

1062   Act V. i. 260-61   Quote: Approximate
  The moment my eye met his, I exclaim'd, / " 'This is
  the man!' "
II Samuel 12:7
  And Nathan said to David, 'Thou art the man. '

1063   Act V. i. 480-82   Quote: Approximate
  My son! mine! who have ever / Abhorr'd both mystery
  and blood, and yet / Am plunged 'into the deepest hell'
  of both!
Deuteronomy 32:22
  For a fire is kindled in mine anger, and shall burn 'unto
  the lowest hell, ' and shall consume the earth with her in-
  crease.

NEW TESTAMENT

THE AGE OF BRONZE

---

1 Lines 183-84   Quote: Approximate
      Thou [Poland] stand'st alone unrivall'd, till 'the fire / To
      come,' in which all empires shall expire.
    Acts 24:25
      He reasoned of righteousness, temperance, and 'judgment
      to come.'

2 Lines 395-99   Reference: Parodic
      The blest Alliance, which says three are all! / An earth-
      ly trinity! which wears the shape / Of heaven's, as man
      in mimick'd by the ape. / A pious unity! in purpose-- /
      To melt three fools to a Napoleon.
    II Corinthians 13:14
      The grace of the Lord Jesus Christ, and the love of God,
      and the communion of the Holy Ghost, be with you all.

3 Lines 602-608   Quote: Exact
      Exalt your notes, / Or else the ministry will lose their
      votes, / And patriotism, so delicately nice, / Her
      'loaves' will lower to the market price; / For ah! " 'the
      loaves and fishes,' " once so high, / Are gone--their
      oven closed, their ocean dry, / And nought remains of
      all the millions spent.
    Matthew 15:36
      And he took 'the' seven 'loaves and the fishes,' and gave
      thanks, and brake them, and gave to his disciples, and
      the disciples to the multitude.

4 Lines 609-701   Quote: Exact
      Where now, oh pope! is thy forsaken toe? / Could it not
      favour Judah with some kicks? / Or has it ceased to
      " 'kick against the pricks?' "
    Acts 9:5
      I am Jesus whom thou [Paul] persecutest: it is hard for
      thee to 'kick against the pricks.'

5 Lines 690-91   Allusion
        Two Jews--but not Samaritans--direct / The world, with
        all the spirit of their sect.
  Luke 10:29-37
        Rf. the parable of the good Samaritan.

6 Lines 693-95   Quote: Exact
        A congress forms their " 'New Jerusalem,' " / Where
        baronies and orders both invite-- / Oh, holy Abraham!
        dost thou see the sight?
  Revelation 3:12
        And I will write upon him [that overcometh] the name of
        my God, and the name of the city of my God, which is
        'New Jerusalem.'

BEPPO

---

7 Lines 41-42   Quote: Approximate
        This feast is named the Carnival, 'which being / Inter-
        preted,' implies "farewell to flesh."
  John 1:41
        We have found the Messias, 'which' is, 'being interpre-
        ted,' the Christ.

8 Lines 626-28   Quote: Parodic
        I have my reasons, you no doubt suppose, / And as, per-
        haps, they would not highly flatter, / I'll keep them for
        my 'life (to come)' in prose.
  I Timothy 4:8
        Godliness is profitable unto all things, having promise of
        the 'life' that now is, and of that which is 'to come.'

THE BLUES

---

9 Eclogue First, 47-51   Quote: Parodic
        I'd inoculate sooner my wife ... than listen two hours /
        To the torrent of trash which around him he pours, ...
        disgorged with such labour, / That--come--do not make
        me 'speak ill of one's neighbour.'
  Romans 13:10
        Love 'worketh no ill to his neighbour.'

10 Eclogue First, 113-16   Reference: Parodic
>And you who're a man of the gay world, no less / Than
>a poet of t'other, may easily guess / That I never could
>mean, 'by a word, to offend' / A genius like you.

James 3:2
>If any man 'offend' not 'in word,' the same is a perfect
>man.

THE BRIDE OF ABYDOS

---

11 Canto I, 95-98   Allusion
>Tamely view old Stambol's wall / Before the dogs of Mos-
>cow fall, / Nor strike one stroke for life and death / A-
>gainst the curs of Nazareth!

Matthew 2:23
>And He [Jesus] came and dwelt in a city called Nazareth;
>that it might be fulfilled which was spoken by the prophets,
>He shall be called a Nazarene.

12 Canto I, 327   Parallelism
>He [Selim] lived--he breathed--he moved--he felt.

Acts 17:28
>For in him [the Lord] we live, and move, and have our
>being.

13 Canto II, 72-75   Parallelism
>And by her [Zuleika's] comboloio lies ... many a bright
>emblazon'd rhyme / By Persian scribes 'redeem'd from
>time.'

Ephesians 5:15-16
>See then that ye walk circumspectly, ... 'Redeeming the
>time.'

14 Canto II, 105-108   Allusion
>She [Zuleika] dream'd what Paradise might be: / Where
>woman's parted soul shall go / Her prophet had disdain'd
>to show; / But Selim's mansion was secure.

John 14:2
>In my [Jesus'] Father's house are many mansions: if it
>were not so, I would have told you. I go to prepare a
>place for you.

15 Canto II, 595-97   Quote: Exact
>There lies a white capote! / 'Tis 'rent in twain'--one
>dark-red stain / The wave yet ripples o'er in vain.

Matthew 27:51
>And, behold, the veil of the temple was 'rent in twain'
>from the top to the bottom.

CAIN

16 Act I, i. 18-21
                                            Parallelism
        Oh, God ... 'Keep us from' further 'evil. '
    Matthew 6:13
        And lead us not into temptation, but 'deliver us from
        evil. '

17 Act I, i. 63-64
                                            Quote: Exact
        'The peace of God' / Be on your [Cain's] spirit, brother!
    Philippians 4:7
        And 'the peace of God, ' which passeth all understanding,
        shall keep your hearts and minds through Christ Jesus.

18 Act I, i. 74-76
                                            Allusion
        They have but / One answer to all questions, " 'Twas his
        [God's] will, / And he is good. " How know I that?
    Matthew 19:17
        And he [Jesus] said unto him, Why callest thou me good?
        there is none good but one, that is, God.

19 Act I, i. 78-79
                                            Reference: Subject
        I [Cain] judge but by the fruits--and they are bitter-- /
        Which I must feed on for a fault not mine.
    Matthew 7:16, 20
        Ye shall know them by their fruits. Do men gather grapes
        of thorns, or figs of thistles?

20 Act I, i. 281-84
                                            Reference: Subject
        What is death ... 'tis denounced against us, / Both them
        who sinn'd and sinn'd not, as an ill.
    Romans 5:14
        Death reigned from Adam to Moses, even over them that
        had not sinned after the similitude of Adam's transgression,
        who is the figure of him that was to come.

21 Act I. i. 298-300
                                            Quote: Exact
        Cain: Wilt thou teach me all? Lucifer: Ay, upon one
        condition. Cain: Name it. Lucifer: That / Thou dost
        'fall down and worship me'--thy Lord.
    Matthew 4:9
        [The devil] saith unto him [Jesus], All these things will I
        give thee, if thou wilt 'fall down and worship me. '

22 Act I. i. 343
                                            Quote: Exact
        I [Cain] must 'away with him' [Lucifer].
    John 19:15
        But they cried out, 'Away with him, away with him, '
        crucify him.

23   Act I. i. 358-60   Allusion
     Adah: Cain! walk not with this spirit. / Bear with what
     we have borne, and love me--I / Love thee.   Lucifer:
     More than thy mother and thy sire?
    Matthew 10:37
     He that loveth father or mother more than me is not wor-
     thy of me: and he that loveth son or daughter more than
     me is not worthy of me.

24   Act I. i. 536-38   Reference: Subject
     Lucifer: Ay, woman! he alone / Of mortals from that
     place (the first and last / Who shall return, save ONE)
     shall come back to thee.
    John 14:3
     And if I go and prepare a place for you, I will come a-
     gain, and receive you unto myself; that where I am, there
     ye may be also.

25   Act I. i. 543-44   Quote: Parodic
     'Where are' / Thy God or Gods--'there am I.'
    Matthew 18:20
     For 'where two or three are' gathered together in my
     name, 'there am I' in the midst of them.

26   Act II. i. 2-3   Reference: Subject
     Have faith in me [Lucifer], and thou shalt be / Borne on
     the air, of which I am the prince.
    Ephesians 2:2
     In time past ye walked according to the course of this
     world, according to the prince of the power of the air.

27   Act II. i. 16-20   Reference: Subject
     There will come / An hour, when, toss'd upon some wa-
     terdrops, / A man shall say to a man, "Believe in me,
     / And walk the waters"; and the man shall walk / The
     billows and be safe.
    Matthew 14:22-33
     Rf. Peter's walk on the water at Jesus' request.

28   Act II. i. 20-22   Quote: Exact
     I will not say, / 'Believe in me,' as a conditional creed
     / To save thee.
    Matthew 18:6
     But whoso shall offend one of these little ones which 'be-
     lieve in me,' it were better for him that a millstone were
     hanged about his neck, and that he were drowned in the
     depth of the sea.

29   Act II. i. 60-64   Reference: Subject
     Spirit! I / Know nought of death, save as a dreadful
     thing / Of which I have heard my parents speak, as of /
     A hideous heritage I owe to them / No less than life.

Romans 5:12
> By one man sin entered into the world, and death by sin;
> and so death passed upon all men, for that all have sinned.

30   Act II. ii. 239-40   Allusion
> What? Hath not he who made ye / Said 'tis another life?

I Corinthians 15:1-58
> Rf. doctrine of the resurrection of the dead.

31   Act II. ii. 395-98   Allusion
> And yon immense / Serpent, ... rears his dripping mane
> and vasty / Head ten times higher than the haughtiest ce-
> dar / Forth from the abyss.

Revelation 9:1-11; 20:1-10
> Rf. Satan enchained in and released from the pit.

32   Act II. ii. 443   Allusion
> I'll not believe it--for I [Cain] thirst for good.

Matthew 5:6
> Blessed are they which do hunger and thirst after right-
> eousness: for they shall be filled.

33   Act II. ii. 619-21   Quote: Exact
> And now I will convey thee to thy world, / Where thou
> shalt multiply the race of Adam, / 'Eat, drink,' toil,
> tremble, laugh, weep, sleep, and die.

Luke 12:19
> Take thine ease, 'eat, drink,' and be merry.

34   Act II. ii. 637-41   Allusion
> Through all eternity, / And the unfathomable gulfs of
> Hades, ... All, all, will I [Lucifer] dispure!

Luke 16:26
> And beside all this, between us [Abraham and Lazarus]
> and you [the rich man] there is a great gulf fixed: so
> that they which would pass from hence to you cannot; nei-
> ther can they pass to us, that would come from thence.

35   Act II. ii. 664-65   Quote: Exact
> One 'good gift' has the fatal apple given-- / Your reason.

James 1:17
> Every 'good gift' and every perfect gift is from above,
> and cometh down from the Father of lights.

36   Act III. i. 23-25   Reference: Subject
> Must the time / Come thou shalt be amerced for sins un-
> known, / Which were not thine nor mine [Cain's]?

Romans 5:12-21
> Rf. universal condemnation through Adam's sin.

37   Act III. i. 79   Quote: Approximate
> Would I Adah could die for them, /'so they might live'!

I John 4:9
> God sent his only begotten Son into the world, 'that we might live' through him.

38   Act III. i. 79   Reference: Subject
> Adah: Would I could die for them, so they might live!

I Thessalonians 5:9-10
> Our Lord Jesus Christ, ... died for us, that ... we should live together with him.

39   Act III. i. 79-92   Reference: Subject
> Adah: Would I could die for them, so they might live!
> Cain: Why, so say I--provided that one victim / Might satiate the insatiable of life. ... Adah: How know we that some such atonement one day / May not redeem our race? Cain: By sacrificing / The harmless for the guilty ... ?

Hebrews 10:12
> But this man [Jesus], after he had offered one sacrifice for sins for ever, sat down on the right hand of God.

40   Act III. i. 80-83   Quote: Approximate
> Why, so say I--provided that ... our little rosy sleeper there / Might never 'taste of death' nor human sorrow.

Hebrews 2:9
> He Jesus by the grace of God should 'taste death' for every man.

41   Act III. i. 85-86   Reference: Subject
> Adah: How know we that some such atonement one day / May not redeem our race?

Romans 5:12-21
> Rf. the death and atonement of Christ.

42   Act III. i. 136   Parallelism
> 'Twere better 'that he never had been born.'

Matthew 26:24
> Woe unto that man by whom the Son of man is betrayed! it had been good for that man 'if he had not been born.'

43   Act III. i. 162-63   Quote: Exact
> My brother, / 'The peace of God' be on thee!

Philippians 4:7
> And 'the peace of God,' which passeth all understanding, shall keep your hearts and minds through Christ Jesus.

44   Act III. i. 202-203   Quote: Exact
> Thy soul seems labouring in / Some 'strong delusion.'

II Thessalonians 2:11
> And for this cause God shall send them a 'strong delusion,' that they should believe a lie.

45 Act III. i. 223-32   Quote: Approximate
        Oh God ... Sole 'Lord of' light! / Of good, and 'glory,'
        and eternity.
    I Corinthians 2:8
        Had they known it, they would not have crucified the 'Lord
        of glory.'

46 Act III. i. 318-20   Quote: Approximate
        Oh, God! receive thy servant [Abel], and / Forgive his
        slayer, 'for he knew not what / He did'--Cain, give me--
        give me thy hand.
    Luke 23:34
        Then said Jesus, Father, forgive them; 'for they know not
        what they do.'

47 Act III. i. 370   Allusion
        Adah!--come hither! Death is in the world!
    Romans 5:12
        Wherefore, as by one man sin entered into the world, and
        death by sin; and so death passed upon all men, for that
        all have sinned.

48 Act III. i. 416-18   Quote: Approximate
        Let it be borne / In such sort as may show our God that
        we / Are 'faithful servants' to his holy will.
    Matthew 25:21
        Well done, thou good and 'faithful servant': thou hast
        been faithful over a few things, I will make thee ruler
        over many things.

49 Act III. i. 486   Quote: Exact
        'Angel of Light' [an angel, not Lucifer]! be merciful
    II Corinthians 11:14
        Satan himself is transformed into an 'angel of light.'

CHILDE HAROLD'S PILGRIMAGE

---

50 "To Ianthe," 10-12   Quote: Exact
        Ah! may'st thou ever be what now thou art, / Nor unbe-
        seem the promise of thy spring, / As fair in form, as
        warm yet 'pure in heart.'
    Matthew 5:8
        Blessed are the 'pure in heart': for they shall see God.

51 Canto I, 16-17   Quote: Exact
        Few 'earthly things' found favour in his sight / Save con-
        cubines and carnal companie.
    John 3:12
        I have told you 'earthly things,' and ye believe not.

52   Canto I, 80-81   Allusion
          Maidens, like moths, are ever caught by glare, / And
          Mammon wins his way where Seraphs might despair.
     Matthew 6:24
          Ye cannot serve God and mammon.

53   Canto I, 338-39   Reference: Subject
          But here the Babylonian whore hath built / A dome, where
          flaunts she in such glorious sheen.
     Revelation 17:4-5
          And the woman was arrayed in purple and scarlet colour,
          ... And upon her forehead was a name written, mystery,
          Babylon the great, the mother of harlots.

54   Canto I, 354-57   Allusion
          Withouten end, / Spain's realms appear whereon her
          shepherds tend / Flocks whose rich fleece right well the
          trader knows-- / Now must the pastor's arm his lambs
          defend.
     Acts 20:28
          Take heed therefore unto yourselves [Ephesian elders],
          and to all the flock, over the which the Holy Ghost hath
          made you overseers, to feed the church of God.

55   Canto I, 421-22   Reference: Subject
          Death rides upon the sulphury Siroc, / Red Battle stamps
          his foot, and Nations feel the shock.
     Revelation 6:8
          And behold a pale horse: and his name that sat on him
          was Death.
     Revelation 6:4
          And there went out another horse that was red: and pow-
          er was given to him that sat thereon to take peace from
          the earth, and that they should kill one another.

56   Canto I, 525-26   Quote: Approximate
          'Woe to the man' that walks in public view / without of
          loyalty this token true!
     Matthew 26:24
          'Woe unto that man' by whom the Son of man is betrayed!

57   Canto I, 553-54   Allusion
          And doth the Power that man adores ordain / Their doom,
          nor heed the suppliant's appeal?
     Romans 13:1
          Let every soul be subject unto the higher powers. For
          there is no power but of God: the powers that be are
          ordained of God.

58   Canto II, 43-44   Reference: Parodic
          Remove yon skull from out the scatter'd heaps: / Is that
          a temple where a God may dwell?

I Corinthians 3:16
> Know ye not that ye are the temple of God, and that the Spirit of God dwelleth in you?

59 Canto II, 64-67   Reference: Subject
> Yet if, as holiest men have deem'd, there be / A land of souls beyond that sable shore, / To shame the doctrine of the Sadducee / And sophists, madly vain of dubious lore.

Matthew 22:23
> The same day came to him the Sadducees, which say that there is no resurrection.

60 Canto II, 68-69   Reference: Subject
> How sweet it were in concert to adore / With those who made our mortal labours light!

Matthew 11:30
> My yoke is easy, and my burden is light.

61 Canto II, 349-51   Quote: Exact
> Could she [Sappho] not live who 'life eternal' gave? / If 'life eternal' may await the lyre, / That only Heaven to which Earth's children may aspire.

John 4:36
> He that reapeth receiveth wages, and gathereth fruit unto 'life eternal.'

62 Canto II, 405   Allusion
> God, was thy globe ordain'd for such ["imperial awards"] to win and lose?

Acts 17:31
> He [God] hath appointed a day, in the which he will judge the world in righteousness by that man whom he hath ordained.

63 Canto II, 550-54   Quote: Exact
> In marble-paved pavilion, where a 'spring / Of living water' from the centre rose, ... All reclined.

John 7:38
> He that believeth on me, as the scripture hath said, out of his belly shall flow 'rivers of living water.'

64 Canto II, 700-701   Allusion
> Oh! who that gallant spirit shall resume, / Leap from Eurotas' banks, and call thee [Spartans who died at Thermopylae] from the tomb?

John 11:43-44
> And when he [Jesus] thus had spoken, he cried with a loud voice, Lazarus, come forth. And he that was dead came forth [from the tomb].

65 Canto II, 708-10   Quote: Approximate
> Nor rise thy sons, but idly rail in vain, ... From birth till death enslaved; 'in word, in deed,' unmann'd.

I John 3:18
> Let us not love 'in word,' ... but 'in deed' and in truth.

66 Canto II, 739-40   Allusion
> That penance which their holy rites prepare / To shrive from man his weight of mortal sin.

Hebrews 12:1
> Let us lay aside every weight, and the sin which doth so easily beset us.

67 Canto III, 14-16   Allusion
> Though the strain'd mast should 'quiver as a reed,' / And the rent canvass fluttering strew the gale, / Still must I on.

Matthew 11:7
> Jesus began to say ... concerning John, What went ye out into the wilderness to see? 'A reed shaken' with the wind.

68 Canto III, 21-23   Quote: Approximate
> Again I seize the theme, then but begun, / And bear it with me, as the 'rushing wind' / Bears the cloud onwards.

Acts 2:2
> There came a sound from a heaven as of a 'rushing' mighty 'wind.'

69 Canto III, 39-42   Quote: Approximate
> Nor below / Can love, or sorrow, fame, ambition, strife, / 'Cut to his heart' again with the keen knife / Of silent, sharp endurance.

Acts 5:33
> They were 'cut to the heart,' and took counsel to slay them.

70 Canto III, 154-55   Quote: Approximate
> And Harold stands upon this 'place of skulls,' / The grave of France, the deadly Waterloo!

Matthew 27:33
> They were come unto a place called Golgotha, that is to say, a 'place of a skull.'

71 Canto III, 275-76   Reference: Subject
> The Archangel's trump, not Glory's, must awake / Those [the dead] whom they [the living] thirst for.

I Thessalonians 4:16
> The Lord himself shall descend from heaven with a shout, with the voice of the archangel, and with the trump of God: and the dead in Christ shall rise first.

72 Canto III, 315   Quote: Exact
> And this [Waterloo] is much, and all which will not 'pass away.'

II Peter 3:10
> The heavens shall 'pass away' with a great noise, and the

elements shall melt with fervent heat, the earth also.

73 Canto III, 635-37   Quote: Exact
    But these are deeds which should not 'pass away,' / And
    names that must not wither, though the earth / Forgets
    her empires with a just decay.
    II Peter 3:10
    The heavens shall 'pass away' with a great noise, and the
    elements shall melt with fervent heat, the earth also.

74 Canto III, 644   Allusion
    Lake Leman woos me with its crystal face.
    Revelation 4:6
    And before the throne there was a sea of glass like unto
    crystal.

75 Canto III, 666-67   Quote: Approximate
    The race of life becomes a hopeless flight / To those that
    'walk in darkness.'
    I John 2:11
    He that hateth his brother is in darkness, and 'walketh in
    darkness.'

76 Canto III. 772-73   Reference: Subject
    The veil they rent, / And what behind it lay, all earth
    shall view.
    Matthew 27:51
    And, behold, the veil of the temple was rent in twain
    from the top to the bottom.

77 Canto III, 855-57   Allusion
    [Early Persians sought] The Spirit, in whose honour
    shrines are weak / Uprear'd of human hands.
    Acts 17:24
    God ... dwelleth not in temples made with hands.

78 Canto III, 856-59   Allusion
    Come, and compare, / Columns and idol-dwellings, ...
    With Nature's realms of worship, earth and air, / Nor
    fix on fond abodes to circumscribe thy pray'r!
    John 4:21-23
    Jesus saith unto her, Woman, ... ye shall neither in this
    mountain, nor yet at Jerusalem, worship the Father ...
    But the hour cometh, and now is, when the true worship-
    pers shall worship the Father in spirit and in truth.

79 Canto III, 945-46   Quote: Approximate
    The bow'd waters meet him [Love], and adore, / 'Kissing
    his feet' with murmurs.
    Luke 7:38
    [A woman] stood at his feet behind him weeping, and be-
    gan to wash his feet with tears, ... and 'kissed his feet.'

80 <u>Canto III, 981-84</u>   Allusion
       They [Gibbon and Voltaire] were gigantic minds, ... daring
       doubts to pile / Thoughts which should call down thunder
       and the flame / Of Heaven.
   <u>Luke 9:54</u>
       And when his disciples James and John saw this, they
       said, Lord, wilt thou that we command fire to come down
       from heaven and consume them?

81 <u>Canto III, 992-93</u>   Quote: Approximate
       [Voltaire] as 'the wind, / Blew where it listed,' laying
       all things prone.
   <u>John 3:8</u>
       'The wind bloweth where it listeth,' and thou hearest the
       sound thereof.

82 <u>Canto III, 1003-1004</u>   Quote: Exact
       Yet, 'peace be with' their [theologians and orthodox his-
       torians] ashes for by them, / If merited, the penalty is
       paid.
   <u>I Peter 5:14</u>
       'Peace be with' you all that are in Christ Jesus.

83 <u>Canto III, 1019-21</u>   Quote: Approximate
       I bend / To their [the Alps] most great and growing re-
       gion, where / The earth to her embrace compels the pow-
       ers of air.'
   <u>Ephesians 2:2</u>
       In time past ye walked according to the course of this
       world, according to the prince of 'the power of the air.'

84 <u>Canto III, 1049</u>   Parallelism
       I have 'not loved the world,' nor the world me.
   <u>I John 2:15</u>
       'Love not the world,' neither the things that are in the
       world.

85 <u>Canto III, 1058-59</u>   Quote: Approximate
       I have 'not loved the world,' nor the world me, -- / But
       let us part fair foes.
   <u>I John 2:15</u>
       'Love not the world,' neither the things that are in the
       world.

86 <u>Canto IV, 17-18</u>   Parallelism
       In purple was she [Venice] robed, and of her feast / Mon-
       archs partook, and deem'd their dignity increased.
   <u>Revelation 17:4</u>
       And the woman was arrayed in purple.

87 <u>Canto IV, 87-88</u>   Reference: Subject
       The thorns which I have reap'd are of the tree / I plant-
       ed,--they have torn me--and I bleed.

Galatians 6:7-8
> Whatsoever a man soweth, that shall he also reap. For
> he that soweth to his flesh shall of the flesh reap corrup-
> tion.

88 Canto IV, 88-90   Reference: Subject
> The thorns which I have reap'd are of the tree / I plant-
> ed,--they have torn me--and I bleed: / I should have
> known what fruit would spring from such a seed.

Matthew 7:16-18
> Ye shall know them by their fruits. Do men gather grapes
> of thorns, or figs of thistles? Even so every good tree
> bringeth forth good fruit; but a corrupt tree bringeth forth
> evil fruit. A good tree cannot bring forth evil fruit, nei-
> ther can a corrupt tree bring forth good fruit.

89 Canto IV, 90   Reference: Subject
> I should have known what fruit would spring from such a
> seed.

Mark 4:26-27
> So is the kingdom of God, as if a man should cast seed
> into the ground; And should sleep, and rise night and day,
> and the seed should spring and grow up, he knoweth not
> how.

90 Canto IV, 103-105   Allusion
> Nations melt / From power's high pinnacle, when they
> have felt / The sunshine for a while.

Matthew 4:5
> The devil taketh him [Jesus] up into the holy city, and
> setteth him on a pinnacle of the temple.

91 Canto IV, 383-85   Quote: Exact
> Nor would the hostile horde / Of many-nation'd spoilers
> from the Po / Quaff 'blood and water. '

John 19:34
> One of the soldiers with a spear pierced his side, and
> forthwith came there out 'blood and water. '

92 Canto IV, 419-20   Reference: Subject
> [Italy,] Parent of our Religion, whom the wide / Nations
> have knelt to for the keys of heaven!

Matthew 16:19
> And I [Jesus] will give unto thee [Peter] the keys of the
> kingdom of heaven.

93 Canto IV, 586-88   Quote: Approximate
> But thou, Clitumnus, in thy sweetest wave / Of the most
> 'living crystal' that was e'er / The haunt of river nymph.

John 4:10
> Jesus answered ... If thou knewest ... , who it is that
> saith to thee, Give me to drink; thou wouldest have asked
> of him, and he would have given thee 'living water. '

94 Canto IV, 880-82   Reference: Subject
    Every good tree bringeth forth good fruit; but a corrupt
    tree bringeth forth evil fruit. A good tree cannot bring
    forth evil fruit, neither can a corrupt tree bring forth
    good fruit.
Matthew 7:17
    Even so every good tree bringeth forth good fruit; but a
    corrupt tree bringeth forth evil fruit.

95 Canto IV, 1072-74   Allusion
    Our young affections run to waste, / Or water but the de-
    sert; whence arise / But weeds of dark luxuriance, tares
    of haste.
Matthew 13:25
    But while men slept, his enemy came and sowed tares
    among the wheat, and went his way.

96 Canto IV, 1081-85   Reference: Subject
    Oh Love! no habitant of earth thou art-- / An unseen
    seraph, we believe in thee ... But never yet hath seen,
    ... thy form, as it should be.
I Corinthians 2:9
    Eye hath not seen, ... the things which God hath prepared
    for them that love him.

97 Canto IV, 1094-96   Allusion
    Where are the charms and virtues which we dare / Con-
    ceive in boyhood and pursue as men, / The unreach'd
    Paradise of our despair.
Luke 23:43
    And Jesus said ... Verily I say unto thee, To day shalt
    thou be with me in paradise.

98 Canto IV, 1195-95   Parallelism
    Thou [time] shalt take / The vengeance, which shall yet
    be 'sought and found.'
Matthew 7:7
    Ask, and it shall be given you; 'seek, and ye shall find';
    knock, and it shall be opened unto you.

99 Canto IV, 1203-1204   Allusion
    Not in the air shall these my words disperse, / Though I
    be ashes.
I Corinthians 14:9
    Except ye utter by the tongue words easy to be understood,
    how shall it be known what is spoken? for ye shall speak
    into the air.

100 Canto IV, 1211-12   Parallelism
    Have I not had my 'brain sear'd,' my heart riven, / Hopes
    sapp'd, name blighted.
I Timothy 4:2
    [Some speak] lies in hypocrisy; having their 'conscience
    seared' with a hot iron.

101 Canto IV, 1230-33   Allusion
     Something unearthly ... shall on their [torture and time]
     soften'd spirits sink, and move / In hearts all rocky now
     the late remorse of love.
     Matthew 13:20-21
     He that received the seed into stony places, the same is
     he that heareth the word, and anon with joy receiveth it;
     Yet hath he not root in himself.

102 Canto IV, 1230-33   Allusion
     Something unearthly ... shall on their [torture and time]
     soften'd spirits sink, and move / In hearts all rocky now
     the late remorse of love.
     Hebrews 3:8
     Harden not your hearts, as in the provocation, in the day
     of temptation in the wilderness.

103 Canto IV, 1234   Allusion
     The seal is set.--Now welcome, thou dread power [death]!
     Revelation 20:2-3
     [An angel] bound him [the Devil] a thousand years, And
     cast him into the bottomless pit, and shut him up, and
     set a seal upon him.

104 Canto IV, 1294-95   Quote: Exact
     When the light shines serene but doth not glare, / Then
     in this magic circle 'raise the dead. '
     Matthew 10:8
     Heal the sick, cleanse the lepers, 'raise the dead, ' cast
     out devils.

105 Canto IV, 1304-1305   Quote: Exact
     Rome and her Ruin past Redemption's skill, / The World,
     the same wide 'den--of thieves, ' or what ye will.
     Matthew 21:13
     It is written, My house shall be called the house of prayer;
     but ye have made it a 'den of thieves. '

106 Canto IV, 1340-41   Parallelism
     She [the mother] sees her little bud put forth its leaves--
     / What may the fruit be yet?
     Matthew 24:32
     Now learn a parable of the fig tree; When his branch is
     yet tender, and putteth forth leaves, ye know that summer
     is nigh.

107 Canto IV, 1369-71   Allusion
     But lo, the dome [St. Peter's], the vast and wondrous
     dome / To which Diana's marvel was a cell, / Christ's
     mighty shrine above his martyr's tomb!
     John 21:18-19
     Another shall gird thee [Peter], and carry thee whither
     thou wouldest not. This spake he [Jesus], signifying by

what death he should glorify God. And when he had spoken this, he saith unto him, Follow me.

108   Canto IV, 1381-82   Reference: Subject
Since Zion's desolation, when that He / forsook his former city
Matthew 24:15-16
When ye therefore shall see the abomination of desolation, spoken of by Daniel the prophet, stand in the holy place. ... Then let them which be in Judaea flee into the mountains.

109   Canto IV, 1381-84   Reference: Subject
Since Zion's desolation, when that He / Forsook his former city, what could be, / Of earthly structures, in his honour piled / Of a sublimer aspect?
Matthew 24:15-16
When ye therefore shall see the abomination of desolation. ... Then let them which be in Judaea flee into the mountains.

110   Canto IV, 1468-70   Quote: Approximate
But where is he, the Pilgrim of my song, / The being who upheld it through the past? / Methinks he cometh late and 'tarries long. '
I Timothy 3:14-15
These things write I unto thee, hoping to come unto thee shortly: But if I 'tarry long, ' that thou mayest know how thou oughtest to behave thyself.

111   Canto IV, 1489-91   Quote: Approximate
[We shall] dream of fame, / And 'wipe the dust from off' the idle name / We never more shall hear.
Matthew 10:14
And whosoever shall not receive you, ... when ye depart out of that house or city, 'shake off the dust' of your feet.

112   Canto IV, 1529-30   Reference: Subject
Her [The Daughter of the Isles] and her hoped-for seed, whose promise seem'd / Like stars to shepherds' eyes.
Hebrew 11:12
Therefore sprang there even of one [Abraham], and him as good as dead, so many as the stars of the sky in multitude.
Luke 2:8-20
Rf. the shepherds who saw the star of Jesus.

113   Canto IV, 1580   Quote: Approximate
Yet not in vain our mortal race hath run.
Hebrews 12:1
Let us lay aside every weight, ... and let us run with patience the race that is set before us.

114   Canto IV, 1580-81   Quote: Approximate
        Yet not in vain our mortal race hath run; / 'We have had
        our reward,' and it is here.
      Matthew 6:2
        When thou doest thine alms, do not sound a trumpet ...
        as the hypocrites do ... that they may have glory of men.
        Verily I say unto you, 'They have their reward.'

115   Canto IV, 1660-61   Quote: Approximate
        The torch shall be extinguish'd which hath lit / My mid-
        night lamp--and 'what is writ, is writ.'
      John 19:22
        Pilate answered, 'What I have written I have written.'

THE CORSAIR

---

116   Canto I, 433-34   Reference: Subject
        But come, the board is spread; our silver lamp / Is
        trimm'd and heeds not the sirocco's damp.
      Matthew 25:7
        Then all those virgins arose, and trimmed their lamps.

117   Canto II, 136-37   Quote: Exact
        What star--what sun is bursting on the bay? / It shines
        a 'lake of fire'!
      Revelation 20:10
        And the devil that deceived them was cast into the 'lake
        of fire' and brimstone.

118   Canto II, 482   Quote: Exact
        'It is enough'--I breathe--and I can bear.
      Luke 22:38
        And they said, Lord, behold, here are two swords. And
        he said unto them, 'It is enough.'

119   Canto III, 193   Quote: Approximate
        'Look to thyself,' nor deem thy falsehood safe!
      II John 8
        'Look to yourselves,' that we lose not those things which
        we have wrought.

120   Canto III, 236-37   Allusion
        The life thou [anyone] leav'st below, denied above / By
        kind monopolists of heavenly love.
      I John 2:15
        Love not the world, neither the things that are in the
        world. If any man love the world, the love of the Father
        is not in him.

121   <u>Canto III, 526</u>   Reference: Subject
      And Heaven must punish on its angry day.
      <u>II Peter 2:9</u>
         The Lord knoweth how to deliver the godly out of temp-
         tations, and to reserve the unjust unto the day of judg-
         ment to be punished.

122   <u>Canto III, 656-57</u>   Quote: Exact
         The sun goes forth, but Conrad's day is dim; / And 'the
         night cometh,' ne'er to pass from him.
      <u>John 9:4</u>
         'The night cometh,' when no man can work.

THE CURSE OF MINERVA

---

123   <u>Lines 46-48</u>   Allusion
         Near Theseus' fane yon solitary palm; / All, tinged with
         varied hues, arrest the eye-- / And dull were his that
         pass'd them heedless by.
      <u>Luke 10:31-33</u>
         And by chance there came down a certain priest that way:
         and when he saw him [the man helped by the good Samar-
         itan] he passed by on the other side.   And likewise a Le-
         vite, ... passed by on the other side.

124   <u>Lines 149-54</u>   Quote: Approximate
         Yet Caledonia claims some native worth, / As dull Boeo-
         tia gave a Pindar birth; / So may her few, ... / 'Shake
         off the' sordid 'dust' of such a land, / And shine like
         children of a happier strand.
      <u>Matthew 10:14</u>
         And whosoever shall not receive you, nor hear your words,
         when ye depart out of that house or city, 'shake off the
         dust' of your feet.

125   <u>Lines 159-60</u>   Quote: Approximate
         This 'vengeance yet is mine,' / To turn my counsels far
         from lands like thine.
      <u>Romans 12:19</u>
         For it is written, 'Vengeance is mine'; I will repay, saith
         the Lord.

THE DEFORMED TRANSFORMED

126 Part I. i. 37-39   Parallelism
   Must I [Arnold] bleed too / Like them? Oh that 'each
   drop which falls to earth' / Would rise a snake to sting
   them, as they have stung me!
   Matthew 10:29
   Are not two sparrows sold for a farthing? and 'one of
   them shall not fall on the ground' without your Father.

127 Part I. i. 458-64   Reference: Subject
   Fire! but in which nought can live, / Save the fabled sal-
   amander, / Or immortal souls, which wander, / Praying
   what doth not forgive, / Howling for a drop of water, /
   Burning in a quenchless lot.
   Luke 16:24
   [The rich man] said, Father Abraham, have mercy on me,
   and send Lazarus, that he may dip the tip of his finger in
   water, and cool my tongue; for I am tormented in this flame.

128 Part I. ii. 605-11   Reference: Subject
   I see ... / That sky whence Christ ascended from the
   cross, / Which his blood made a badge of glory and / Of
   joy (as once of torture unto him, / God and God's Son,
   man's sole and only refuge).
   Acts 1:9
   And when he [Jesus] had spoken these things, while they
   beheld, he was taken up; and a cloud received him out of
   their sight.

129 Part I. ii. 715-16   Allusion
   Up! up with the lily! [i. e. the Bourbons] / And down with
   the keys! [i. e. Rome].
   Matthew 16:19
   And I [Jesus] will give unto thee [Peter] the keys of the
   kingdom of heaven: and whatsoever thou shalt bind on
   earth shall be bound in heaven: and whatsoever thou shalt
   loose on earth shall be loosed in heaven.

130 Part I. ii. 715-18   Allusion
   Up! with the lily! / And down with the keys! / In old
   Rome, the seven'hilly, / We'll revel at ease.
   Matthew 16:19
   And I [Jesus] will give unto thee [Peter] the keys of the
   kingdom of heaven: and whatsoever thou shalt bind on
   earth shall be bound in heaven.

131 Part II. ii. 232-34   Reference: Parodic
   Meantime, pursue thy sport as I [Stranger] do mine; /
   Which is just now to gaze, since all these labourers [sol-

diers] / Will reap my harvest gratis.

Matthew 9:37-38

Then saith he [Jesus] unto his disciples, The harvest
truly is plenteous, but the labourers are few; Pray ye
therefore the Lord of the harvest, that he will send forth
labourers into his harvest.

132 Part II. iii. 242-44   Reference: Subject

Lutheran Soldier: Yonder stands Anti-Christ! Caesar
(interposing): How now, schismatic? / What wouldst thou?
Luthern Soldier: In the holy name of Christ, / Destroy
proud Anti-Christ. I am a Christian.

I John 2:18, 22

And as ye have heard that antichrist shall come, even now
are there many antichrists ... Who is a liar but he that
denieth that Jesus is Christ? He is antichrist, that de-
nieth the Father and the Son.

133 Part II. iii. 253-54   Quote: Approximate

You had far best be quiet; / 'His hour is not yet come. '

John 7:30

No man laid hands on him [Jesus], because 'his hour was
not yet come. '

134 Part II. iii. 256-57   Quote: Approximate

You know that " 'Vengeance is the Lord's' ": / You see
he loves no interlopers.

Romans 12:19

For it is written, 'Vengeance is mine'; I will repay, saith
the Lord.

135 Part II. iii. 261-64   Reference: Subject

'Tis / A glorious triumph still; proud Babylon's / No
more; the Harlot of the Seven Hills / Hath changed her
scarlet raiment for sackcloth / And ashes!

Revelation 17:3-9

And the woman was arrayed in purple and scarlet colour.
... And upon her forehead was a name written, mystery,
Babylon the great, the mother of harlots ... The seven
heads are seven mountains, on which the woman sitteth.

136 Part II. iii. 307-309   Reference: Subject

Great God! through thy redeeming Son, / And thy Son's
Mother, now receive me as / I would approach thee, wor-
thy her, and him, / And thee!

Matthew 1:18

Now the birth of Jesus Christ was on this wise: When as
his mother Mary was espoused to Joseph, before they
came together, she was found with child of the Holy Ghost.

137 Part II. iii. 335-36   Quote: Approximate

'Get you [soldiers] hence'! / Hence to your quarters!

Matthew 4:10

Then saith Jesus unto him, 'Get thee hence, ' Satan.

138   Part II. iii. 350-52   Quote: Exact
      No! Thou hast only sack'd my native land, -- / No in-
jury!--and made my father's house / 'A den of thieves'!
Matthew 21:13
      [Jesus] said unto them, It is written, My house shall be
called the house of prayer; but ye have made it 'a den of
thieves. '

DOMESTIC PIECES

"The Dream"

139   Lines 199-201   Allusion
      To him [the Wanderer] the book of Night was open'd wide,
/ And voices from the deep abyss reveal'd / A marvel
and a secret--Be it so.
Revelation 20:12
      And I saw the dead, small and great, stand before God;
and the books were opened: and another book was opened;
which is the book of life: and the dead were judged out
of those things which were written in the books.

"Lines: On Hearing That Lady Byron Was Ill"

140   Lines 39-41   Reference: Subject
      All the better life / Which, but for this cold treason of
thy heart, / Might still have risen from out the grave....
John 12:17
      He [Jesus] called Lazarus out of his grave, and raised
him from the dead.

"A Sketch"

141   Lines 95-96   Reference: Subject
      Then, when thou fain wouldst weary Heaven with prayer,
/ Look on thine earthly victims--and despair!
Luke 18:1-8
      And he [Jesus] spake a parable unto them ... that men
ought always to pray, and not to faint; ... a judge ...
said within himself, ... because this widow troubleth me,
I will avenge her, lest by her continual coming she weary me.

"Stanzas to Augusta: When All Around Grew Drear"

142   Lines 35-36   Allusion
      For Heaven in sunshine will require / The kind--and thee
the most of all.
Matthew 5:45
      [God] maketh his sun to rise on the evil and on the good,
and sendeth rain on the just and on the unjust.

DON JUAN

143 Dedication, 41-43   Allusion: Parodic
    I would not imitate the petty thought, ... For all the
glory your [Wordsworth's and Southey's] conversion brought.
Luke 15:7
    I say unto you, that likewise joy shall be in heaven over
one sinner that repenteth, more than over ninety and nine
just persons, which need no repentance.

144 Canto I, 6-8   Reference: Parodic
    I'll therefore take our ancient friend Don Juan-- / We
all have seen him, in the pantomime, / Sent to the devil
somewhat ere his time.
Matthew 25:41
    Then shall he say also unto them on the left hand, Depart
from me, ye cursed, into everlasting fire, prepared for
the devil and his angels.

145 Canto I, 43-48   Reference: Parodic
    And then your hero tells, whene'er you please, / What
went before ... Beside his mistress in some soft abode,
/ Palace, or garden, paradise, or cavern.
Luke 23:43
    And Jesus said unto him, Verily I say unto thee, To day
shalt thou be with me in paradise.

146 Canto I, 97   Reference: Parodic
    She knew the Latin--that is, 'the Lord's prayer. "
Matthew 6:9-13
    Our Father which art in heaven, Hallowed be thy name....

147 Canto I, 113-15   Quote: Parodic
    Some women use their tongues--she [Donna Inez] look'd a
lecture, / Each eye a sermon, and her brow a homily, /
An 'all-in-all' sufficient self-director.
I Corinthians 15:28
    Then shall the Son also himself be subject unto him that
put all things under him, that God may be 'all in all. '

148 Canto I, 129-32   Reference: Parodic
    She [Donna Inez] was perfect past all parallel-- / Of any
modern female saint's comparison; / So far above the cun-
ning powers of hell, / Her guardian angel had given up
his garrison.
Hebrews 1:14
    Are they [angels] not all ministering spirits, sent forth to
minister for them who shall be heirs of salvation?

149 Canto I, 197-200   Quote: Approximate
    Had they been but both in / Their senses, they'd have sent

young master forth ... To teach him manners for 'the
time to come.'

Luke 18:29-30

There is no man that hath left house, or parents, ... Who
shall not receive manifold more in this present time and
in 'the world to come' life everlasting.

150   Canto I, 265-66   Quote: Approximate

But, ah! [Don Jose] died; and buried' with him lay / The
public feeling and the lawyers' fees.

Luke 16:22

The 'rich man died, and was buried.'

151   Canto I, 372-75   Reference: Parodic

He [Don Juan] did not take such studies for restraints; /
But 'how faith is acquired,' and then ensured, / So well
not one of the aforesaid paints / As Saint Augustine in his
fine Confessions.

Romans 10:17

So then 'faith cometh by hearing,' and hearing by the word
of God.

152   Canto I, 377   Reference: Parodic

This [acquiring faith], too, was a seal'd book to little Juan.

Revelation 5:1

And I saw in the right hand of him that sat on the throne
a book written within and on the backside, sealed with
seven seals.

153   Canto I, 385   Quote: Approximate

Young Juan 'wax'd in goodliness and grace.'

Luke 2:40

And the child [Jesus] grew, and 'waxed' strong 'in spirit,
... and' the 'grace' of God was upon him.

154   Canto I, 406-407   Quote: Parodic

But scandal's my aversion--I protest / Against 'all evil
speaking,' even in jest.

Ephesians 4:31

Let 'all' bitterness, and wrath, ... and 'evil speaking,'
be put away from you, with all malice.

155   Canto I, 502   Quote: Approximate

'The flesh is frail,' and so the soul undone.

Matthew 26:41

The spirit indeed is willing, but 'the flesh is weak.'

156   Canto I, 663-64   Reference: Parodic

Christians have burnt each other, quite persuaded / That
all the Apostles would have done as they did.

Matthew 10:2-5

Now the names of the twelve apostles are these ... These
twelve Jesus sent forth.

157   Canto I, 732-36   Quote: Exact
    And then he [Don Juan] thought ... of the many bars to
    'perfect knowledge' of the boundless skies;-- / And then
    he thought of Donna Julia's eyes.
    Acts 24:22
    And when Felix heard these things, having more 'perfect
    knowledge' ... he deferred them.

158   Canto I, 1005   Allusion: Parodic
    Sweet is old wine in bottles, ale in barrels.
    Matthew 9:17
    Neither do men put new wine into old bottles: else the
    bottles break, ... but they put new wine into new bottles.

159   Canto I, 1060-61   Allusion
    Pleasure's a sin, and sometimes sin's a pleasure; / Few
    mortals know what end they would be at.
    Romans 7:15, 19
    For that which I do I allow not: for what I would, that
    do I not; but what I hate, that do I ... For the good that
    I would I do not: but the evil which I would not, that I do.

160   Canto I, 1082-84   Reference: Parodic
    At her [Donna Julia's] door / Arose a clatter might awake
    the dead, / If they had never been awoke before, / And
    that they have been so we all have read.
    Matthew 27:50-53
    Jesus, ... yielded up the ghost ... And the graves were
    opened; and many bodies of the saints which slept arose.

161   Canto I, 1082-86   Reference: Parodic
    At her [Donna Julia's] door / Arose a clatter might awake
    the dead, / If they had never been awoke before, / And
    that they have been so we all have read, / And are to
    be so, at the least, once more.
    I Corinthians 15:51-52
    We shall not all sleep, but we shall all be changed, In a
    moment, ... and the dead shall be raised incorruptible,
    and we shall be changed.

162   Canto I, 1314-15   Quote: Parodic
    Oh womankind! / How can you do such things and keep
    your fame, / Unless 'this world,' and t'other too, be
    blind.
    Matthew 12:32
    Whosoever speaketh against the Holy Ghost, it shall not
    be forgiven him, neither in 'this world,' neither in the
    world to come.

163   Canto I, 1548-49   Quote: Approximate
    Sword, gown, gain, glory, 'offer in exchange' / Pride,
    fame, ambition, to fill up his heart.
    Matthew 16:26
    What shall a man 'give in exchange' for his soul?

164   Canto I, 1755-56
                                        Quote: Approximate
      All things that have been born were born to die, / And
      'flesh' (which Death mows down to hay) 'is grass.'
      I Peter 1:24
         For all 'flesh is as grass,' and all the glory of man as
         the flower of grass. The grass withereth, and the flower
         thereof falleth away.

165   Canto II, 68-70
                                        Reference: Parodic
      And though Inez grieved / (As every kind of parting has
      its stings), / She hoped he would improve.
      I Corinthians 15:55-56
         O death, where is thy sting? O grave, where is thy vic-
         tory? The sting of death is sin; and the strength of sin
         is the law.

166   Canto II, 185-86
                                        Reference: Parodic
      The ship, call'd the most 'holy "Trinidada",' / Was steer-
      ing duly for the port Leghorn.
      Matthew 28:19
         Go ye therefore, and teach all nations, baptizing them in
         the name of the 'Father,' and of the 'Son, and' of the
         Holy Ghost.'

167   Canto II, 311
                                        Quote: Approximate
         'Tis true that 'man can only die once.'
      Hebrews 9:27
         It is appointed unto 'men once to die.'

168   Canto II, 355-56
                                        Parallelism
      Some cursed the day on which they saw the sun, / And
      gnash'd their teeth, and, howling, tore their hair.
      Matthew 8:12
         But the children of the kingdom shall be cast out into out-
         er darkness: there shall be weeping and gnashing of teeth.

169   Canto II, 583-84
                                        Quote: Exact
      And out they [the shipwrecked] spoke of lots for 'flesh and
      blood,' / And who should die to be his fellow's food.
      Matthew 16:17
         Blessed art thou, Simon ... for 'flesh and blood' hath not
         revealed it unto thee, but my Father.

170   Canto II, 600
                                        Quote: Parodic
         'The lot [to be cannibalized] fell on' Juan's luckless tutor.
      Acts 1:26
         And 'the lot fell upon' Matthias.

171   Canto II, 683-88
                                        Reference: Subject
      Their [the shipwrecked men's] throats were ovens, their
      swoln tongues were black, / As the rich man's in hell,
      who vainly scream'd / To beg the beggar, who could not
      rain back a drop of dew.

Luke 16:24
And he [the rich man] cried and said, Father Abraham, have mercy on me, and send Lazarus, that he may dip the tip of his finger in water, and cool my tongue; for I am tormented in this flame.

172   Canto II, 731-32   Parallelism
[The sun was] 'brought forth' in purple, 'cradled' in vermillion, / Baptized in molten gold, and 'swathed' in dun.

Luke 2:7
And she [Mary] 'brought forth' her firstborn son, and wrapped him in 'swaddling' clothes, and 'laid him in' a manger.

173   Canto II, 732   Parallelism
[The sun was] baptized in molten gold.

Matthew 3:11
I indeed baptize you with water: but ... he shall baptize you with the Holy Ghost, and with fire.

174   Canto II, 1001-1003   Reference: Parodic
A fisher, therefore, was he [Lambro],--though of men, / Like Peter the Apostle,--and he fish'd / For wandering merchant-vessels, now and then.

Matthew 4:19
And he [Jesus] saith unto them, Follow me, and I will make you fishers of men.

175   Canto II, 1030-31   Quote: Parodic
[Haidee] deem'd herself in common pity bound, / 'As far as in her lay,' "to take him in."

Romans 12:18
If it be possible, 'as much as lieth in you,' live peaceably with all men.

176   Canto II, 1030-32   Quote: Parodic
Yet deem'd herself in common pity bound, / As far as in her lay, "to 'take him in, / A stranger' " dying, with so white a skin.

Matthew 25:35, 43
I was 'a stranger,' and 'ye took me in.'

177   Canto II, 1039-40   Reference: Parodic
He [Lambro] would have hospitably cured the stranger, / And sold him instantly when out of danger.

Luke 10:34
And [the Good Samaritan] went to him, and bound up his wounds, pouring in oil and wine, ... and brought him to an inn, and took care of him.

178   Canto II, 1045-48   Reference: Parodic
Their [Haidee's and her maid's] charity increased about their guest; / And their compassion grew to such a size, /

It open'd half the turnpike-gates to heaven / (St. Paul
says, 'tis the toll which must be given).

I Corinthians 13:1-13

Though I speak with the tongues of men and of angels, and
have not charity, I am become as sounding brass. ... And
now abideth faith, hope, charity, these three; but the great-
est of these is charity.

179 Canto II, 1265-66
                                        Quote: Approximate
And so she took the liberty to state, / Rather by 'deeds'
than 'words.'

Colossiams 3:17

And whatsoever ye do in 'word or deed,' do all in the
name of the Lord Jesus.

180 Canto II, 1355-56
                                        Quote: Exact
Ceres presents a plate of vermicelli, -- / For love must
be sustain'd like 'flesh and blood.'

Matthew 16:17

Blessed art thou, Simon ... for 'flesh and blood' hath
not revealed it unto thee, but my Father.

181 Canto II, 1383-84
                                        Quote: Approximate
He was her own, her ocean-treasure, cast / Like a rich
wreck--'her first love,' and her last.

Revelation 2:4

Nevertheless I have somewhat against thee, because thou
hast left 'thy first love.'

182 Canto II, 1421-22
                                        Reference: Subject
And they may preach / Who please,--the more because
they preach in vain.

I Corinthians 15:14

And if Christ be not risen, then is our preaching vain.

183 Canto II, 1505-1507
                                        Quote: Exact
They fear'd no eyes nor ears on that lone beach, / They
felt no terrors from the night, they were / 'All in all'
to each other.

I Corinthians 15:28

Then shall the Son also himself be subject unto him ...
that God may be 'all in all.'

184 Canto II, 1509-11
                                        Allusion
And all the 'burning tongues' the passions teach / Found
in one sigh the best interpreter / Of nature's oracle.

Acts 2:3

And there appeared unto them 'cloven tongues like as of
fire,' and it sat upon each of them.

185 Canto II, 1530-36
                                        Quote: Parodic
The hour ... pays off moments in an endless shower / Of
hell-fire--all 'prepared for people' giving / Pleasure or
pain to one another living.

Matthew 25:41
Then shall he say also unto them on the left hand, Depart
from me, ye cursed, into everlasting fire, 'prepared for
the devil' and his angels.

186   Canto II, 1585-86   Quote: Parodic
Alas! the love of women! it is known / To be a lovely
and 'a fearful thing.'
Hebrews 10:31
It is 'a fearful thing' to fall into the hands of the living
God.

187   Canto II, 1655   Quote: Parodic
'Eat, drink, and love,' what can the rest avail us?
Luke 12:19
Soul, thou hast much goods laid up for many years; take
thine ease, 'eat, drink, and be merry.'

188   Canto III, 54   Reference: Parodic
Both [man and wife] are tied till one shall have expired.
I Corinthians 7:39
The wife is bound by the law as long as her husband liv-
eth; but if her husband be dead, she is at liberty to be
married to whom she will: only in the Lord.

189   Canto III, 68-70   Quote: Exact
The future states of both are left to faith, / For authors
fear description might disparage / 'The worlds to come'
of both, or fall beneath, / And then both worlds would
punish their miscarriage.
Luke 18:29-30
Verily I say unto you, There is no man that hath left
house, or parents, ... for the kingdom of God's sake,
Who shall not receive manifold more in this present time,
and in 'the world to come' life everlasting.

190   Canto III, 159-60   Quote: Exact
All hands were busy 'beyond measure,' / In getting out
goods, ballast, guns, and treasure.
Mark 7:37
And [the people] were 'beyond measure,' astonished, say-
ing, He [Jesus] hath done all things well.

191   Canto III, 307-308   Quote: Exact
The servants all were getting drunk or idling, / A life
which made them happy 'beyond measure.'
Mark 7:36-37
But the more he charged them, so much the more a great
deal they published it; And were 'beyond measure' aston-
ished.

192   Canto III, 369-73   Reference: Subject
Now in a person used to much command-- / To bid men

come, and go, and come again-- / To see his orders
done ... It may seem strange to find his manners bland.
Matthew 8:9
> For I [the centurion] am a man under authority, having
> soldiers under me: and I say to this man, Go, and he
> goeth; and to another, Come, and he cometh; and to my
> servant, Do this, and he doeth it.

193 Canto III, 393-400   Reference: Parodic
> If all the dead could now return to life / (Which God for-
> bid!) or some, or a great many, / For instance, if a
> husband or his wife ... Tears shed into the grave of the
> connection / Would share most probably its resurrection.
Matthew 27:52-53
> And the graves were opened; and many bodies of the saints
> which slept arose, And came out of the graves after his
> [Jesus'] resurrection.

194 Canto III, 425-31   Quote: Approximate
> 'The love of power, ' and rapid gain of gold ... Had cost
> his enemies a long repentance.
I Timothy 6:10
> For 'the love of money' is the root of all evil.

195 Canto III, 767-68   Quote: Exact
> Trust not for freedom to the Franks-- / They have a king
> who 'buys and sells. '
James 4:13
> Go to now, ye that say, To day or to morrow we will go
> ... and 'buy and sell, ' and get gain.

196 Canto III, 853-54   Allusion: Parodic
> Things which in this country don't strike / The public
> mind, --so few are the elect.
Romans 8:33
> Who shall lay any thing to the charge of God's elect? It
> is God that justifieth.

197 Canto III, 855-56   Reference: Parodic
> [Of Wordsworth and Joanna Southcote] And the new births
> of both their stale virginities / Have proved but dropsies,
> taken for divinities.
Matthew 1:18, 23
> Now the birth of Jesus Christ was on this wise: When as
> his mother Mary was espoused to Joseph, before they
> came together, she was found with child of the Holy Ghost
> ... Behold, a virgin shall be with child, and shall bring
> forth a son, and they shall call his name Emmanuel.

198 Canto III, 913-14   Quote: Exact
> Ave Maria! 'tis 'the hour of prayer'! / Ave Maria! 'tis
> the hour of love!

Acts 3:1
Now Peter and John went up together into the temple at 'the hour of prayer.'

199   Canto III, 915-16   Reference: Subject
Ave Maria! may our spirits dare / Look up to thine and to thy Son's above!
Matthew 1:21
And she shall bring forth a son, and thou shalt call his name Jesus.

200   Canto III, 917-18   Reference: Subject
Ave Maria! oh that face so fair! / Those downcast eyes beneath the Almighty dove.
Matthew 3:16
And Jesus, ... saw the Spirit of God descending like a dove, and lighting upon him.

201   Canto IV, 239-40   Allusion
Strange state of being! (for 'tis still to be) / Senseless to feel, and with seal'd eyes to see.
Matthew 13:14
By hearing ye shall hear, and shall not understand; and seeing ye shall see, and shall not perceive.

202   Canto IV, 279-80   Quote: Approximate
Oh! 'Powers of Heaven'! what dark eye meets she there? / 'Tis--'tis her father's--fix'd upon the pair!
Matthew 24:29
And the stars shall fall from heaven, and 'the powers of the heavens' shall be shaken.

203   Canto IV, 300-302   Parallelism
Dearest father [Lambro], ... I 'kiss / Thy garment's hem' with transport.
Matthew 9:20
A woman, which was diseased ... came behind him, and 'touched the hem of his garment.'

204   Canto IV, 304   Quote: Exact
Deal with me [Haidee] 'as thou wilt,' but spare this boy [Don Juan].
Matthew 15:28
O woman, great is thy faith: be it unto thee even 'as thou wilt.'

205   Canto IV, 315-17   Quote: Approximate
The old man's cheek grew pale, but not with dread, / And drawing from his belt a pistol, he / Replied, " 'Your blood be then on your own head.' "
Acts 18:6
[Paul] said unto them, 'Your blood be upon your own heads.'

206   Canto IV, 425-26   Quote: Parodic
           I leave Don Juan for the present, 'safe-- / Not sound, '
           poor fellow, but severely wounded.
       Luke 15:27
           And he said unto him, Thy brother [the prodigal son] is
           come; and thy father hath killed the fatted calf, because
           he hath received him 'safe and sound. '

207   Canto IV, 440   Reference: Subject
           And as the soil is, so the heart of man.
       Matthew 13:23
           But he that received seed into the good ground is he that
           heareth the word, and understandeth it.

208   Canto IV, 444-45   Reference: Subject
           The Moorish blood partakes the planet's hour, / And like
           the soil beneath it will bring forth.
       Matthew 13:23
           But he that received seed into the good ground is he that
           heareth the word, and understandeth it; which also bear-
           eth fruit, and bringeth forth, some an hundredfold, some
           sixty, some thirty.

209   Canto IV, 489-90   Reference: Subject
           She woke at length, but not as sleepers wake, / Rather
           the dead, for life seem'd something new.
       John 11:13
           Howbeit Jesus spake of his death [death of Lazarus]: but
           they thought that he had spoken of taking of rest in sleep.

210   Canto IV, 773-76   Reference: Parodic
           Therefore I'll make Don Juan leave the ship soon, / Be-
           cause the publisher declares, in sooth, / Through need-
           les' eyes it easier for the camel is / To pass, than those
           two cantos into families.
       Matthew 19:24
           And again I say unto you, It is easier for a camel to go
           through the eye of a needle, than for a rich man to en-
           ter into the kingdom of God.

211   Canto IV, 805-807   Quote: Exact
           The wide destruction ... Leaves nothing till " 'the coming
           of the just' "-- / Save change.
       Acts 7:52
           The prophets ... shewed before of 'the coming of the
           Just' One.

212   Canto IV, 810-12   Quote: Parodic
           And tomb inherits tomb, / Until the memory of an age is
           'fled, / And, buried, ' sinks beneath its offspring's doom.
       Acts 2:29
           The patriarch David, ... is both 'dead and buried. '

213 Canto IV, 851-53   Quote: Exact
     Men, who partake all passions as they pass, / Acquire
     the deep and bitter power to give / Their images again
     'as in a glass. '
     II Corinthians 3:18
     We all, with open face beholding 'as in a glass' the glory
     of the Lord, are changed into the same image.

214 Canto IV, 919-20   Reference: Subject
     The virtues, even the most exalted, Charity, / Are sav-
     ing--vice spares nothing for a rarity.
     I Corinthians 13:13
     And now abideth faith, hope, charity, these three; but the
     greatest of these is charity.

215 Canto V, 235-38   Quote: Exact
     Methinks at meals some odd thoughts might intrude, / And
     conscience ask a curious sort of question, / About the
     right divine how far we should / Sell 'flesh and blood.'
     Matthew 16:17
     Blessed art thou, Simon ... for 'flesh and blood' hath not
     revealed it unto thee, but my Father.

216 Canto V, 285-86   Reference: Subject
     He [military commandant] said, as the centurion saith, /
     "Go, " and he goeth; "come, ' and forth he stepp'd.
     Matthew 8:9
     For I the [centurion] am a man under authority, having
     soldiers under me: and I say to this man, Go, and he
     goeth; and to another, Come, and he cometh; and to my
     servant, Do this, and he doeth it.

217 Canto V, 421-24   Quote: Parodic
     And divers smoked superb pipes decorated / With amber
     'mouths of greater price or less'; / And several strutted,
     others slept, and some / Prepared for supper with a
     glass of rum.
     Matthew 13:45-46
     The kingdom of heaven is like unto a merchant man, seek-
     ing goodly pearls: Who, when he had found one 'pearl of
     great price, ' went and sold all that he had, and bought it.

218 Canto V, 492-96   Allusion
     They [infidels] won't ... Believe the Jews, those unbe-
     lievers.
     Acts 14:2
     The unbelieving Jews stirred up the Gentiles.

219 Canto V, 515-16   Allusion
     But in this one [chamber] / The movables were prodigally
     rich.
     Luke 15:11-32
     Rf. the Prodigal Son.

220 Canto V, 595-96   Quote: Approximate
        This spirit's well, but it may 'wax' too 'bold,' / And you
        will find us not too fond of joking.
     Acts 13:46
        Then Paul and Barnabas 'waxed bold' [and preached].

221 Canto V, 750-51   Parallelism
        Great lustre, there is much to be forgiven; / Groups of
        bad statues, tables, chairs, and pictures.
     Luke 7:41-47
        Which of them will love him most? I suppose that he, to
        whom he forgave most ... Her sins which are many, are
        forgiven; for she loved much.

222 Canto V, 766-78   Quote: Parodic
        She sign'd to Baba, who first 'kiss'd the hem' / Of her
        deep purple robe, and speaking low, / Pointed to Juan
        who remain'd below.
     Matthew 9:20
        And, behold, a woman, which was diseased with an issue
        of blood twelve years, came behind him, and 'touched the
        hem' of his garment.

223 Canto V, 869-70   Reference: Parodic
        The sun himself was scarce more free from specks / Than
        she from aught at which the eye could cavil.
     Matthew 7:3
        And why beholdest thou the mote that is in thy brother's
        eye, but considerest not the beam that is in thine own eye?

224 Canto V, 878-80   Reference: Parodic
        Our souls at least are free, and 't is in vain / We would
        against them make the flesh obey-- / The spirit in the
        end will have its way.
     Matthew 26:41
        The spirit indeed is willing, but the flesh is weak.

225 Canto V, 955-58   Reference: Parodic
        Female hearts are such a genial soil / For kinder feel-
        ings, whatsoe'er their nation, / They naturally pour the
        'wine and oil," / Samaritans in every situation.
     Luke 10:34
        And [the good Samaritan] went to him, and bound up his
        wounds, pouring in oil and wine, ... and took care of
        him.

226 Canto V, 1015-16   Parallelism
        Heads bow, knees bend, 'eyes watch around a throne,' /
        And hands obey.
     Revelation 4:6
        And before the 'throne' there was a sea of glass like unto
        crystal: and in the midst of the throne, and round about
        the throne, were four beasts full of 'eyes before and be-
        hind.'

227 Canto V, 1097   Quote: Exact
        [Humiliation] teaches them that they are 'flesh and blood. '
     Matthew 16:17
        Blessed art thou, Simon ... for 'flesh and blood' hath not
        revealed it unto thee, but my Father.

228 Canto V, 1098-1112   Reference: Subject
        Others, / Although of clay, are yet not quite of mud; /
        That urns and pipkins are but fragile brothers, / And
        works of the same pottery, bad or good, / Though not
        all born of the same sires and mothers.
     Romans 9:20-21
        Shall the thing formed say to him that formed it, Why hast
        thou made me thus? Hath not the potter power over the
        clay, of the same lump to make one vessel unto honour,
        and another unto dishonour?

229 Canto VI, 36-38   Allusion
        I had no great plenty / Of worlds to lose, yet still, to
        pay my court, I / Gave what I had--a heart.
     Revelation 12:7-9
        And there was war in heaven ... and the great dragon
        was cast out, that old serpent, called the Devil, ... he
        was cast out into the earth.

230 Canto VI, 41-42   Reference: Subject
        [My heart] was the boy's "mite," and, like the "widow's, "
        may / Perhaps be weigh'd hereafter, if not now.
     Mark 12:42-44
        And there came a certain poor widow, and she threw in
        two mites, which make a farthing ... even all her living.

231 Canto VI, 45-46   Quote: Exact
        'God is love, ' they say, / And Love's a god.
     I John 4:8
        He that loveth not knoweth not God; for 'God is love. '

232 Canto VI, 292-93   Reference: Parodic
        They all found as few, or fewer, 'specks' / In the fair
        form of their companion [Don Juan] new.
     Matthew 7:3
        And why beholdest thou the 'mote' that is in thy brother's
        eye, but considerest not the beam that is in thine own eye?

233 Canto VI, 441-43   Allusion: Parodic
        I think it [the age] may be of "Corinthian Brass, " / Which
        was a mixture of all metals, but / The brazen uppermost.
     I Corinthians 13:1
        Though I speak with the tongues of men ... and have not
        charity, I am become as sounding brass, or a tinkling
        cymbal.

234 Canto VI, 486-88   Quote: Parodic
        She rather suffer'd, / Pricking her fingers with those

cursed pins, / Which surely were invented 'for our sins. '
I Corinthians 15:3
    Christ died 'for our sins' according to the scriptures.

235 Canto VI, 761-64   Quote: Parodic
      His Highness had to hold / His daily council upon ways
      and means / How to encounter ... This modern Amazon
      and 'queen of queens. '
I Timothy 6:16
      He [God] ... is the blessed and only Potentate, the 'King
      of kings, ' and Lord of lords.

236 Canto VI, 801-802   Quote: Parodic
      Gulbeyaz was no model of true patience, / Nor much
      disposed to wait 'in word or deed. '
Colossians 3:17
      And whatsoever ye do 'in word or deed, ' do all in the
      name of the Lord Jesus.

237 Canto VII, 172-73   Parallelism
      'I'd rather tell ten lies than say a word' / Of truth;--such
      truths are treason.
I Corinthians 14:19
      In the church 'I had rather speak five words' with my un-
      derstanding, ... 'than ten thousand words' in an unknown
      tongue.

238 Canto VII, 323-26   Parallelism
      The fiat of this spoil'd 'child of the Night' ... could de-
      cree / More evil in an hour, than thirty bright / Sum-
      mers could renovat.
Ephesians 5:8
      For ye were sometimes darkness, but now are ye light
      in the Lord: walk as 'children of light. '

239 Canto VII, 665-67   Reference: Parodic
      Medals, rank, ribands, lace, embroidery, scarlet, / Are
      things immortal to immortal man, / As purple to the Ba-
      bylonian harlot.
Revelation 17:4-5
      And the woman was arrayed in purple and scarlet colour,
      ... And upon her forehead was a name written, mystery,
      Babylon the great, the mother of harlots and abominations
      of the earth.

240 Canto VIII, 70-72   Allusion: Parodic
      "Carnage" (so Wordsworth tells you) "is God's daughter:"
      / If he speak truth, she is Christ's sister, and / Just
      now behaved as in the Holy Land.
Matthew 12:50
      For whosoever shall do the will of my Father which is in
      heaven, the same is my brother, and sister, and mother.

241 Canto VIII, 153-54   Quote: Parodic
        Thus on they [Don Juan and Johnson] 'wallowed in the
        bloody mire' / Of dead and dying thousands.
     II Peter 2:22
        But it is happened unto them according to the true pro-
        verb, ... the sow that was washed [is turned] to her 'wal-
        lowing in the mire. '

242 Canto VIII, 162-67   Quote: Approximate
        The nightly muster and the silent march ... might make
        him [Don Juan] shiver, yawn, or throw / A glance on
        the dull clouds ... as if he 'wish'd for day. '
     Acts 27:29
        They cast four anchors out of the stern, and 'wished for
        the day. '

243 Canto VIII, 206-208   Reference: Parodic
        Those ancient good intentions, which once shaved / And
        smooth'd the brimstone of that street of hell / Which
        bears the greatest likeness to Pall Mall.
     Revelation 14:10
        And he shall be tormented with fire and brimstone in the
        presence of the holy angels.

244 Canto VIII, 207-208   Allusion: Parodic
        And smooth'd the brimstone of that street of hell / Which
        bears the greatest likeness to Pall Mall.
     Revelation 19:20
        These both [the beast and the false prophet] were cast
        alive into a lake of fire burning with brimstone.

245 Canto VIII, 217-20   Quote: Exact
        I don't know how the thing occurr'd--it might / Be that
        'the greater part' were kill'd or wounded, / And that the
        rest had faced unto the right / About.
     I Corinthians 15:6
        He [Jesus] was seen of above five hundred brethren at
        once; of whom 'the greater part' remain unto this present,
        but some are fallen asleep.

246 Canto VIII, 238-40   Quote: Parodic
        He stumbled on ... to add his own slight arm and forces
        / To corps, 'the greater part' of which were corses.
     I Corinthians 15:6
        He was seen of above five hundred brethren at once; of
        whom 'the greater part' remain unto this present, but
        some are fallen asleep.

247 Canto VIII, 417-18   Parallelism
        And here he was--who upon woman's breast, / Even from
        a child, felt like a child.
     I Corinthians 13:11
        When I was a child, I spake as a child, I understood as
        a child, I thought as a child.

248 Canto VIII, 532   Allusion
         Corruption could not make their [a sylvan tribe's] hearts
         her soil.
     Matthew 13:19, 23
         When any one heareth the word of the kingdom ... then
         cometh the wicked one, and catcheth away that which was
         sown in his heart ... But he that received seed into the
         good ground is he that heareth the word.

249 Canto VIII, 683-88   Reference: Parodic
         There is little art / In leaving verse more free from the
         restriction / Of truth than prose, unless to suit the mart
         for ... that outrageous 'appetite for lies' / Which Satan
         angles with for souls, like flies.
     John 8:44
         Ye are of your father the devil, ... for 'he is a liar,'
         and the father of it.

250 Canto VIII, 687-88   Reference: Parodic
         Lies / Which Satan angles with for souls, like flies.
     Matthew 4:19
         And he [Jesus] saith unto them [disciples], Follow me,
         and I will make you fishers of men.

251 Canto VIII, 713-16   Reference: Subject
         And one good action in the midst of crimes / Is "quite
         refreshing," in the affected phrase / Of these ambrosial,
         Pharisaic times, / With all their pretty milk-and-water
         ways.
     Matthew 23:1-3
         Then spake Jesus ... , Saying, The scribes and the Phar-
         isees sit in Moses' seat: All therefore whatsoever they
         bid you observe, that observe and do; but do not ye after
         their works.

252 Canto VIII, 881-83   Allusion: Parodic
         The eldest [son of the Sultan] was a true and tameless
         Tartar, / As great a scorner of the Nazarene / As ever
         Mahomet pick'd out for a martyr.
     Matthew 2:23
         And he [Jesus] came and dwelt in a city called Nazareth:
         that it might be fulfilled which was spoken by the prophets,
         He shall be called a Nazarene.

253 Canto VIII, 908-912   Reference: Subject
         If all be true we hear of heaven / And hell, there must
         at least be six or seven.
     II Corinthians 12:2
         I knew a man in Christ ... caught up to the third heaven.

254 Canto VIII, 932-34   Allusion
         He did not heed / Their pause nor signs: his heart was
         out of joint, / And shook (till now unshaken) like a reed.

Matthew 11:7
>   Concerning John, What went ye out into the wilderness to
>   see? A reed shaken with the wind?

255 Canto VIII, 933-34   Allusion
>   His heart was out of joint, / And shook (till now unshaken)
>   like a reed.

Matthew 11:7
>   And as they departed, Jesus began to say unto the multi-
>   tudes concerning John, What went ye out into the wilder-
>   ness to see? A reed shaken with the wind?

256 Canto VIII, 972-74   Reference: Subject
>   The crescent's silver bow / Sunk, and the crimson cross
>   glared o'er the field, / But red with no redeeming gore.

Colossians 1:20
>   And, having made peace through the blood of his cross,
>   ... to reconcile all things unto himself.

257 Canto VIII, 1045-46   Quote: Parodic
>   It was not their [ravished women] fault, but only fate, /
>   'To bear these crosses.'

Matthew 27:32
>   They found a man of Cyrene, Simon by name: him they
>   compelled 'to bear his cross.'

258 Canto VIII, 1063   Quote: Exact
>   'Glory to God' and to the Empress!

Luke 2:14
>   'Glory to God' in the highest.

259 Canto VIII, 1076-77   Parallelism
>   For I will teach, if possible, the stones / To rise against
>   earth's tyrants.

Matthew 3:9
>   For I say unto you, that God is able of these stones to
>   raise up children unto Abraham.

260 Canto VIII, 1081-84   Allusion
>   That hour [of the world's freedom] is not for us, but 'tis
>   for you: / And as, in the great joy of your millennium, /
>   You hardly will believe such things were true / As now
>   occur.

Revelation 20:2-7
>   And he laid hold on the dragon, ... which is the Devil,
>   and Satan, and bound him a thousand years ... And when
>   the thousand years are expired, Satan shall be loosed out
>   of his prison.

261 Canto IX, 41-44   Reference: Parodic
>   Now go and dine from off the plate / Presented by the
>   Prince of the Brazils, / And send the sentinel before your
>   [Duke of Wellington's] gate / A slice or two from your
>   luxurious meals.

Luke 16:19-21

There was a certain rich man, which ... fared sumptu-
ously every day: And there was a certain beggar named
Lazarus, which was laid at his gate, full of sores, And
desiring to be fed with the crumbs which fell from the
rich man's table.

262   Canto IX, 79-80   Allusion

You did great things; but not being great in mind, / Have
'left undone the greatest'--and mankind,

Matthew 23:23

Woe unto you, scribes and Pharisees, hypocrites! for ye
pay tithe of mint and anise and cummin, and have omitted
the weightier matters of the law, judgment, mercy, and
faith: these ought ye to have done, and not to 'leave the
other undone. '

263   Canto IX, 85-87   Reference: Subject

'Death' laughs at all you weep for:--look upon / This hour-
ly dread of all! whose threaten'd 'sting' / Turns life to
terror, even though in its sheath.

I Corinthians 15:55-56

O death, where is thy sting? O grave, where is thy vic-
tory? The sting of death is sin; and the strength of sin
is the law.

264   Canto IX, 123-24   Parallelism

'Tis true we speculate both far and wide, / And deem,
because 'we see, ' we are all-seeing.

John 9:40-41

Some of the Pharisees ... said unto him, Are we blind
also? Jesus said unto them, If ye were blind, ye should
have no sin: but now ye say, 'We see'; therefore your
sin remaineth.

265   Canto IX, 146-48   Reference: Parodic

We have / Souls to save, since Eve's slip and Adam's
fall, / Which tumbled all mankind into the grave.

Romans 5:12

By one man [Adam] sin entered into the world, and death
by sin; and so death passed upon all men, for that all
have sinned.

266   Canto IX, 147-50   Reference: Parodic

Eve's slip ... tumbled all mankind into the grave, / Be-
sides fish, beasts, and birds. "The sparrow's fall / Is
special providence. "

Matthew 10:29

Are not two sparrows sold for a farthing? and one of them
shall not fall on the ground without your Father.

267   Canto IX, 149-51   Reference: Parodic

"The sparrow's fall / Is special providence, " though how
it gave / Offence, we know not.

Matthew 10:29
>Are not two sparrows sold for a farthing? and one of them shall not fall on the ground without your Father.

268   Canto IX, 185-87   Quote: Approximate
>And I will war, at least 'in words (and'--should / My chance so happen--'deeds'), with all who war / With Thought.

Colossians 3:17
>And whatsoever ye do 'in word or deed,' do all in the name of the Lord Jesus, giving thanks to God and the Father by him.

269   Canto IX, 197-99   Reference: Parodic
>Whether they [demagogues and infidels] may sow scepticism to reap hell, / As is the Christian dogma rather rough, / I do not know.

Galatians 6:7
>For whatsoever a man soweth, that shall he also reap.

270   Canto IX, 205-206   Reference: Parodic
>He / Who neither wishes to be bound nor bind, / May still expatiate freely [without fear of offending].

Matthew 16:19
>And whatsoever thou shalt bind on earth shall be bound in heaven: and whatsoever thou shalt loose on earth shall be loosed in heaven.

271   Canto IX, 266-67   Reference: Parodic
>One life saved, especially if young / Or pretty, is a thing to recollect.

Luke 15:4
>What man of you, having an hundred sheep, if he lose one of them, doth not leave the ninety and nine in the wilderness, and go after that which is lost, until he find it.

272   Canto IX, 271-72   Allusion
>Though hymn'd by every harp, unless within / Your heart joins chorus, Fame is but a din.

Ephesians 5:19
>[Speak] to yourselves in psalms ... singing and making melody in your heart to the Lord.

273   Canto IX, 397-98   Quote: Exact
>That monstrous hieroglyphic--that long spout / Of 'blood and water,' leaden Castlereagh!

John 19:34
>But one of the soldiers with a spear pierced his side, and forthwith came there out 'blood and water.'

274   Canto IX, 424-28   Parallelism
>Catherine, ... 'loved all things' ... and pass'd for much / Admiring those ... Gigantic gentlemen.

I Corinthians 13:7
> [Charity] 'Beareth all things,' believeth all things, hopeth all things, endureth all things.

275   Canto IX, 471-72   Reference: Parodic
> As fall the dews on quenchless sands, / Blood only serves to wash Ambition's hands!

Matthew 27:24
> When Pilate saw that he could prevail nothing, but that rather a tumult was made, he took water, and washed his hands before the multitude, saying, I am innocent of the blood of this just person [Jesus]: see ye to it.

276   Canto IX, 585-92   Quote: Exact
> Besides Platonic love, besides 'the love / Of God,' the love of sentiment, ... there are those things which words name senses.

Luke 11:42
> For ye tithe mint and rue and all manner of herbs, and pass over judgment and 'the love of God.'

277   Canto IX, 612   Allusion
> I cannot stop to alter words once written.

John 19:22
> Pilate answered, What I have written I have written.

278/9   Canto IX, 637-40   Quote: Parodic
> She had a cursed taste for war, / And was not the best wife, unless we call / Such Clytemnestra, though perhaps 'tis better / 'That one should die,' than two drag on the fetter.

John 11:50
> It is expedient for us, 'that one' man [Jesus] 'should die' for the people, and that the whole nation perish not.

280   Canto X, 202-206   Quote: Exact
> Waste, and haste, and glare, and gloss, and glitter, ... Peep out sometimes, when things are in a flurry, / Through all the " 'purple and fine linen.' "

Luke 16:19
> There was a certain rich man, which was clothed in 'purple and fine linen,' and fared sumptuously every day.

281   Canto X, 206-208   Reference: Parodic
> All the "purple and fine linen,' [are] fitter / For Babylon's than Russia's royal harlot-- / And neutralize her outward show of scarlet.

Revelation 17:4-5
> And the woman was arrayed in purple and scarlet colour, ... And upon her forehead was a name written, mystery, Babylon the great, the mother of Harlots.

282   Canto X, 249-50   Allusion
          She [Donna Inez] also recommended him to God, / And
          no less To God's Son, as well as Mother.
      Matthew 1:23
          Behold, a virgin shall be with child, and shall bring forth
          a son, and they shall call his name Emmanuel, which be-
          ing interpreted is, God with us.

283   Canto X, 249-50   Quote: Approximate
          She [Donna Inez] also 'recommended him to God,' / And
          no less to God's Son, as well as Mother.
      Acts 20:32
          And now, brethren, I 'commend you to God,' and to the
          word of his grace.

284   Canto X, 268-69   Reference: Parodic
          Oh for trumps of cherubim! / Or the ear-trumpet of my
          good old aunt.
      I Corinthians 15:52
          In the twinkling of an eye, at the last trump: for the
          trumpet shall sound, and the dead shall be raised incor-
          ruptible, and we shall be changed.

285   Canto X, 273-77   Reference: Parodic
          She [Donna Inez] was no hypocrite at least, poor soul, /
          But went to heaven in as sincere a way /
          As any body on the elected roll, /
          Which portions out upon the judgment day /
          Heaven's freeholds.
      Revelation 20:12
          And I saw the dead, small and great, stand before God;
          and the books were opened: and another book was opened,
          which is the book of life: and the dead were judged out
          of those things which were written in the books, accord-
          ing to their works.

286   Canto X, 306-10   Reference: Parodic
          Her [Catherine's] physician ... found the tick of his
          [Don Juan's] fierce pulse betoken a condition /
          Which augur'd of 'the dead,' however 'quick' /
          Itself.
      Acts 10:42
          It is he [Jesus] which was ordained of God to be the Judge
          of quick and dead.

287   Canto X, 376-80   Reference: Parodic
          But time, the comforter, will come at last; / And four-
          and-twenty hours, and twice that number / Of candidates
          requesting to be placed, / Made Catherine taste next
          night a quiet slumber.

John 14:16-17, 26
> And I will pray the Father, and he shall give you another Comforter, that he may abide with you for ever ... The Comforter, ... is the Holy Ghost.

288   Canto X, 377   Allusion
> But time, the comforter, will come at last.

John 15:26
> But when the Comforter is come, whom I will send unto you from the Father, even the Spirit of truth, which proceedeth from the Father, he shall testify of me.

289   Canto X, 437-40   Allusion
> Her [Leila] salvation / Through his [Don Juan's] means and the church's might be paved. / But one thing's odd, which here must be inserted, / The little Turk refused to be converted.

Acts 15:3
> They passed through ... declaring the conversion of the Gentiles.

290   Canto X, 594-97   Allusion: Parodic
> [Leila] wonder'd how / He [God] suffered Infidels in his homestead, / The cruel Nazarenes, who had laid low / His holy temples.

Matthew 2:23
> He [Jesus] came and dwelt in a city called Nazareth: that it might be fulfilled which was spoken by the prophets, He shall be called a Nazarene.

291   Canto X, 612-15   Quote: Exact
> Juan admired these highways of free millions; / A country [England] in all senses the most dear / To foreigner or native, save some silly ones, / Who " 'kick against the pricks' " just at this juncture.

Acts 9:5 (and 26:14)
> And the Lord said, I am Jesus whom thou persecutest: it is hard for thee to 'kick against the pricks. '

292   Canto XI, 29-32   Reference: Subject
> Our days are too brief for affording / Space to dispute what no one ever could / Decide, and every body one day will / Know very clearly -- or at least lie still.

I Corinthians 13:12
> For now we see through a glass, darkly; but then face to face: now I know in part; but then shall I know even as also I am known.

293/94   Canto XI, 41-43   Reference: Parodic
         The first attack at once proved the Divinity / (But that I
         never doubted, nor the Devil); / The next, the Virgin's
         mystical virginity.
    Matthew 1:18
         Now the birth of Jesus Christ was on this wise; When as
         his mother Mary was espoused to Joseph, before they
         came together, she was found with child of the Holy Ghost.

295   Canto XI, 45-47   Allusion: Parodic
         The fourth [attack] at once establish'd the whole Trinity /
         On so uncontrovertible a level, / That I devoutly wish'd
         the three were four.
    Matthew 28:19
         Go ye therefore, and teach all nations, baptizing them in
         the name of the Father, and of the Son, and of the Holy
         Ghost.

296   Canto XI, 70-71   Allusion
         Here peals the people's voice, nor can entomb it / Racks,
         prisons, inquisitions; resurrection / Awaits it.
    Matthew 16:21
         [Jesus] must go unto Jerusalem, and suffer many things
         ... and be killed, and be raised again the third day.

297   Canto XI, 85-88   Quote: Parodic
         The heedless gentleman ... May find himself within that
         isle of riches [England] / Exposed to 'lose his life' as
         well as breeches.
    Matthew 10:39
         He that findeth his life shall lose it; and he that 'loseth
         his life' for my sake shall find it.

298   Canto XI, 118-20   Reference: Subject
         But what is to be done? I can't allow / The fellow to
         lie groaning on the road: / So take him up.
    Luke 10:31-32
         There came down a certain priest that way: and when he
         saw him, he passed by on the other side.   And likewise
         a Levite, ... passed by on the other side.   But a cer-
         tain Samaritan as he journeyed, came where he was: and
         when he saw him, he had compassion on him.   And went
         to him, and bound up his wounds, pouring in oil and wine,
         and set him on his own beast, and brought him to an inn,
         and took care of him.

299   Canto XI, 222-23   Parallelism
         'What I can, / I've done' to find the same [an honest man]
         throughout life's journey.
    Mark 14:8
         'She hath done what she could': she is come aforehand
         to anoint my body.

300   Canto XI, 353-55   Quote: Exact
       The great world, --'which, being interpreted,' / Meaneth
       the west or worst end of a city, / And about twice two
       thousand people bred.
       John 1:38, 41
       They said unto him, Rabbi, (which is to say, 'being inter-
       preted,' Master,) where dwellest thou ... We have found
       the Messias, 'which' is, 'being interpreted,' the Christ.

301   Canto XI, 366   Reference: Parodic
       A rib's a thorn in a wed gallant's side.
       II Corinthians 12:7
       And lest I should be exalted above measure through the
       abundance of the revelations, there was given to me a
       thorn in the flesh, the messenger of Satan to buffet me,
       lest I should be exalted above measure.

302   Canto XII, 71-72   Quote: Parodic
       He [the miser], despising every sensual call, / Commands
       --the intellectual 'lord of all.'
       Acts 10:36
       He [Jesus] is 'Lord of all.'

303   Canto XII, 97-98   Quote: Parodic
       "For love / Is heaven, and 'heaven is love:' "--so sings
       the bard.
       I John 4:8
       He that loveth not knoweth not God; for 'God is love.'

304   Canto XII, 111-12   Quote: Parodic
       And as for "Heaven being Love," why not say honey / Is
       wax? 'Heaven is not Love,' 'tis Matrimony.
       I John 4:8
       He that loveth not knoweth not God; for 'God is love.'

305   Canto XII, 137-42   Reference: Parodic
       Some persons ... / Baptize posterity, or future clay,--
       / To me seems but a dubious kind of reed / To lean on
       for support.
       Matthew 28:19
       Go ye therefore, and teach all nations, baptizing them in
       the name of the Father, and of the Son, and of the Holy
       Ghost.

306   Canto XII, 197-98   Quote: Exact
       When tired of play, he [Juan] flirted 'without sin' / With
       some of those fair creatures.
       John 8:7
       He that is 'without sin' among you, let him first cast a
       stone at her.

307   Canto XII, 389   Allusion: Parodic
       And how he had been toss'd, he [Don Juan] scarce knew
       whither.

Ephesians 4:14
That we henceforth be no more children, tossed to and fro, and carried about with every wind of doctrine.

308   Canto XII, 401   Parallelism
'How far it [war] profits' is another matter.
Mark 8:36
For 'what shall it profit' a man, if he shall gain the whole world, and lose his own soul?

309   Canto XII, 469-70   Quote: Parodic
Many [ladies] have a method more reticular-- / " 'Fishers for men,' " like sirens with soft lutes.
Mark 1:17
And Jesus said unto them, Come ye after me, and I will make you to become 'fishers of men.'

310   Canto XII, 492-96   Reference: Parodic
I meant and mean not to disparage / The show of virtue even in the vitiated ... But to denounce the amphibious sort of harlot, "Coleur de rose," who's neither white nor scarlet.
Revelation 17:3-5
I saw a woman sit upon a scarlet coloured beast ... And the woman was arrayed in purple and scarlet colour ... And upon her forehead was a name written, mystery, Babylon the great, the mother of harlots.

311   Canto XII, 573-75   Quote: Parodic
This reflection brings me to plain physics, / And to the beauties of a foreign dame, / Compared with those of our pure 'pearls of price.'
Matthew 13:45-46
The kingdom of heaven is like unto a merchant man, seeking goodly pearls: Who, when he had found one 'pearl of great price,' went and sold all that he had, and bought it.

312   Canto XII, 624-26   Quote: Exact
For Fame's a Carthage not so soon rebuilt. / Perhaps this is as it should be;--it is / A comment on the Gospel's " 'Sin no more.' "
John 8:11
Jesus said unto her, ... go and 'sin no more.'

313   Canto XII, 624-27   Quote: Approximate
For Fame's a Carthage not so soon rebuilt. / Perhaps this is as it should be; it is a comment on the Gospel's ... 'be thy sins forgiven.'
Matthew 9:2
And Jesus ... said unto the sick of the palsy; Son, be of good cheer; 'thy sins be forgiven thee.'

313a Canto XII, 629-31   Quote: Parodic
Though doubtless they [saints] do much amiss, / An erring

woman finds 'an opener door' / For her return to Virtue.
Revelation 3:8

Behold, I have set before thee [the church in Philadelphia]
'an open door, ' and no man can shut it.

314 Canto XIII, 173-76; 194-97   Reference: Parodic

He knew the world, and would not see depravity / In
faults which sometimes show the soil's fertility, / If that
the weeds o'erlive not the first crop-- / For then they
are very difficult to stop ... men are so censorious, /
And apt to sow an author's wheat with tares, / Reaping
allusions private and inglorious, / Where none were
dreamt of.
Matthew 13:25

But while men slept, his enemy came and sowed tares
among the wheat, and went his way.

315 Canto XIII, 290-94   Parallelism

What say you to a bottle of champagne? / Frozen into a
very vinous ice ... in the very centre, 'past all price, '
/ About a liquid glassful will remain; ... And your cold
people are 'beyond all price. '
Matthew 13:45-46

A merchant man, seeking goodly pearls: Who, when he
had found one pearl 'of great price, ' went and sold all
that he had, and bought it.

316 Canto XIII, 329-31   Reference: Parodic

The English winter--ending in July, / To recommence in
August--now was done. / 'Tis the postilion's paradise.
Luke 23:43

And Jesus said ... To day shalt thou be with me in par-
adise.

317 Canto XIII, 417-19   Parallelism

Who doubts the Morning Post? / (Whose articles are like
the "Thirty-nine," / Which those most swear to who 'be-
lieve them most')
Luke 7:42

Tell me therefore, which of them will 'love him most'?

318 Canto XIII, 481-83   Reference: Subject

But in a higher niche, alone, but crown'd, / The Virgin
Mother of the God-born Child, / With her Son in her
blessed arms, look'd round.
Matthew 1:23

Behold, a virgin shall be with child, and shall bring forth
a son, and they shall call his name Emmanuel, which be-
ing interpreted is, God with us.

319 Canto XIII, 517-20   Quote: Exact

The spring gush'd ... in a thousand bubbles, / Like man's
'vain glory, ' and his vainer troubles.

Galatians 5:26
Let us not be desirous of 'vain glory.'

320 Canto XIII, 567-68   Quote: Approximate
Spagnoletto tainted / His brush with all 'the blood of all
the sainted.'
Revelation 16:6
They have shed 'the blood of saints' and prophets, and
thou hast given them blood to drink.

321/2 Canto XIII, 577-79   Quote: Parodic
O reader! 'if that thou canst read,'--and know, / 'Tis
not enough to spell, or even to read, / To constitute a
reader.
Mark 9:22-23
'If thou canst do' any thing, have compassion on us, and
help us. Jesus said unto him, 'If thou canst believe,' all
things are possible to him that believeth.

323 Canto XIII, 795-96   Quote: Exact
We have added since, 'the love of money,' / The only
sort of pleasure which requites.
I Timothy 6:10
For 'the love of money' is the root of all evil.

324 Canto XIII, 834-35   Reference: Parodic
The earth has nothing like a she epistle, / And hardly
heaven--because it never ends.
Acts 15:30
Rf. New Testament epistles.

325 Canto XIV, 6-8   Quote: Approximate
Old Saturn ate his progeny; / For when his pious consort
'gave him stones' / In lieu of sons, of these he made no
bones.
Matthew 7:9
What man is there of you, whom if his son ask bread,
will he 'give him a stone'?

326 Canto XIV, 113-15   Quote: Exact
The portion of 'this world' which I at present / Have ta-
ken up to fill the following sermon, / Is one of which
there's no description recent.
Matthew 13:22
The care of 'this world,' and the deceitfulness of riches,
choke the word.

327 Canto XIV, 125-27   Allusion
[The world has] factitious passions, wit without much
salt, / A want of that true nature which sublimes / What-
e'er it shows with truth.
Colossians 4:6
Let your speech be alway with grace, seasoned with salt.

328   Canto XIV, 241-42   Quote: Approximate
        Juan--in this respect, at least, like saints-- / Was 'all
        things unto people of all sorts. '
    I Corinthians 9:23
        'I am made all things to all men, ' that I might by all
        means save some.

329   Canto XIV, 241-44   Reference: Subject
        Juan ... lived contentedly, without complaints, / In camps,
        in ships, in cottages, or courts.
    Philippians 4:11
        I have learned, in whatsoever state I am, therewith to be
        content.

330   Canto XIV, 279-80   Parallelism
        [Don Juan] rode beyond all price, / Ask'd next day, "If
        men ever hunted twice? "
    Matthew 13:45-46
        A merchant man, seeking goodly pearls: ... when he had
        found one pearl of great price, went and sold all that he
        had, and bought it.

331   Canto XIV, 341   Quote: Approximate
        'Woe to the man' who ventures a rebuke [to a woman]!
    Mark 14:21
        'Woe to that man' by whom the Son of man is betrayed!

332   Canto XIV, 363-64   Quote: Parodic
        My 'Dian of the Ephesians, ' Lady Adeline, / Began to
        think the duchess' conduct free.
    Acts 19:28
        They [of Ephesus] ... cried out, saying, Great is 'Diana
        of the Ephesians. '

333   Canto XIV, 523-24   Quote: Approximate
        [Lord Henry] 'never judged from what appear'd, ' / with-
        out strong reason.
    John 7:24
        'Judge not according to the appearance, ' but judge right-
        eous judgment.

334   Canto XIV, 677-78   Allusion
        A wavering spirit may be easier wreck'd, / Because 'tis
        frailer, doubtless, than a stanch one.
    James 1:6
        Let him ask in faith, nothing wavering, for he that waver-
        eth is like a wave of the sea driven with the wind and
        tossed.

335   Canto XV, 126-28   Allusion: Parodic
        If once their [women's] phantasies be brought to bear /
        Upon an object, whether sad or playful, / They can trans-
        figure brighter than a Raphael.

Matthew 17:1-2
>
And after six days Jesus taketh Peter, James, and John his brother, and bringeth them up into an high mountain apart, And was transfigured before them: and his face did shine as the sun, and his raiment was white as the light.

336 Canto XV, 137-40   Reference: Subject
>
Was it not so, ... thou, Diviner still, / Whose lot it is by man to be mistaken, / And thy pure creed made sanction of all ill?

Matthew 16:13-14
>
Jesus came ... , saying Whom do men say that I the Son of man am? And they said, Some say ... John the Baptist: some, Elias; and others, Jeremias, or one of the prophets.

337 Canto XV, 140   Reference: Subject
>
And thy [Christ's] pure creed [is] made sanction of all ill?

I Corinthians 1:18
>
For the preaching of the cross is to them that perish foolishness; but unto us which are saved it is the power of God.

338 Canto XV, 182-83   Quote: Approximate
>
I should 'turn the other way, ' / And wax ultra-royalist in loyalty.

Matthew 5:39
>
But whosoever shall smite thee on thy right cheek, 'turn' to him 'the other' also.

339 Canto XV, 403-406   Quote: Parodic
>
If bad, the best way's certainly to tease on, / And amplify: you lose much by concision, / Whereas insisting 'in or out of season' / Convinces all men, even a politician.

II Timothy 4:2
>
Preach the word; be instant 'in season, out of season. '

340 Canto XV, 701-702   Quote: Parodic
>
He who 'doubts all things' nothing can deny: / Truths fountains may be clear--her streams are muddy.

I Corinthians 13:7
>
[Charity] beareth all things, 'believeth all things, ' hopeth all things, endureth all things.

341 Canto XV, 705-707   Reference: Parodic
>
Apologue, fable, poesy, and parable, / Are false, but may be render'd also true, / By those who sow them in a land that's arable.

Matthew 13:3-30
>
Rf. the parable of the sower and the soils.

342 Canto XVI, 42-43   Reference: Subject
        Believe:--if 'tis improbable you must, / And if it is im-
        possible, you shall.
     Hebrews 11:6
        But without faith it is impossible to please him: for he
        that cometh to God must believe that he is.

343 Canto XVI, 45-46   Allusion
        I do not speak profanely, to recall / Those holier mys-
        teries which the wise and just receive as gospel.
     Matthew 13:11
        It is given unto you to know the nysteries of the kingdom
        of heaven.

344 Canto XVI, 49-52   Reference: Parodic
        Johnson said, / That in the course of some six thousand
        years, / All nations have believed that from the dead / A
        visitant at intervals appears。
     Matthew 28
        Rf. the resurrection of Jesus.

345 Canto XVI, 459-60   Allusion: Parodic
        A thing quite necessary to the elect, / Who wish to take
        the tone of their society.
     Romans 8:33
        Who shall lay any thing to the charge of God's elect?   It
        is God that justifieth.

346 Canto XVI, 549-50   Allusion: Parodic
        Of all things, excepting tithes and leases, / Perhaps
        these [morals] are most difficult to tame.
     James 3:7-8
        Every kind of beasts, and of birds, and of serpents, and
        of things in the sea, is tamed, and hath been tamed of
        mankind: But the tongue can no man tame.

347 Canto XVI, 564-68   Reference: Parodic
        She was not a sentimental mourner / Parading all her
        sensibility, / Nor insolent enough to scorn the scorner,
        / But stood in trembling, 'patient tribulation,' / To be
        call'd up for her examination.
     Romans 12:12
        [Be] 'patient in tribulation.'

348 Canto XVI, 610-11   Quote: Exact
        He [Lord Henry] was 'all things to all men,' and dis-
        pensed / To some civility, to others bounty.
     I Corinthians 9:22
        I am made 'all things to all men,' that I might by all
        means save some.

349 Canto XVI, 635-36   Allusion: Parodic
        But could he [Lord Henry] quit his king in times of strife,

/ Which threaten'd the whole country with perdition?

Hebrews 10:39
But we are not of them who draw back unto perdition: but of them that believe to the saving of the soul.

350   Canto XVI, 732-33   Quote: Parodic
Bacchus and Ceres being, as we know / Even 'from our grammar upwards, ' friends of yore.

Matthew 19:20
The young man saith unto him [Jesus], All these things have I kept 'from my youth up'; what lack I yet?

351   Canto XVI, 766-68   Reference: Parodic
One scarce knew at what to marvel most / Of two things --how (the question rather odd is) / Such bodies could have souls, or souls such bodies.

I Thessalonians 5:23
I pray God your whole spirit and soul and body be preserved blameless.

352   Canto XVI, 958-60   Allusion: Parodic
For immaterialism's a serious matter; / So that even those whose faith is the most great / In souls immortal, shun them tete-a-tete.

Romans 2:7
To them who by patient continuance in well doing seek for glory and honour and immortality, eternal life.

353   Canto XVI, 989-92   Allusion: Parodic
His [Don Juan's] own internal ghost began to awaken / Within him, and to quell his corporal quaking-- / Hinting that soul and body on the whole / Were odds against a disembodied soul.

I Thessalonians 5:23
I pray God your whole spirit and soul and body be preserved blameless.

354   Canto XVI, 1025-28   Quote: Exact
The ghost, ... A dimpled chin, a neck of ivory, stole / Forth into something much like 'flesh and blood. '

I Corinthians 15:50
Now this I say, brethren, that 'flesh and blood' cannot inherit the kingdom of God.

ENGLISH BARDS AND SCOTCH REVIEWERS

---

355   Lines 177-178   Parallelism
Let such forego the poet's sacred name, / Who rack their brains for lucre, not for fame.

I Timothy 3:2-3
>A bishop then must be ... not greedy of filthy lucre.

356 Lines 279-80   Reference: Parodic
>If tales like thine [Lewis and Scott] may please, / St.
>Luke alone can vanquish the disease.

Colossians 4:14
>Luke, the beloved physician, and Demas, greet you.

357 Line 294   Quote: Parodic
>She [the muse] bids thee "mend thy line, 'and sin no
>more. ' "

John 8:11
>Jesus said ... Go, 'and sin no more. '

358 Lines 301-302   Quote: Parodic
>Learn, 'if thou [Percy Clinton Sydney Smythe, sixth Vis-
>count Strangford] canst, ' to yield thine author's sense, /
>Nor vend thy sonnets on a false pretence.

Mark 9:22-23
>But 'if thou [Jesus] canst' do any thing, have compassion
>on us, and help us. Jesus said unto him, 'If thou canst'
>believe.

359 Lines 377-78   Reference: Parodic
>Write, as if St. John's soul could still inspire, / And do
>from hate what Mallet did for hire.

Revelation 1:9-11
>I [John] was in the Spirit ... and heard behind me a great
>voice, ... Saying, ... What thou seest, write in a book.

360 Lines 741-43   Quote: Parodic
>With you, ye Druids! rich in native lead, / Who daily
>scribble for 'your daily bread'; / With you I war not.

Matthew 6:11
>Give us this day 'our daily bread. '

361 Lines 799-800   Reference: Parodic
>To the famed throng now paid the tribute due, / Neglected
>genius!

Matthew 22:17-21
>Is it lawful to give tribute unto Caesar ... ? Then saith
>he unto them, Render therefore unto Caesar the things
>which are Caesar's' and unto God the things that are God's.

362 Lines 873-76   Reference: Subject
>But doubly blest is he whose heart expands / With hallow'd
>feelings for those classic lands; / Who 'rends the veil' of
>ages long gone by, / And views their remnants with a
>poet's eye!

Matthew 27:51
>And, behold, 'the veil' of the temple was 'rent in twain'
>from the top to the bottom; and the earth did quake, and
>the rocks rent.

363   Lines 874-76   Reference: Parodic
          With hallow'd feelings for those classic lands; / Who rends
          the veil of ages long gone by, / And views their remnants
          with a poet's eye!
      Matthew 27:51
          And, behold, the veil of the temple was rent in twain
          from the top to the bottom; and the earth did quake, and
          the rocks rent [at the death of Jesus].

364   Lines 893-98   Reference: Parodic
          Flimsy Darwin's pompous chime, ... whose gilded cym-
          bals, ... fatigued the ear; / In show the simple lyre
          could once surpass, / But now, worn down, appear in
          native brass.
      I Corinthians 13:1
          Though I speak with the tongues of men and of angels, and
          have not charity, I am become as sounding brass, or a
          tinkling cymbal.

365   Lines 1042-44   Parallelism
          My page, though nameless, never disavow'd; / And now
          at once I tear 'the veil away':-- / Cheer on the pack!
          the quarry stands at bay.
      II Corinthians 3:13-16
          Until this day remaineth 'the' same 'vail' untaken 'away'
          in the reading of the old testament ... Nevertheless when
          it shall turn to the Lord, 'the vail shall be taken away.'

EPHEMERAL VERSES

"To Dives (William Beckford).   A Fragment"

366   Entire poem   Reference: Parodic
      Luke 16:19-31
          Rf. the rich man and Lazarus.

367   Line 4   Reference: Parodic
          Wrath's vial on thy lofty head hath burst.
      Revelation 16:1
          And I heard a great voice out of the temple saying to the
          seven angels, Go your ways, and pour out the vials of the
          wrath of God upon the earth.

"What Matter the Pangs of a Husband and Father"

368   Lines 1-3   Allusion
          What matter the pangs of a husband and father, / If his
          sorrows in exile be great or be small, / So the Pharisee's

glories around her [the wife] she gather [i. e. at her ball].
Matthew 23:13
But woe unto you, scribes and Pharisees, hypocrites!

THE GIAOUR

---

369   Lines 374-79   Quote: Approximate
The calm wave rippled to the bank; / I watch'd it as it
sank, ... 'twas but the beam / That checker'd o'er the
'living stream. '
John 4:11
Sir, thou [Jesus] hast nothing to draw with, and the well
is deep: from whence then hast thou that 'living water'?

370   Lines 747-52   Quote: Approximate
But thou, false Infidel! shalt writhe / Beneath avenging
Monkie's scythe; / And from its torment 'scape alone /
To wander round lost Eblis' throne; / And 'fire unquench'd,
unquenchable, ' / Around, within, thy heart shall dwell.
Matthew 3:12
[Jesus] will thoroughly purge his floor, and gather his
wheat into the garner; but he will burn up the chaff with
'unquenchable fire. '

371   Lines 1040-41   Reference: Subject
The very name of Nazarene / Was wormwood to his Pay-
nim spleen.
Matthew 2:23
And he [Jesus] came and dwelt in a city called Nazareth:
that it might be fulfilled which was spoken by the prophets,
He shall be called a Nazarene.

372   Lines 1127-30   Quote: Exact
She was ... 'The Morning-star' of Memory!
Revelation 2:28
And I [God] will give him [Jesus] 'the morning star. '

373   Lines 1149-51   Quote: Exact
'Why marvel ye, ' if they who lose / This present joy,
this future hope, / No more with sorrow meekly cope?
Acts 3:12
[Peter] answered unto the people, ... 'why marvel ye' at
this? or why look ye so earnestly on us, as though by our
own power or holiness we had made this man to walk?

374   Lines 1165-66   Allusion
But this was taught me by the dove, / To die--and know
no 'second love. '

Revelation 2:4
Nevertheless I have somewhat against thee, because thou
hast left thy 'first love.'

HEAVEN AND EARTH

---

375 Part I, i. 58-59   Quote: Approximate
He hath made me 'of the least / Of those' cast out from
Eden's gate.
Matthew 25:40
Verily I say unto you, Inasmuch as ye have done it unto
one of the least of these' my brethren, ye have done it
unto me [Jesus].

376 Part I, i. 120-22   Reference: Subject
We are / Of as eternal essence, and must war / With
him [God] if he will war with us.
Revelation 12:7
And there was war in heaven: Michael and his angels
fought against the dragon [the Devil]; and the dragon fought
and his angels.

377 Part I, ii. 237   Quote: Approximate
How would I Japhet have adored thee God, but 'thou
wouldst not.'
Matthew 23:37
O Jerusalem, Jerusalem, ... how often would I [Jesus]
have gathered thy children together, even as a hen gath-
ereth her chickens under her wings, and 'ye would not'!

378 Part I, ii. 262-63   Allusion
All evil things are powerless on the man / Selected by
Jehovah.
I Peter 3:12
For the eyes of the Lord are over the righteous, and his
ears are open unto their prayers: but the face of the Lord
is against them that do evil.

379 Part I, iii. 273-75   Parallelism
Yet, in a few days, / Perhaps even hours, ye will be
changed, / rent, hurl'd / Before the mass of waters.
I Corinthians 15:51-52
We shall not all sleep, but we shall all be changed. In a
moment, in the twinkling of an eye, at the last trump.

380 Part I, iii. 297-300   Allusion
And can those words "no more" / Be meant for thee, for
all things, save for us, / And the predestined creeping

things reserved / By my sire to Jehovah's bidding?
Romans 8:29-30
>   For whom he [God] did foreknow, he also did predestinate
>   to be conformed to the image of his Son, that he might be
>   the firstborn among many brethren. Moreover whom he
>   did predestinate, them he also called: and whom he called,
>   them he also justified.

381   Part I, iii. 459-62   Allusion
>   The eternal will / Shall ... redeem / Unto himself all
>   times.
Ephesians 5:15-16
>   See then that ye walk circumspectly, ... Redeeming the
>   time.

382   Part I, iii. 459-64   Reference: Subject
>   The eternal will / Shall ... redeem / Unto himself all
>   times, all things; / And, gather'd under his almighty
>   wings, / Abolish hell!
Matthew 23:37
>   O Jerusalem, Jerusalem, ... how often would I have
>   gathered thy children together, even as a hen gathereth
>   her chickens under her wings, and ye would not!

383   Part I, iii. 625-26   Allusion
>   If they love as they are loved, they will not shrink / More
>   to be mortal.
John 15:12
>   This is my [Jesus'] commandment, That ye love one ano-
>   ther, as I have loved you.

384   Part I, iii. 725-26   Quote: Exact
>   I have ever hail'd our Maker, Samiasa, / As thine, and
>   mine: a 'God of love, ' not sorrow.
II Corinthians 13:11
>   The 'God of love' and peace shall be with you.

385   Part I, iii. 755-56   Quote: Approximate
>   Not ye Azaziel 'in all your glory' can redeem / What he
>   who made you glorious hath condemn'd.
Matthew 6:29
>   And yet I say unto you, That even Solomon 'in all his
>   glory' was not arrayed like one of these.

386   Part I, iii. 820-21   Quote: Exact
>   I came to call ye back to your fit sphere, / In the great
>   name and at 'the word of God. '
I Thessalonians 2:13
>   When ye received the word of God which ye heard of us,
>   he received it not as the word of men, but as it is in
>   truth, 'the word of God. '

387   Part I. iii. 853-54   Allusion
          He [Satan] cannot tempt / The angels, from his further
          snares exempt.
      I Timothy 3:7
          Moreover he must have a good report ... lest he fall in-
          to reproach and the snare of the devil.

388   Part I. iii. 869-72   Reference: Subject
          Why partake / The agony to which they must be heirs--
          / Born to be plough'd with years, and sown with cares,
          / And reap'd by Death, lord of the human soil?
      Matthew 13:1-23
          Rf. the parable of the sower and the soils.

389   Part I. iii. 1071-73   Allusion
          Some clouds sweep on as vultures for their prey, / While
          others, fix'd as rocks, await the word / At which their
          wrathful vials shall be pour'd.
      Revelation 16:1
          And I heard a great voice out of the temple saying to the
          seven angels, Go your ways, and pour out the vials of
          the wrath of God upon the earth.

390   Part I. iii. 1142-43   Quote: Exact
          Fly, son of Noah, fly! and 'take thine ease' / In thine
          allotted ocean-tent.
      Luke 12:19
          And I will say to my soul, Soul, thou hast much goods
          laid up for many years; 'take thine ease,' eat, drink, and
          be merry.

391   Part I. iii. 1148-49   Quote: Exact
          'Blessed are the dead / Who die in the Lord'!
      Revelation 15:13
          And I heard a voice from heaven saying unto me, Write,
          'Blessed are the dead which die in the Lord' from hence-
          forth.

HEBREW MELODIES

"The Destruction of Sennacherib"

392   Line 1   Allusion
          The Assyrian came down like the wolf on the fold.
      John 10:12-16
          But he that is an hireling, ... seeth the wolf coming, ...
          and fleeth ... And other sheep I have, which are not of
          this fold.

"Herod's Lament for Mariamne"

393   Title   Allusion
      Matthew 2:12
            And being warned of God in a dream that they [the wise
            men] should not return to Herod [the Great], they depart-
            ed into their own country another way.

"If That High World"

394   Lines 1-4   Reference: Subject
            If that high world, which lies beyond ... If there the cher-
            ish'd heart be fond, / The eye the same, except in tears.
      Revelation 7:17
            And God shall wipe away all tears from their eyes.

"Oh! Weep for Those"

395   Lines 11-12   Reference: Subject
            The wild-dove hath her nest, the fox his cave, / Mankind
            their country--Israel but the grave!
      Matthew 8:20
            Jesus saith ... , The foxes have holes, and the birds of
            the air have nests; but the Son of man hath not where to
            lay his head.

"On the Day of the Destruction of Jerusalem by Titus"

396   Entire poem   Reference: Subject
      Matthew 24
            Rf. the promised destruction of Jerusalem, A.D. 70.

"Thy Days Are Done"

397   Lines 7-8   Quote: Exact
            Though thou art fall'n, while we are free / Thou 'shalt
            not taste of death'!
      Matthew 16:28
            There be some standing here, which 'shall not taste of
            death,' till they see the Son of man coming in his king-
            dom.

"Vision of Belshazzar"

398   Lines 41-42   Quote: Approximate
            Belshazzar's grave is made, / His kingdom 'pass'd away.'
      Matthew 24:35
            Heaven and earth shall 'pass away,' but my words shall
            not pass away.

"The Wild Gazelle"

399   Lines 23-24   Reference: Subject
            Our temple hath not left a stone, / And Mockery sits on
            Salem's throne.

Matthew 24:2
>   Verily I [Jesus] say unto you, There shall not be left here one stone [of the temple] upon another, that shall not be thrown down.

HINTS FROM HORACE

---

400   Lines 380-82   Quote: Parodic
>   Faith cants, perplex'd apologist of sin! / While the 'Lord's servant chastens whom he loves,' / And Simeon kicks, where Baxter only "shoves."

Hebrews 12:6
>   For 'whom the Lord loveth he chasteneth,' and scourgeth every son whom he receiveth.

401   Lines 585-86   Reference: Parodic
>   But poesy between the best and worst / No medium knows; you must be last or first.

Matthew 19:30
>   But many that are first shall be last; and the last shall be first.

402   Lines 593-94   Quote: Parodic
>   Some, worse than Turks, / Would rob poor Faith to decorate " 'good works.' "

Matthew 5:16
>   Let your light so shine before men, that they may see your 'good works,' and glorify your Father which is in heaven.

HOURS OF IDLENESS

"Answer to Some Elegant Verses ..."

403   Lines 37-39   Allusion
>   For me, I fain would please the 'chosen few,' / Whose souls, to feeling and to nature true, / Will spare the childish verse.

Matthew 20:16
>   For many be called, but 'few chosen.'

"Elegy on Newstead Abbey"

404   Lines 78-80
                                      Allusion
       Far different incense now ascends to heaven, / Such vic-
       tims wallow on the glory ground.
       Revelation 8:4
       The smoke of the incense, which came with the prayers
       of the saints, ascended up before God out of the angel's
       hand.

"The Episode of Nisus and Euryalus"

405   Line 134
                                      Parallelism
       Internal virtues are the gift of Heaven.
       Hebrews 6:4-6
       It is impossible for those who ... have tasted of the hea-
       venly gift, ... If they shall fall away, to renew them
       again unto repentance.

406   Lines 375-76
                                      Reference: Subject
       He pray'd in vain; the dark assassin's sword / Pierced
       the fair side, the snowy bosom gored.
       John 19:34
       But one of the soldiers with a spear pierced his [Jesus']
       side, and forthwith came there out blood and water.

"Oscar of Alva"

407   Lines 231-32
                                      Reference: Subject
       Come, drink remembrance of the dead, / And raise thy
       cup with firmer hand.
       Luke 22:19
       This is my body which is given for you: this do in re-
       membrance of me.

"The Prayer of Nature"

408   Lines 1-2
                                      Quote: Exact
       'Father of Light'! great God of Heaven! / Hear'st thou
       the accents of despair?
       James 1:17
       Every good gift and every perfect gift is from above, and
       cometh down from the 'Father of lights.'

409   Lines 17-18
                                      Allusion
       Shall man confine his Maker's sway / To Gothic domes
       of mouldering stone?
       Act 17:24
       He is Lord of heaven and earth, [and] dwelleth not in
       temples made with hands.

"To Caroline: When I hear"

410 Lines 27-29   Reference: Subject
       Our breasts, which alive with such sympathy glow, / Will
       sleep in the grave till the blast shall wake us, / When
       calling the dead, in earth's bosom laid low.

    I Corinthians 15:51-52
       We shall not all sleep, but we shall all be changed, In a
       moment, in the twinkling of an eye, at the last trump:
       for the trumpet shall sound, and the dead shall be raised.

"To M--"

411 Lines 13-16   Allusion
       Therefore, to guard her dearest work, / 'Lest angels
       might dispute the prize,' / She bade a secret lightning
       lurk / Within those once celestial eyes.

    Jude 9
       Yet 'Michael the archangel, when contending with the de-
       vil he disputed' about the body of Moses.

"To Romance"

412 Lines 59-61   Reference: Subject
       E'en now the gulf appears in view, / Where unlamented
       you must lie: / Oblivion's blackening lake is seen.

    Luke 16:26
       And beside all this, between us and you there is a great
       gulf fixed: so that they which would pass from hence to
       you cannot.

"To the Duke of Dorset"

413 Lines 111-12   Allusion
       The guardian seraph who directs thy fate / Will leave
       thee glorious, as he found thee great.

    Hebrews 1:14
       Are they [angels] not all ministering spirits, sent forth to
       minister for them who shall be heirs of salvation?

"To the Earl of Clare"

414 Lines 25-30   Allusion
       Our vital streams of weal or woe, ... distinctly flow, ...
       Till death's unfathom'd gulf appear, / And both shall quit
       the shore

    Luke 16:26
       And beside all this, between us and you there is a great
       gulf fixed: so that they which would pass from hence to
       you cannot.

THE ISLAND

415   Canto II, 156   Quote: Exact
      'Root up' the spring, and trample on the wave.
      Matthew 13:29
      But he [Jesus] said, Nay; lest while ye gather up the
      tares, ye 'root up' also the wheat with them.

416   Canto IV, 353-54   Reference: Subject
      And they / Who doom to hell, themselves are on the way.
      Matthew 7:2
      For with what judgment ye judge, ye shall be judged: and
      with what measure ye mete, it shall be measured to you again.

THE LAMENT OF TASSO

417   Lines 21-28   Allusion
      For I have ... pour'd my spirit over Palestine, / In
      honour of the sacred war for Him, / 'The God who was
      on earth and is in heaven. '
      Matthew 1:18-25
      Rf. the incarnation of Jesus.

418   Lines 124-25   Parallelism
      I told it not, I breathed it not, it was / Sufficient to it-
      self, its own reward.
      Matthew 6:34
      Take therefore no thought for the morrow ... Sufficient
      unto the day is the evil thereof.

419   Lines 172-73   Reference: Subject
      The world was past away, / Thou didst annihilate the
      earth to me!
      Revelation 21:1
      And I saw a new heaven and a new earth: for the first
      heaven and the first earth were passed away; and there
      was no more sea.

LARA

420   Canto II, 49-50   Quote: Exact
      'I know him not'--but me it seems he knew / In lands

where, but I must not trifle too.

John 8:55

If I [Jesus] should say, 'I know him [God] not,' I shall be a liar.

---

421 Canto II, 161-62   Parallelism

Long 'war without' and frequent 'broil within' / Had made a path for blood and giant sin.

II Corinthians 7:5

For, when we were come ... we were troubled on every side; 'without were fightings, within were fears.'

---

422 Canto II, 228-29   Parallelism

Now was the hour for faction's rebel growth, / The Serfs 'contemn'd the one, and hated both.'

Matthew 6:24

No man can serve two masters: for either he will 'hate the one, and love the other'; or else he will hold to the one, and despise the other. Ye cannot serve God and mammon.

---

423 Canto II, 280-81   Quote: Parodic

The torch was lighted, and the flame was spread, / And Carnage smiled upon 'her daily dead.'

Matthew 6:11

Give us this day 'our daily bread.'

---

424 Canto II, 402-405   Reference: Subject

That panting thirst which scorches in the breath / Of those that die the soldier's fiery death, / In vain impels the burning mouth to crave / One drop--the last--to cool it for the grave.

Luke 16:22-24

The rich man also died, ... And in hell ... he cried and said, Father Abraham, have mercy on me, and send Lazarus, that he may dip the tip of his finger in water, and cool my tongue; for I am tormented in this flame.

MANFRED

---

425 Act I, i, 13-15   Quote: Approximate

Philosophy and science, and the springs / Of wonder, and 'the wisdom of the world,' / I have essay'd.

I Corinthians 1:20

Hath not God made foolish 'the wisdom of this world'?

426   Act I. i. 38-40   Allusion
       By this sign, / Which makes you [spirits] tremble; by the
       claims of him / Who is undying,--Rise!
       James 2:19
       The devils also believe and tremble.

427   Act I. i. 60-63   Parallelism
       Mont Blanc is the monarch of mountains; / They crown'd
       him long ago / On a throne of rocks, in a robe of clouds,
       / With a diadem of snow.
       John 19:2
       And the soldiers platted a crown of thorns, and put it on
       his [Jesus'] head, and they put on him a purple robe.

428   Act I. i. 140-42   Allusion
       Ask of us seven spirits subjects, sovereignty, ... or a
       sign / Which shall control the elements.
       Matthew 12:38-39
       Then certain of the scribes and of the Pharisees answered,
       saying, Master, we would see a sign from thee. But he
       answered and said unto them, An evil and adulterous gen-
       eration seeketh after a sign.

429   Act I. i. 224-25   Allusion
       And a spirit of the air / Hath begirt thee with a snare.
       Ephesians 2:2
       Wherein in time past ye walked according to the course of
       this world, according to the prince of the power of the air,
       the spirit that now worketh in the children of disobedience.

430   Act I. ii. 309-11   Allusion
       The natural music of the mountain reed / (For here the
       patriarchal days are not / A pastoral fable) pipes in the
       liberal air.
       Acts 7:8-9
       And Jacob begat the twelve patriarchs. And the patri-
       archs, moved with envy, sold Joseph into Egypt.

431   Act II. ii. 95-102   Reference: Subject
       The sunbow's rays still arch / The torrent with the many
       hues of heaven, / And roll the sheeted silver's waving
       column / O'er the crag's head-long perpendicular, / And
       fling its lines of foaming light along, / And to and fro,
       like the pale courser's tail, / The Giant steed, to be be-
       strode by Death, / As told in the Apocalypse.
       Revelation 6:8
       And I looked, and behold a pale horse: and his name that
       sat on him was Death, and Hell followed with him.

432   Act II. ii. 144-45   Quote: Approximate
       'From my youth upwards' / My spirit walk'd not with the
       souls of men.

Matthew 19:20
The young man saith unto him, All these things have I
kept 'from my youth up. '

433   Act II. ii. 225-27   Allusion
I [Manfred] have gnash'd / My teeth in darkness till re-
turning morn, / Then cursed myself till sunset.
Matthew 8:12
But the children of the kingdom shall be cast out into out-
er darkness: there shall be weeping and gnashing of teeth.

434   Act II. iii. 314-19   Reference: Subject
The Captive Usurper, / Hurl'd down from the throne, /
Lay buried in torpor, / Forgotten and lone; / I [a super-
natural voice] broke through his slumbers, / I shiver'd
his chain.
Revelation 20:1-2
And I saw an angel come down from heaven, having the
key of the bottomless pit and a great chain in his hand.
And he laid hold on the dragon, that old serpent, which
is the Devil, and Satan, and bound him a thousand years.

435   Act II. iii. 346-48   Parallelism
'The blest are the dead, ' / Who see not the sight / Of
their own desolation.
Revelation 14:13
'Blessed are the dead' which die in the Lord.

436   Act II. iv. 371   Allusion
Hail to our Master!--Prince of Earth and Air!
Ephesians 2:2
In time past ye walked according to the course of this
world, according to the prince of the power of the air.

437   Act II. iv. 393   Parallelism
'Sovereign of Sovereigns [Arimanes]! we are thine.
I Timothy 6:16
[Jesus] is the blessed and only Potentate, the 'King of
kings, ' and Lord of lords.

438   Act II. iv. 420-22   Quote: Approximate
Hence! Avaunt!--he's mine [First Destiny of Manfred].
/ 'Prince of the Powers invisible. ' This man / Is of no
common order.
Ephesians 2:2
Wherein in time past ye walked according to the course
of this world, according to the 'prince of the power of
the air, ' the spirit that now worketh in the children of
disobedience.

439   Act II. iv. 481-82   Quote: Approximate
My [Nemesis's] power extends no further. / 'Prince of
air'! / It rests with thee alone.

Ephesians 2:2
> Wherein in time past ye walked according to the course of this world, according to the 'prince of the power of the air,' the spirit that now worketh in the children of disobedience.

440 Act II. iv. 501   Quote: Approximate
> 'I [Manfred] know not what I ask,' nor what I seek.

Matthew 20:21-22
> She [mother of Zebedee's children] saith unto him, Grant that these my two sons may sit, the one on thy right hand, and the other on the left, in thy kingdom. But Jesus answered and said, 'Ye know not what ye ask.'

441 Act III. i. 47-48   Parallelism
> 'I come to save, and not destroy.' / I would not pry into thy secret soul.

Matthew 5:17
> Think not that I [Jesus] am come to destroy the law, or the prophets: 'I am not come to destroy, but to fulfill.'

442 Act III. i. 54-55   Allusion
> I [Manfred] shall not choose a mortal / To be my mediator.

I Timothy 2:5
> For there is one God, and one mediator between God and men, the man Christ Jesus.

443 Act III. i. 169-70   Parallelism
> And my [the Abbot's] duty / Is to 'dare all things' for a righteous end.

I Corinthians 13:7
> [Charity] 'beareth all things,' believeth all things.

444 Act III. iv. 314   Reference: Subject
> My [Manfred's] days are number'd, and my deeds recorded.

Revelation 20:12
> And the dead were judged out of those things which were written in the books, according to their works.

445 Act III. iv. 344-46   Quote: Exact
> I have commanded / Things of an essence greater far than thine, / And striven with thy masters. 'Get thee hence'!

Matthew 4:10
> Then saith Jesus unto him, 'Get thee hence,' Satan.

446 Act III. iv. 370-71   Parallelism
> My life is in its last hour,--that I know, / Nor would 'redeem a moment' of that hour.

Ephesians 5:15-16
> See then that ye walk circumspectly, ... 'Redeeming the time,' because the days are evil.

447 Act III. iv. 372-73   Reference: Subject
     I [Manfred] do not combat against death, but thee / And
     thy surrounding angels.

Ephesians 6:12
     For we wrestle not against flesh and blood, but against
     principalities, against powers, against the rulers of the
     darkness of this world, against spiritual wickedness in
     high places.

MARINO FALIERO, DOGE OF VENICE

---

448 Act I. ii. 288-89   Reference: Subject
     Hollow bauble; / Beset with all the thorns that line a
     crown.

Matthew 27:29
     And when they had platted a crown of thorns, they put it
     upon his head, ... saying, Hail, King of the Jews!

449 Act I. ii. 600-602   Allusion
     At the midnight hour, then, / Near to the church where
     sleep my sires; the same, / Twin-named from the apos-
     tles John and Paul.

Matthew 10:2
     Now the names of the twelve apostles are these; The first,
     Simon, ... and John.

I Corinthians 15:8-9
     And last of all he Jesus was seen of me Paul also, as of
     one born out of due time. For I am the least of the apos-
     tles.

450 Act II. i. 111-12   Quote: Approximate
     And then he has been rash 'from his youth upwards,' /
     Yet temper'd by redeeming nobleness.

Matthew 19:20
     The young man saith unto him, All these things have I
     kept 'from my youth up.'

451 Act II. i. 182-85   Parallelism
     You know what daily cares oppress all those / Who gov-
     ern this precarious commonwealth, / Now suffering from
     the 'Genoese without,' / And 'malcontents within.'

II Corinthians 7:5
     For when we were come ... we were troubled on every
     side; 'without were fightings, within were fears.'

452 Act II. i. 193-99   Allusion
     'Tis not / In hostile states, nor perils, thus to shake you;
     / You, who have stood all storms and never sunk, / And
     climb'd up to the pinnacle of power / And never fainted

by the way, and stand / Upon it, and can look down
steadily / Along the depth beneath, and ne'er feel dizzy.
Matthew 4:5

Then the devil taketh him [Jesus] up into the holy city
and seeeth him on a pinnacle of the temple.

453   Act II. i. 206-209

                                          Parallelism
Doge: Pride, Angiolina? Alas! none is left me.   Angi-
olina: Yes--the same sin that overthrew the angels, /
And 'of all sins most easily besets / Mortals' the near-
est to the angelic nature.
Hebrews 12:1

Let us lay aside every weight, and 'the sin which doth so
easily beset us. '

454   Act II. ii. 260-61

                                   Reference: Subject
Angiolina: Heaven bids us to forgive our enemies.   Doge:
Doth Heaven forgive her own?
Matthew 6:14-15

For if ye forgive men their trespasses, your heavenly Fa-
ther will also forgive you: But if ye forgive not men their
trespasses, neither will your Father forgive your trespass-
es.

455   Act II. ii. 524-26

                                      Quote: Exact
These same 'drops of blood, ' / Shed shamefully, shall
have the whole of his [the Doge] / For their requital.
Luke 22:44

And his [Jesus] sweat was as it were great 'drops of
blood' falling down to the ground.

456   Act III. ii. 381-85

                                   Reference: Parodic
All the patricians flocking to the Council ... Will then be
gather'd in unto the harvest, / And we will reap them
with the sword for sickle.
John 4:35

Say not ye, There are yet four months, and then cometh
harvest? behold, I say unto you, Lift up your eyes, and
look on the fields; for they are white already to harvest.

457   Act III. ii. 640

                                   Reference: Parodic
But there is hell within me [the Doge] and around.
Luke 17:21

For, behold, the kingdom of God is within you.

458   Act IV. i. 153-54

                                      Parallelism
I 'come / To save' patrician blood, and 'not to shed it'!
Luke 9:56

For the Son of man is 'not come to destroy' men's lives,
but 'to save' them.

459   Act IV. i. 156-57

                                   Quote: Exact
Time / Has changed his slow scythe for the 'two-edged
sword. '

Hebrews 4:12
    For the word of God is quick, and powerful, and sharper
    than any 'two-edged sword,' piercing even to the dividing
    asunder of soul and spirit.

460 Act IV. i. 276-77   Quote: Approximate
    Venice, and all that she inherits, are / 'Divided like a
    house against itself.'
Matthew 12:25-26
    Every kingdom divided against itself is brought to desola-
    tion; and every city or 'house diveded against itself' shall
    not stand: And if Satan cast out Satan, he is divided
    against himself.

461 Act IV. ii. 482-83   Reference: Subject
    Now the destroying Angel hovers o'er / Venice, and pau-
    ses ere he pours the vial.
Revelation 16:1
    And I heard a great voice out of the temple saying to the
    seven angels, Go your ways, and pour out the vials of
    the wrath of God upon the earth.

462 Act IV. ii. 504-505   Reference: Subject
    But this day, black within the calendar, / Shall be suc-
    ceeded by a bright millennium.
Revelation 20:2-3
    [An angel] laid hold on ... Satan, and bound him a thou-
    sand years, ... that he should deceive the nations no
    more, till the thousand years should be fulfilled.

463 Act IV. ii. 602-603   Quote: Exact
    Thou hast done a worthy deed, and earn'd 'the price /
    Of blood,' and they who use thee will reward thee.
Matthew 27:6
    And the chief priests took the silver pieces [earlier given
    to Judas], and said, It is not lawful for to put them into
    the treasury, because it is 'the price of blood.'

464 Act IV. ii. 640   Reference: Subject
    Doge: Who hath been our Judas.
Matthew 26:14-25
    Rf. Judas' betrayal of Jesus.

465 Act V. i. 30-32   Reference: Subject
    On the verge / Of that dread gulf which none repass, the
    truth / Alone can profit you on earth or heaven.
Luke 16:26
    And beside all this, between us and you there is a great
    gulf fixed: so that they which would pass from hence to
    you cannot.

466 Act V. i. 387-88   Allusion
    They will cry unto their God / For mercy, and be an-
    swer'd as they answer.

Matthew 5:7
    Blessed are the merciful: for they shall obtain mercy.
James 2:13
    For he shall have judgment without mercy, that hath
    shewed no mercy; and mercy rejoiceth against judgment.

467   Act V. i. 396-98   Quote: Exact
    I would not take / A 'life eternal,' granted at the hands
    / Of wretches.
   Matthew 25:46
    And these shall go away into everlasting punishment: but
    the righteous into 'life eternal.'

468   Act V. iii. 712-15   Allusion
    There's not a history / But shows a thousand crown'd
    conspirators / Against the people; but to set them free
    / One sovereign only died, and one is dying.
   John 11:50
    It is expedient for us, that one man [Jesus] should die
    for the people, and that the whole nation perish not.

MAZEPPA

---

469   Lines 577-78   Reference: Subject
    My sight return'd, though dim, alas! / And thicken'd, as
    it were with glass.
   I Corinthians 13:12
    For now we see through a glass, darkly; but then face to
    face.

470   Lines 783-86   Reference: Subject
    I know no more--my latest dream / Is something of a
    lovely star / Which fix'd my dull eyes from afar, / And
    went and came with wandering beam.
   Jude 12-13
    [These are] raging waves of the sea, foaming out their
    own shame; wandering stars.

MISCELLANEOUS POEMS

"The Adieu"

471   Lines 112-13   Quote: Exact
    'Father of Light'! to Thee I call, / My soul is dark within.

James 1:17
>Every good gift and every perfect gift is from above, and cometh down from the 'Father of lights. '

472   Lines 113-20   Quote: Exact
>Thou, who canst guide the 'wandering star, ' ... Instruct me how to die.

Jude 13
>[These are] raging waves of the sea, ... 'wandering stars, ' to whom is reserved the blackness of darkness for ever.

473/4   Lines 113-14   Reference: Subject
>Thou, who canst mark the sparrow's fall, / Avert the death of sin.

Matthew 10:29
>Are not two sparrows sold for a farthing? and one of them shall not fall on the ground without your Father.

"Condolatory Address"

475   Lines 25-27   Allusion
>What can his vaulted gallery now disclose? / A garden with all flowers--except the rose;-- / A fount that only wants its living stream.

Revelation 7:17
>For the Lamb which is in the midst of the throne shall feed them, and shall lead them unto living fountains of waters.

"Darkness"

476   Lines 2-3   Reference: Subject
>The bright sun was extinguish'd, and the stars / Did wander darkling in the eternal space.

Jude 13
>[These people are] Raging waves of the sea, ... wandering stars, to whom is reserved the blackness of darkness for ever.

"Fill the Goblet"

477   Line 31   Quote: Exact
>We must die--who shall not?--May our 'sins be forgiven. '

Matthew 9:2
>Jesus ... said unto the sick of the palsy; Son, be of good cheer; thy 'sins be forgiven' thee.

"Inscription on the Monument of a Newfoundland Dog"

478   Lines 1-3   Reference: Subject
>When some proud son of man returns to earth, / Unknown to glory, but upheld by birth, / The sculptor's art exhausts the pomp of woe.

Matthew 24:30
> And then shall appear the sign of the Son of man in hea-
> ven: and then shall all the tribes of the earth mourn,
> and they shall see the Son of man coming in the clouds
> of heaven with power and great glory.

"The Irish Avatar"

479   Line 17   Reference: Parodic
> But he [George IV] comes! the Messiah of royalty comes!

John 4:25
> The woman saith unto him [Jesus], I know that Messias
> cometh, which is called Christ: when he is come, he
> will tell us all things.

480   Line 73   Reference: Parodic
> Ay! "Build him [George IV] a dwelling!" let each give
> his mite!

Mark 12:41-44
> And Jesus sat over against the treasury, and beheld how
> the people cast money into the treasury ... And there
> came a certain poor widow, and she threw in two mites,
> even all her living.

481   Lines 73-74   Reference: Subject
> Ay! "Build him [George IV] a dwelling!" let each give
> his mite! / Till, ... the new royal dome hath arisen!

Mark 12:42-44
> And there came a certain poor widow, and she threw in
> two mites, ... all that she had, even all her living.

"Lines to Mr. Hodgson"

481a   Lines 59-60   Quote: Parodic
> "Help!"--"A couplet?"--"No, 'a cup / Of warm water--.' "

Matthew 10:42
> And whosoever shall give to drink unto one of these little
> ones 'a cup of cold water' only in the name of a disciple,
> verily I say unto you, he shall in no wise lose his re-
> ward.

"Monody on the Death of the Right Hon. R. B. Sheridan"

482   Lines 97-100   Allusion
> Ours be the gentler wish, the kinder task, / To give the
> tribute Glory need not ask, / To mourn the vanish'd beam
> and add our mite / Of praise in payment of a long delight.

Mark 12:41-43
> And many that were rich cast in much. And there came
> a certain poor widow, and she threw in two mites ... all
> that she had.

"Ode from the French"

483   Lines 13-14   Quote: Exact
        When 'tis [freedom] full 't will 'burst asunder'-- / Never
        yet was heard such thunder.
        Acts 1:18
        And falling headlong, he [Judas] 'burst asunder' in the midst,
        and all his bowels gushed out.

484   Lines 16-18   Reference: Subject
        Never yet was seen such lightning / As o'er heaven shall
        then be bright'ning! / Like the Wormwood Star foretold.
        Revelation 8:10-11
        And the third angel sounded, and there fell a great star
        from heaven, ... And the name of the star is called
        Wormwood: and the third part of the waters became
        wormwood; and many men died of the waters, because
        they were made bitter.

485   Lines 101-102   Quote: Exact
        When once more her hosts assemble, / Tyrants shall
        'believe and tremble.'
        James 2:19
        Thou believest that there is one God; thou doest well: the
        devils also 'believe, and tremble.'

"On a Cornelian Heart Which Was Broken"

486   Lines 1-2   Quote: Exact
        Ill-fated Heart! and can it be / That thou shouldst thus
        be 'rent in twain'!
        Matthew 27:51
        And, behold, the veil of the temple was 'rent in twain'
        from the top to the bottom; and the earth did quake, and
        the rocks rent.

"One Struggle More, and I Am Free"

487   Lines 11-12   Parallelism
        I'll be that light, unmeaning thing / That smiles with all,
        and 'weeps with none.'
        Romans 12:15
        Rejoice with them that do rejoice, and 'weep with them'
        that weep.

"On the Star of 'The Legion of Honour' "

488/9 Lines 1-2   Quote: Exact
        Star of the brave!--whose beam hath shed / Such glory
        o'er the 'quick and dead.'
        Acts 10:42
        It is he [Jesus] which was ordained of God to be the Judge
        of 'quick and dead.'

"There Was a Time, I Need Not Name"

490   Lines 5-7   Allusion
        And from that hour when first thy tongue / Confess'd a
        love which equall'd mine, ... None, none hath sunk so
        deep as this.
      Romans 14:11
        As I live, saith the Lord, every knee shall bow to me,
        and every tongue shall confess to God.

"To Anne"

491   Lines 1-2   Quote: Approximate
        Oh, Anne! your offences to me have been grievous; / I
        thought 'from my wrath' no atonement could 'save you. '
      Romans 5:9
        Much more then, being now justified by his blood, 'we
        shall be saved from wrath' through him [Jesus].

"To a Vain Lady"

492   Lines 15-16   Quote: Approximate
        Thy peace, thy hope, thy all is lost, / 'If thou canst'
        venture to 'believe. '
      Mark 9:22-23
        If thou canst do any thing, have compassion on us, and
        help us. Jesus said unto him, 'If thou canst believe, '
        all things are possible to him that believeth.

"A Very Mournful Ballad"

492a Lines 56-57   Parallelism
        He who holds no laws in awe, / He must 'perish by the
        law. '
      Romans 2:12
        For as many as have sinned without law shall also 'per-
        ish without law': and as many as have sinned in the law
        shall be 'judged by the law. '

THE MORGANTE MAGGIORE

---

493   Lines 1-2   Quote: Exact
        'In the beginning was the Word' next God; / God was the
        Word, the Word no less was he.
      John 1:1
        'In the beginning was the Word, ' and the Word was with
        God, and the Word was God.

494   Lines 1-4   Quote: Approximate
     In the beginning was the Word next God; / God was the
Word, the Word no less was he: / This was in the be-
ginning, to my mode / Of thinking, 'and without him
nought could be. '
John 1:1-3
     In the beginning was the Word, and the Word was with
God, and the Word was God. The same was in the be-
ginning with God. All things were made by him; 'and
without him was not anything made that was made. '

495   Lines 9-10   Reference: Subject
     And thou, oh Virgin! daughter, mother, bride, / Of the
same Lord.
Matthew 1:18, 23
     Now the birth of Jesus Christ was on this wise: When as
his mother Mary was espoused to Joseph, before they
came together, she was found with child of the Holy Ghost
... Behold, a virgin shall be with child, and shall bring
forth a son, and they shall call his name Emmanuel.

496   Lines 9-11   Allusion
     And thou, oh Virgin! daughter, mother, bride, / Of the
same Lord, who gave to you each key / Of heaven and
hell and every thing beside.
Matthew 16:19
     And I [Jesus] will give unto thee [Peter] the keys of the
kingdom of heaven: and whatsoever thou shalt bind on
earth shall be bound in heaven: and whatsoever thou shalt
loose on earth shall be loosed in heaven.

497   Lines 37-40   Parallelism
     He [Emperor Charles] in the cabinet being always ready,
... for the church and Christian faith had wrought, / Cer-
tes, far more than yet is 'said or thought. '
Ephesians 3:20-21
     Now unto him that is able to do exceeding abundantly a-
bove all that we 'ask or think, ' ... Unto him be glory in
the church.

498   Lines 165-66   Reference: Subject
     [Orlando] said that he was taught to adore / Him who was
born of Mary's holiest blood.
Matthew 1:18
     Now the birth of Jesus Christ was on this wise: When as
his mother Mary was espoused to Joseph, before they
came together, she was found with child of the Holy Ghost.

499   Lines 197-99   Allusion
     But here 'tis fit we keep on the alert in / Our bounds,
or taste the stones shower'd down for bread / From off
yon mountain daily raining faster.

Matthew 7:9
    What man is there of you, whom if his son ask bread,
    will he give him a stone?
Exodus 16:4
    Then said the Lord unto Moses, Behold, I will rain bread
    from heaven for you; and the people shall go out and ga-
    ther a certain rate every day.

500   Lines 260-62
                                    Reference: Subject
    But Christ his servants ne'er abandons long, / Especially
    Orlando, such a knight / As to desert would almost be a
    wrong.
Hebrews 13:5
    Be content with such things as ye have: for he hath said,
    I will never leave thee, nor forsake thee.

501   Lines 279-80
                                    Allusion
    But while his [Macon's] crude, rude blasphemies he heard,
    / Orlando thank'd the Father and the Word.
John 1:14
    And the Word was made flesh, and dwelt among us.

502   Line 283
                                    Reference: Subject
    I know my life was saved by thee from heaven.
John 6:33
    [Jesus] ... cometh down from heaven, and giveth life un-
    to the world.

503   Lines 316-17
                                    Quote: Exact
    But praying blessed Jesu, he [the giant] was 'set / At
    liberty' from all the fears which rack'd him.
Hebrews 13:23
    Know ye that our brother Timothy is 'set at liberty.'

504   Line 335
                                    Reference: Subject
    Christ I adore, who is the genuine Lord.
Acts 2:36
    God hath made that same Jesus ... both Lord and Christ.

505   Lines 341-42
                                    Reference: Subject
    Hence to thy God, who for ye did atone / Upon the cross,
    preferr'd I my petition.
Hebrews 5:11
    We also joy in God through our Lord Jesus Christ, by
    whom we have now received the atonement.

506   Lines 349-50
                                    Quote: Exact
    And, if you please, as friends we [Orlando and Baron]
    will ally us, / And I will love you with a 'perfect love.'
I John 4:18
    There is no fear in love; but 'perfect love' casteth out
    fear: because fear hath torment. He that feareth is not
    made perfect in love.

507 Lines 353-54   Reference: Subject
        The Lord descended to the virgin breast / Of Mary Mo-
        ther, sinless and divine.
     Matthew 1:18
        Now the birth of Jesus Christ was on this wise: When
        as his mother Mary was espoused to Joseph, before they
        came together, she was found with child of the Holy Ghost.

508 Line 359   Reference: Subject
        Baptize yourself with zeal, since you repent.
     Acts 2:38
        Then Peter said unto them, Repent, and be baptized every
        one of you in the name of Jesus Christ for the remission
        of sins, and ye shall receive the gift of the Holy Ghost.

509 Lines 390-92   Allusion
        And our true Scripture soundeth openly, / Good is reward-
        ed, and chastised the ill, / Which the Lord never faileth
        to fulfil.
     I Peter 3:12
        For the eyes of the Lord are over the righteous, and his
        ears are open unto their prayers: but the face of the
        Lord is against them that do evil.

510 Line 409   Reference: Subject
        But they in Christ have firmest hope.
     I Corinthians 15:19
        If in this life only we have hope in Christ, we are of all
        men most miserable.

511 Lines 420-22   Allusion
        And if the will of God seem good to me, / Just as you
        tell me 'tis in heaven obey'd-- / Ashes to ashes,--merry
        let us be!
     Matthew 6:10
        Thy kingdom come, thy will be done in earth, as it is in
        heaven.

512 Lines 420-22   Allusion
        And if the will of God seem good to me, ... merry let
        us be!
     John 1:13
        [They] were born, not of blood, nor of the will of the
        flesh, nor of the will of man, but of God.

513 Lines 442-43   Quote: Approximate
        'Be thou of good cheer'; / He [in] Christ believes [and]
        as Christian must be rated.
     John 16:33
        In the world ye shall have tribulation: but 'be of good
        cheer'; I have overcome the world.

514   Lines 455-56   Reference: Subject
      You [Morgante] now a true and perfect friend will show /
      Yourself to Christ, as once you were a foe.
      Galatians 1:13-18
      Rf. Paul's conversion.

515   Lines 457-60   Quote: Approximate
      And one of our apostles, Saul once named, / Long per-
      secuted sore the faith of Christ, / Till, one day, by the
      Spirit being inflamed, / " 'Why dost thou persecute me
      thus?' " said Christ.
      Acts 9:4
      And he [Paul] fell to the earth, and heard a voice saying
      unto him, Saul, Saul, 'why persecutest thou me?'

516   Lines 457-60   Reference: Subject
      And one of our apostles, Saul once named, / Long per-
      secuted sore the faith of Christ, / Till, one day, by the
      Spirit being inflamed, / "Why dost thou persecute me
      thus?" said Christ.
      Acts 9:1-4
      Saul, yet breathing out threatenings and slaughter against
      the disciples of the Lord. ... came near Damascus: and
      suddenly there shined round about him a light from heaven:
      And he fell to the earth, and heard a voice saying unto
      him, Saul, Saul, why persecutest thou me?

517   Lines 457-64   Reference: Subject
      And one of our apostles, Saul once named, / Long per-
      secuted sore the faith of Christ, / Till, one day, by the
      Spirit being inflamed, / "Why dost thou persecute me
      thus?" said Christ; / And then from his offence he was
      reclaim'd, / And went for ever after preaching Christ, /
      And of the faith became a trump, whose sounding / O'er
      the whole earth is echoing and rebounding.
      Acts 9-28
      Rf. the conversion, preaching career, and subsequent in-
      fluence of Paul.

518   Lines 461-62   Quote: Approximate
      And then from his offence he [Paul] was reclaim'd, / And
      went for ever after 'preaching Christ.'
      I Corinthians 1:23
      But we 'preach Christ' crucified.

519   Lines 466-67   Reference: Subject
      He who repents--thus writes the Evangelist-- / Occasions
      more rejoicing in the skies / Than ninety-nine of the ce-
      lestial list.
      Matthew 18:12-13
      If a man have an hundred sheep, and one of them be gone
      astray, doth he not leave the ninety and nine, and goeth
      into the mountains, and seeketh that which is gone astray?

And if so be that he find it, verily I say unto you, he re-
joiceth more of that sheep, than of the ninety and nine
which went not astray.

520   Lines 493-96   Quote: Exact
And lo! a monstrous 'herd of swine' appears, / And on-
ward rushes with tempestuous tread, / And to the foun-
tain's brink precisely pours, / So that the giant's join'd
by all the boars.

Matthew 8:31-32
So the devils besought him, saying, If thou cast
us out, suffer us to go away into the 'herd of
swine' ... they went into the herd of swine: and,
behold, the whole herd of swine ran violently down
a steep place into the sea, and perished in the
waters.

521   Lines 566-68   Parallelism
Morgante, do not undertake / To lift or carry this dead
courser, who, / 'As you have done to him, will do to you. '

Matthew 7:12
Therefore all things 'whatsoever ye would that men should
do to you, do ye even so to them': for this is the law
and the prophets.

522   Lines 642-44   Reference: Subject
The way was lost / By which we could pursue a fit ca-
reer / In search of Jesus and the saintly host.

Matthew-John
Rf. Jesus and the saints.

523   Lines 649-53   Reference: Subject
But to bear arms and wield the lance; indeed, / With
these as much is done as with this cowl; / In proof of
which the Scripture you may read. / This giant up to
heaven may bear his soul / By your compassion: now
in peace proceed.

I John 5:16
If any man see his brother sin a sin which is not unto
death, he shall ask, and he shall give him life for them
that sin not unto death: I do not say that he shall pray
for it.

524   Lines 682-83   Quote: Exact
Oh God, who in the sky / 'Know'st all things'!

John 21:17
And he [Peter] said unto him, Lord, thou 'knowest all
things'; thou knowest that I love thee.

ODE ON VENICE

525 Lines 94-96   Quote: Approximate
     Momentary starts from Nature's laws, ... smite / 'But
     for a term, ' then pass.
     Mark 4:17
        [They] have no root in themselves, and so endure 'but
        for a time. '

526 Lines 103-105   Quote: Approximate
     The league of mightiest nations, in those hours / When
     Venice was an envy, might abate, / But did 'not quench,
     her spirit. '
     I Thessalonians 5:19
        'Quench not the spirit. '

PARISINA

527 Lines 83-87   Reference: Subject
     Why doth Prince Azo start, / As if the Archangel's voice
     he heard? / And well he may--a deeper doom / Could
     scarcely thunder o'er his tomb, / When he shall wake to
     sleep no more.
     I Thessalonians 4:16
        For the Lord himself shall descend from heaven with a
        shout, with the voice of the archangel, and with the trump
        of God: and the dead in Christ shall rise first.

528 Lines 276-79   Parallelism
     I will not plead the cause of crime, / Nor sue thee to
     'redeem from time' / A few brief hours or days that
     must / At length roll o'er my reckless dust.
     Ephesians 5:15-16
        See than that ye walk circumspectly, not as fools, but as
        wise, 'Redeeming the time. '

529 Lines 405-406   Allusion
     The crowd in a speechless circle gather / To see the
     Son fall by the doom of the Father !
     John 3:16
        For God so loved the world, that he gave his only be-
        gotten Son.

POEMS ON VARIOUS OCCASIONS

"Answer to a Beautiful Poem, Entitled 'The Common Lot' "

530 Lines 43-44   Reference: Subject
     Some few who ne'er will be forgot / Shall burst the bon-
     dage of the grave.

     John 11:43-44
     He [Jesus] cried with a loud voice, Lazarus, come forth.
     And he that was dead came forth, bound hand and foot
     with graveclothes.

     Mark 28:6
     He [Jesus] is not here: for he is risen, as he said.
     Come, see the place where the Lord lay.

THE PRISONER OF CHILLON

531 Lines 176-78   Quote: Exact
     Oh, God! 'it is a fearful thing' / To see the human soul
     take wing / In any shape, in any mood.

     Hebrews 10:31
     'It is a fearful thing' to fall into the hands of the living
     God.

532 Lines 368-69   Reference: Subject
     I had no hope my eyes to raise, / And clear them of
     their dreary mote.

     Matthew 7:3-4
     And why beholdest thou the mote that is in thy brother's
     eye, but considerest not the beam that is in thine own eye?

THE PROPHECY OF DANTE

533 Canto I, 2-6   Parallelism
     I feel ... too soon bereft / Of the immortal vision which
     could ... Lift me from that 'deep gulf' without repeal.

     Luke 16:26
     Between us and you there is a 'great gulf' fixed.

534   Canto I, 43-44
                                        Quote: Exact
        But the sun, though not overcast, must set, / And 'the
        night cometh'; I am old in days.
        John 9:4
        I must work the works of him that sent me, while it is
        day: 'the night cometh, ' when no man can work.

535   Canto I, 60-65
                                        Reference: Subject
        O Florence! Florence! unto me thou wast / Like that
        Jerusalem which the almight He / Wept over, "but thou
        wouldst not!' As the bird / Gathers its young, I would
        have gather'd thee / Beneath a parent pinion, hadst thou
        heard / My voice.
        Matthew 23:37
        O Jerusalem, Jerusalem, thou killest the prophets, and
        stonest them which are sent unto thee, how often would
        I have gathered thy children together, even as a hen ga-
        thereth her chickens under her wings, and ye would not!

536   Canto II, 30-32
                                        Quote: Approximate
        All present speech to thine [Italy's] shall seem / The note
        of meaner birds, 'and every tongue / Confess' its barbar-
        ism when compared with thine.
        Romans 14:11
        For it is written, As I live, saith the Lord, every knee
        shall bow to me, 'and every tongue shall confess' to God.

537   Canto II, 35-36
                                        Reference: Subject
        Woe! woe! the veil of coming centuries / Is rent.
        Matthew 27:51
        And, behold, the veil of the temple was rent in twain
        from the top to the bottom.

538   Canto II, 133-35
                                        Allusion
        But how vain the toil, / While still Division sows the
        seeds of woe / And weakness, till the stranger reaps the
        spoil.
        John 4:37
        And herein is that saying true, One soweth, and another
        reapeth.

539   Canto II, 134-35
                                        Reference: Subject
        While still Division sows the seeds of woe / And weakness,
        till the stranger reaps the spoil.
        I Corinthians 3:3, 6
        For ye are yet carnal: for whereas there is among you
        envying, and strive, and divisions, are ye not carnal, ...
        I have planted, Apollos watered; but God gave the increase.

540   Canto III, 1-4
                                        Quote: Approximate
        From out the mass of never-dying ill, / The Plague, the
        Prince, the Stranger, and the Sword, / 'Vials of wrath'
        but emptied to refill / And flow again.

Revelation 16:1
    And I heard a great voice out of the temple saying to the
    seven angels, Go your ways, and pour out the 'vials of'
    the 'wrath' of God upon the earth.

541 Canto III, 9-12   Reference: Parodic
    There where the farthest suns and stars have birth, /
    Spread like a banner at the gate of heaven, / The bloody
    scroll of our millenial wrongs / Waves.
Revelation 20:1-15
    Rf. the millenium.

542 Canto III, 52-53   Reference: Subject
    Oh! more than these illustrious far shall be / The being--
    and even yet he may be born-- / The mortal saviour who
    shall set thee free.
Luke 2:11
    For unto you is born this day in the city of David a Sav-
    iour, which is Christ the Lord.
John 8:31-32
    Then said Jesus ... ye shall know the truth, and the
    truth shall make you free.

543 Canto III, 119-20   Reference: Subject
    [Art] of a tenderer, sadder mood, / Shall pour his soul
    out o'er Jerusalem.
Matthew 23:37
    O Jerusalem, Jerusalem, thou that killest the prophets,
    and stonest them which are sent unto thee, how often
    would I have gathered thy children together, even as a
    hen gathereth her chickens under her wings, and ye would
    not!

544 Canto III, 121-22   Reference: Subject
    [Art] shall sing of arms and Christian blood / Shed where
    Christ bled for man.
Mark 14:24
    And he [Jesus] said unto them, This is my blood of the
    new testament, which is shed for many.

545 Canto III, 127-29   Reference: Subject
    Wave / The red-cross banners where the first red Cross
    / Was crimson'd from his [Jesus] veins who died to save.
Matthew 18:11
    For the Son of man is come to save that which was lost.

546 Canto III, 128-30   Reference: Subject
    The red-cross banners where the first red Cross / Was
    crimson'd from his veins who died to save,-- / Shall be
    his sacred argument.
II Corinthians 5:14-15
    He [Jesus] died for all, that they which live should not
    henceforth live unto themselves, but unto him which died
    for them, and rose again.

547   Canto III, 136-37   Reference: Subject
       [Dante] was sent / To be Christ's Laureate.
       Matthew-John
              Rf. Jesus Christ.

548   Canto IV, 28-33   Allusion
       A whole life may glow, ... for high heaven is there /
       Transfused, transfigurated.
       Matthew 17:1-2
              And after six days Jesus ... bringeth them up into an
              high mountain apart, And was transfigured before them:
              and his face did shine as the sun.

549   Canto IV, 119-24   Allusion
       For such sway is not limited to kings, ... all that springs
       / From Death the Sin-born's incest with his mother.
       James 1:15
              When lust hath conceived, it bringeth forth sin: and sin,
              when it is finished, bringeth forth death.

       _____

                         SARDANAPALUS

       _____

550   Act I, ii. 168-69   Parallelism
       I [Sardanapalus] understand thee--thou wouldst have me go
       / Forth as a conqueror.
       Revelation 6:2
              And he [the one on a white horse] went forth conquering
              and to conquer.

551   Act I, ii. 260-61   Quote: Approximate
       I married her as monarchs wed--for state, / And 'loved
       her as' most 'husbands love their wives. '
       Ephesians 5:25
              'Husbands, love your wives, ' even 'as Christ also loved'
              the church, and gave himself for it.

552   Act I, ii. 299   Quote: Parodic
       'Eat, drink, and love'; the rest's not worth a fillip.
       Luke 12:19
              Soul, thou hast much goods laid up for many years; take
              thine ease, 'eat, drink, and be merry. '

553   Act I, ii. 303-305   Quote: Exact
       Obey the king ... 'Fall down and worship, ' or get up and
       toil.
       Matthew 4:9
              [The devil] saith unto him [Jesus], All these things will
              I give thee, if thou wilt 'fall down and worship' me.

554   Act I. ii. 533   Reference: Subject
      For he who loves another loves himself.

      Luke 10:27
      Thou shalt love ... thy neighbour as thyself.

555   Act I. ii. 693-94   Quote: Exact
      'The hour is coming' when he'll need all love, / And
      find none.

      John 5:25
      'The hour is coming,' and now is, when the dead shall
      hear the voice of the Son of God.

556   Act II. i. 36-39   Reference: Subject
      Beleses, why / So rapt in thy devotions? Dost thou stand
      / Gazing to trace thy disappearing god / Into some realm
      of undiscover'd day?

      Acts 1:11
      Ye men of Galilee, why stand ye gazing up into heaven?
      this same Jesus, which is taken up from you into heaven,
      shall so come in like manner as ye have seen him go into
      heaven.

557   Act II. i. 112-14   Allusion
      His [the monarch's] slaves / Will take the crumbs he
      deigns to scatter from / His royal table at the hour.

      Matthew 15:27
      And she [a woman of Canaan] said, Truth, Lord: yet the
      dogs eat of the crumbs which fall from their master's
      table.

      Luke 16:20-21
      And there was a certain beggar named Lazarus, which
      was laid at his [the rich man's] gate, full of sores, And
      desiring to be fed with the crumbs which fell from the
      rich man's table.

558   Act II. i. 371-72   Reference: Subject
      As it is, / I [Arbaces] must forgive you, even as he for-
      gave us.

      Colossians 3:12-13
      Put on ... bowels of mercies, ... forgiving one another,
      ... even as Christ forgave you, so also do ye.

559   Act II. i. 599   Quote: Exact
      Grief cannot come where 'perfect love' exists.

      I John 4:18
      There is no fear in love; but 'perfect love' casteth out fear.

560   Act IV. i. 41-42   Quote: Exact
      'Be of good cheer'; / All will go well.

      Matthew 9:2
      Jesus seeing their faith said unto the sick of the palsy;
      Son, 'be of good cheer'; thy sins be forgiven thee.

561   Act IV. i. 73   Quote: Approximate
        I [Myrrha] can 'bear all things,' dreams of life or death.
      I Corinthians 13:7
        [Charity] 'Beareth all things,' believeth all things.

562   Act IV. i. 160-61   Reference: Subject
        I [Sardanapalus] was dead, yet feeling-- / Buried, and
        raised again.
      I Corinthians 15:3-4
        Christ died for our sins according to the scriptures, And
        ... he was buried, and ... he rose again the third day.

563   Act V. i. 266-67   Quote: Exact
        No, Pania! that must not be; 'get thee hence,' / And
        leave me [Sardanapalus] to my fate.
      Matthew 4:10
        Then saith Jesus unto him, 'Get thee hence,' Satan: for
        it is written, Thou shalt worship the Lord thy God.

564   Act V. i. 268-70   Allusion
        So all men / Dare beard me [Sardanapalus] now, and In-
        solence within / Apes Treason from without.
      II Corinthians 7:5
        We were troubled on every side; without were fightings,
        within were fears.

565   Act V. i. 280-81   Allusion
        Bring frankincense and myrrh, too, for it is / For a
        great sacrifice I [Sardanapalus] build the pyre!
      Matthew 2:11
        And when they had opened their treasures, they presented
        unto him [the infant Jesus] gifts; gold, and frankincense,
        and myrrh.

THE SIEGE OF CORINTH

---

566   Lines 1-3   Reference: Subject
        In the year since Jesus died for men, / Eighteen hundred
        years and ten, / We were a gallant company.
      II Corinthians 5:14-15
        If one died for all, then were all dead: And that he died
        for all, that they which live should not henceforth live un-
        to themselves, but unto him which died for them, and
        rose again.

567   Lines 95-100   Quote: Exact
        But near and nearest to the wall / Of those who wish and
        work its fall, / With deeper skill in war's black art /

Than Othman's sons, and high of heart / As any chief
that ever stood / Triumphant in 'the fields of blood.'

Acts 1:19

And it [circumstances of Judas' suicide] was known unto
all the dwellers at Jerusalem; insomuch as that field is
called ... 'The field of blood.'

568   Lines 222-24   Allusion

And ere that faithless truce was broke / Which freed her
[Greece] from the unchristian yoke, / With him [the Doge]
his gentle daughter came.

Matthew 11:29-30

Take my yoke upon you, and learn of me; ... For my
yoke is easy, and my burden is light.

569   Lines 318-19   Allusion

He, their mightiest chief, had been / In youth a bitter
Nazarene.

Matthew 2:23

[Joseph] came and dwelt in a city called Nazareth: that
it might be fulfilled which was spoken by the prophets,
He shall be called a Nazarene.

570   Lines 575-76   Reference: Subject

Thou hast done a fearful deed / In falling away from thy
father's creed.

II Thessalonians 2:3

Let no man deceive you by any means: for that day [se-
cond coming] shall not come, except there come a falling
away first.

571   Lines 717-18   Parallelism

He who first downs with the red cross may crave / His
heart's dearest wish; let him 'ask it, and have'!

Matthew 7:7

'Ask, and it shall be given' you.

572   Lines 926-27   Quote: Approximate

For 'narrow the way that led to' the spot / Where still
the Christians yielded not.

Matthew 7:14

Strait is the gate, and 'narrow is the way, which leadeth
unto' life, and few there be that find it.

573   Lines 954-56   Reference: Subject

We kneeling see / Her [the Madonna], and the boy-God
on her knee.

Matthew 2:11

And when they [the wise men] were come into the house,
they saw the young child with Mary his mother, and fell
down, and worshipped him.

574   Lines 1002-1005   Reference: Subject

That morn it held the holy wine, / Converted by Christ

to his blood so divine, / Which his worshippers drank at
the break of day, / To shrive their souls ere they join'd
in the fray.

Matthew 26:27-28

And he [Jesus] took the cup, ... saying, Drink ye all of
it; For this is my blood of the new testament, which is
shed for many for the remission of sins.

SONNET ON CHILLON

---

575   Lines 1-2
                                          Quote: Exact
'Eternal Spirit' of the chainless Mind! / Brightest in dun-
geons, Liberty!

Hebrews 9:14

How much more shall the blood of Christ, who through
the 'eternal Spirit' offered himself without spot to God,
purge your conscience from dead works to serve the liv-
ing God?

THE TWO FOSCARI

---

576   Act II. i. 125-26
                                          Quote: Approximate
I [the Doge] forgive this, 'for / You know not what you
say. '

Luke 23:34

Then said Jesus, Father, forgive them; 'for they know
not what they do. '

577   Act II. i. 154
                                          Quote: Approximate
Better for him [the son of the Doge] 'he never had been
born'

Matthew 26:24

Woe unto that man by whom the Son of man is betrayed!
it had been good for that man if 'he had not been born. '

578   Act III. i. 312-14
                                          Reference: Subject
I [Marina] have probed his [Loredano's] soul / A moment,
as the eternal fire ere long / Will reach it always.

Matthew 18:8

It is better for thee to enter into life halt or maimed,
rather than having two hands or two feet to be cast into
everlasting fire.

579   Act IV. i. 218-21   Quote: Exact
         Avaunt! / Incarnate Lucifer [Loredano] ... Get thee back
         to thy 'place of torment'!
      Luke 16:27-28
         Send him [Lazarus] to my [the rich man's] father's house:
         for I have five brethren; that he may testify unto them,
         lest they also come into this 'place of torment.'

580   Act V. i. 156-57   Reference: Subject
         Now the rich man's hell-fire upon your tongue, / Un-
         quench'd, unquenchable!
      Luke 16:19-24
         There was a certain rich man ... And in hell he lift up
         his eyes, being in torments ... And he cried and said,
         Father Abraham, have mercy on me, and send Lazarus,
         that he may dip the tip of his finger in water, and cool
         my tongue; for I am tormented in this flame.

581   Act V. i. 360-61   Quote: Parodic
         Well, sirs, 'your will be done'! as one day, / I [Marina]
         trust, Heaven's will be done too.
      Matthew 6:10
         'Thy will be done' in earth, as it is in heaven.

THE VISION OF JUDGMENT

---

582   Entire poem   Allusion
      Jude 9
         Michael the archangel, when contending with the devil he
         disputed about the body of Moses.

583   Lines 1-2   Reference: Parodic
         Saint Peter sat by the celestial gate: / His keys were
         rusty and the lock was dull.
      Matthew 16:18-19
         Thou art Peter ... And I will give unto thee the keys of
         the kingdom of heaven: and whatsoever thou shalt bind on
         earth shall be bound in Heaven: and whatsoever thou shalt
         loose on earth shall be loosed in heaven.

584   Line 4   Allusion: Parodic
         Not that the place [heaven] by any means was full.
      Matthew 7:14
         Strait is the gate, and narrow is the way, which leadeth
         unto life, and few there be that find it.

585   Line 17   Allusion: Parodic
         The guardian seraphs had retired on high.

Hebrews 1:14
> Are they [angels] not all ministering spirits, sent forth
> to minister for them who shall be heirs of salvation?

586   Lines 19-20   Reference: Parodic
> Terrestrial business fill'd nought in the sky / Save the re-
> cording angel's black bureau.

Revelation 20:12
> And I saw the dead, small and great, stand before God;
> and the books were opened: and another book was opened,
> which is the book of life: and the dead were judged out
> of those things which were written in the books, accord-
> ing to their works.

587   Lines 26-28   Allusion: Parodic
> [Peter] was ... (Just like those cherubs, earthly minis-
> ters).

Hebrews 1:14
> Are they [angels] not all ministering spirits, sent forth
> to minister for them who shall be heirs of salvation?

588   Lines 53-54   Reference: Subject
> Meantime they [years] increase, / "With seven heads
> and ten horns," and all in front.

Revelation 12:3
> And there appeared another wonder in heaven; and behold
> a great red dragon, having seven heads and ten horns,
> and seven crowns upon his heads.

589   Lines 53-56   Quote: Parodic
> [Years] increase, / "With 'seven heads and ten horns,' "
> and all in front, / Like Saint John's foretold beast; but
> ours are born / Less formidable in the head than horn.

Revelation 17:7
> I will tell thee the mystery of the woman, and of the beast
> that carrieth her, which hath the 'seven heads and ten
> horns.'

590   Lines 118-20   Quote: Parodic
> Not that I'm fit for such a noble dish, / As one day will
> be that 'immortal fry' / Of almost every body born to die.

Matthew 18:8
> It is better ... to enter into life halt or maimed, ... than
> having two hands or two feet to be cast into 'everlasting
> fire.'

591   Lines 121-22   Reference: Parodic
> Saint Peter sat by the celestial gate, / And nodded o'er
> his 'keys.'

Matthew 16:18-19
> Thou art Peter ... And I will give unto thee the 'keys' of
> the kingdom of heaven: and whatsoever thou shalt bind on
> earth shall be bound in heaven: and whatsoever thou shalt
> loose on earth shall be loosed in heaven.

592   Lines 121-22   Reference: Parodic
        Saint Peter sat by the celestial gate, / And 'nooded' o'er
        his keys.
    Matthew 26:40
        And he [Jesus] cometh unto the disciples, and findeth
        them 'asleep,' and saith unto Peter, What, could ye not
        watch with me one hour?
    Luke 9:22
        But Peter and they that were with him [Jesus] were heavy
        with 'sleep': and when they were awake, they saw his glory

593   Lines 121-22   Allusion: Parodic
        Saint Peter sat by the celestial 'gate,' / And nodded o'er
        his keys.
    Revelation 21:12-13
        [The New Jerusalem] had twelve 'gates,' and at the 'gates'
        twelve angels.

594   Lines 122-24   Quote: Approximate
        Lo! there came / A wondrous noise he had not heard of
        late-- / 'A rushing sound of wind,' and stream, and
        flame.
    Acts 2:2-3
        And suddenly there came 'a sound' from heaven as 'of a
        rushing mighty wind,' and it filled all the house where
        they were sitting. And there appeared unto them ... like
        as of fire.

595   Lines 131-32   Allusion: Parodic
        Saint Peter yawn'd, and rubb'd his nose: / "Saint 'por-
        ter,' " said the angel, "prithee rise!"
    Matthew 16:18-19
        Thou art Peter, ... And I will give unto thee the 'keys'
        of the kingdom of heaven: and whatsoever thou shalt
        bind of earth shall be bound in heaven: and whatsoever
        thou shalt loose on earth shall be loosed in heaven.

596   Line 138   Reference: Parodic
        "And who is George the Third?" replied the apostle.
    Matthew 10:2
        Now the names of the twelve apostles are these; The first,
        Simon, who is called Peter.

597   Lines 149-50   Reference: Parodic
        If I [Peter] had my sword, as I had once / When I cut
        ears off, I had cut him [King of France] down.
    John 18:10
        Then Simon Peter having a sword drew it, and smote the
        high priest's servant, and cut off his right ear.

598   Lines 151-52   Reference: Parodic
        But having but my [Peter's] keys, ... / I only knock'd
        his [King of France's] head from out his hand.

Matthew 16:18-19
> Thou art Peter, ... And I will give unto thee the keys of
> the kingdom of heaven: and whatsoever thou shalt bind on
> earth shall be bound in heaven: and whatsoever thou shalt
> loose on earth shall be loosed in heaven.

599 Lines 151-52   Reference: Parodic
> But having but my [Peter's] keys, and not my brand, /
> I only knock'd his [King of France's] head from out his
> hand.

John 18:10
> Then Simon Peter having a sword drew it, and smote the
> high priest's servant, and cut off his right ear. The ser-
> vant's name was Malchus.

600 Lines 155-56   Reference: Parodic
> And there he [King of France] sits by St. Paul, cheek by
> jowl; / That fellow Paul--the parvenu!

I Corinthians 15:8
> And last of all [the apostles] he [Jesus] was seen of me
> [Paul] also, as of one born out of due time. [Ed.: An
> apostle had to witness Jesus. Paul did so only after the
> ascension.]

601 Lines 177-83   Quote: Parodic
> While thus they spake, the angelic caravan, / Arriving
> 'like a rush of mighty winds', ... Halted before the gate.

Acts 2:2
> And suddenly there came a sound from heaven 'as of a
> rushing mighty wind,' and it filled all the house where
> they were sitting.

602 Lines 181-83   Reference: Subject
> An old man ... Halted before the gate.

Revelation 21:12
> [The New Jerusalem] had twelve gates, and at the gates
> twelve angels.

603 Lines 193-94   Reference: Subject
> As he [Lucifer] drew near, he gazed upon the gate / Ne'er
> to be enter'd more by him or sin.

Revelation 12:7-9
> And there was war in heaven ... and the great dragon was
> cast out, that old serpent, called the Devil.

604 Line 197   Reference: Parodic
> He [Peter] patter'd with his keys at a great rate.

Matthew 16:18-19
> Thou art Peter, ... And I will give unto thee the keys
> of the kingdom of heaven: and whatsoever thou shalt bind
> on earth shall be bound in heaven: and whatsoever thou
> shalt loose on earth shall be loosed in heaven.

605   Lines 209-12   Allusion
          The gate flew / Asunder, and the flashing of its hinges /
          Flung over space an universal hue / Of many colour'd
          flame.
      Revelation 21:12
          [The New Jerusalem] had twelve gates, and at the gates
          twelve angels.

606   Lines 217-19   Reference: Subject
          And from the gate thrown open issued beaming / A beau-
          tiful and mighty Thing of Light, / Radiant with glory.
      Revelation 21:23
          And the city [the New Jerusalem] had no need of the sun,
          neither of the moon, to shine in it: for the glory of God
          did lighten it, and the Lamb is the light thereof.

607   Lines 241-42, 281, 297, 305, 381, 401,
      481, 517, 537, 550, 659, 690, 753   Reference: Subject
          Rf. Michael the archangel.
      Jude 9
          Yet Michael the archangel, when contending with the devil
          he disputed about the body of Moses, durst not bring a-
          gainst him a railing accusation, but said, The Lord re-
          buke thee.

608   Lines 305-307   Quote: Approximate
          "Michael!" replied 'the Prince of Air,' "even here, / Be-
          fore the Gate of him thou servest, must / I claim my
          subject."
      Ephesians 2:2
          In time past ye walked according to the course of this
          world, according to 'the prince of' the power of the 'air,'
          the spirit that now worketh in the children of disobedience.

609   Lines 305-307   Allusion
          "Michael!" replied the Prince of Air, 'even here, / Be-
          fore the Gate of him thou servest, must / I claim my
          subject."
      Revelation 21:12
          [The New Jerusalem] had twelve gates, and at the gates
          twelve angels.

610   Lines 377-81   . Reference: Subject
          Five millions of the primitive, ... implored ... Freedom
          to worship--not alone your Lord, / Michael, but you, and
          you, Saint Peter!
      Acts 10:25-26
          And as Peter was coming in, Cornelius ... fell down at
          his feet, and worshipped him. But Peter took him up,
          saying, Stand up; I myself also am a man.

611   Lines 377-78   Quote: Approximate
          Five millions of the primitive, ... 'hold / The faith.

I Timothy 3:8-9
>   Likewise must the deacons be grave, ... 'holding' the
>   mystery of 'the faith' in a pure conscience.

612   Line 385   Quote: Exact
>   True! he [George III] allow'd them to 'pray God.'

Acts 8:22
>   Repent therefore of this thy wickedness, and 'pray God.'

613   Lines 457-59   Quote: Exact
>   And then it grew a cloud; / And so it was--'a cloud of
>   witnesses.' / But such a cloud!

Hebrews 12:1
>   Wherefore seeing we also are compassed about with so
>   great 'a cloud of witnesses,' let us lay aside every weight.

614   Lines 497-501   Reference: Parodic
>   I [Michael] did not mean / That you [Satan] should half
>   of earth and hell produce; / 'Tis even superfluous, since
>   two honest, clean, / True testimonies are enough.

Hebrews 10:28
>   He that despised Moses' law died without mercy under
>   two or three witnesses.

615   Line 665   Quote: Exact
>   'What I [Junius] have written, I have written.'

John 19:22
>   Pilate answered, 'What I have written I have written.'

616   Lines 665-66   Parallelism
>   "Let / The rest 'be on his head' or mine!" So spoke /
>   [Junius].

Matthew 27:25
>   Then answered all the people, and said, His [Jesus']
>   blood 'be on us,' and on our children.

Acts 18:6
>   He [Paul] ... said unto them, Your blood 'be upon your
>   own heads'; I am clean.

617   Lines 681-83   Quote: Parodic
>   I have sprain'd / My left wing, he's so heavy; one would
>   think / Some of his [Junius'] works 'about his neck were
>   chain'd.'

Matthew 18:6
>   But whoso shall offend one of these little ones ... , it
>   were better for him that millstone 'were hanged about his
>   neck' and that he were drowned in the depth of the sea.

618   Lines 735-36   Quote Parodic
>   The monarch, mute till then, exclaim'd, "What! what! /
>   Pye 'come again'? No more--no more of that!"

Luke 10:35
>   Whatsoever thou spendest more, when I [the good Samari-
>   tan] 'come again,' I will repay thee.

619 Lines 743-44   Reference: Parodic
          The bard Saint Peter pray'd to interpose / (Himself an
          author) only for his prose.
     I Peter and II Peter
          Rf. writings of Peter.

620 Lines 797-800   Reference: Parodic
          Mine [Satan's] is a pen of all work; not so new / As it
          was once, but I would make you shine / Like your own
          trumpet. By the way, my own / Has more of brass in it.
     I Corinthians 13:1
          Though I speak with the tongues of men and of angels,
          and have not charity, I am becoming as sounding brass,
          or a tinkling cymbal.

621 Lines 803-804   Allusion: Parodic
          Judge with my [Satan's] judgment, and by my decision /
          Be guided who shall enter heaven or fall.
     Romans 2:3
          And thinkest thou this, O Man, that judgest them which
          do such things, and doest the same, that thou shalt es-
          cape the judgment of God?

622 Lines 807-808   Allusion: Parodic
          When I [Satan] thus see double, / I save the Deity some
          worlds of trouble.
     Matthew 6:22
          The light of the body is the eye: if therefore thine eye
          be single, thy whole body shall be full of light.

623 Lines 825-27   Reference: Parodic
          Saint Peter, who has hitherto been known / For an im-
          petuous saint, upraised his keys, / And at the fifth line
          knock'd the poet down.
     John 18:10
          Then Simon Peter having a sword drew it, and smote the
          high priest's servant, and cut off his right ear. The ser-
          vant's name was Malchus.

624 Lines 825-27   Reference: Parodic
          Saint Peter, who has hitherto been known / For an im-
          petuous saint, upraised his keys, / And at the fifth line
          knock'd the poet down.
     Matthew 16:18-19
          Thou art Peter, ... And I will give unto thee the keys of
          the kingdom of heaven: and whatsoever thou shalt bind
          on earth shall be bound in heaven: and whatsoever thou
          shalt loose on earth shall be loosed in heaven.

THE WALTZ

625 Lines 87-90   Reference: Parodic
     Not soft Herodias, when, with winning tread, / Her nim-
     ble feet danced off another's head; / Not Cleopatra on her
     galley's deck / Display'd so much of leg, or more of neck.
     Matthew 14:1-12
          Rf. Salome's dance for the head of John the Baptist.

WERNER; OR, THE INHERITANCE

626 Act I. i. 504-506   Allusion
     If it is he, he is so changed, / His father, rising from
     his grave again, / Would pass him by unknown.
     Luke 24:13-35
          Rf. the resurrected Jesus unrecognized by disciples.

627 Act I. i. 747-50   Parallelism
     Josephine: Yet one question-- / What hast thou done?
     Werner (fiercely): 'Left one thing undone which / Had
     made all well.
     Matthew 23:23
          Ye pay tithe of mint and anise and cummin, and have
          omitted the weightier matters of the law, judgment, mer-
          cy, and faith: these ought ye to have done, and not to
          'leave the other undone. '

628 Act II. i. 85-87   Reference: Subject
     A prodigal son, beneath his father's ban / For the last
     twenty years; for whom his sire / Refused to kill the
     fatted calf; and, therefore, / If living he must chew the
     husks still.
     Luke 15:11-32
          Rf. the parable of the prodigal son.

629 Act II. i. 332-33   Allusion
     And now he storms at half a dozen wretches, / Because
     they love their lives too!
     John 12:25
          He that loveth his life shall lose it; and he that hateth
          his life in this world shall keep it unto life eternal.

630 Act II. ii. 724-26   Reference: Subject
     Ulric: Hath he no right? Stralenheim: Right! none; A
     disinherited prodigal / Who for these twenty years dis-
     graced his lineage / In all his acts.

Luke 15:11-32
Rf. the parable of the prodigal son.

631   Act III. i. 70-71   Allusion
Oh, just God! / Thy hell is not hereafter!
Matthew 10:28
And fear not them which kill the body, but are not able
to kill the soul: but rather fear him which is able to
destroy both soul and body in hell.

632   Act III. i. 147-48   Reference: Subject
And one base sin hath done me less ill than / The leav-
ing undone one far greater.
Matthew 23:23
Ye pay tithe of mint ... and have omitted the weightier
matters of the law, judgment, mercy, and faith: these
ought ye to have done, and not to leave the other undone.

633   Act III. i. 339-42   Allusion
I am, methinks, already / A little king, a lucky alchy-
mist! / A wise magician, who has bound the devil / With-
out the forfeit of his soul.
Revelation 20:2
[An angel] laid hold on ... the Devil, ... and bound him
a thousand years.

634   Act III. iii. 394-97   Allusion
Each stroke / Peals for a hope the less; the funeral
note / Of Love deep-buried without resurrection / In
the grave of Possession.
Matthew 16:21
He must go unto Jerusalem, and suffer many things ... ,
and be killed, and be raised again the third day.

635   Act III. iv. 510-11   Quote: Approximate
Ulric: That's well; but had been better, if / You ne'er
had turn'd it [secret passage] to 'a den for'--Werner:
'Thieves!'
Mark 11:17
Is it not written, My house shall be called of all nations
the house of prayer? but ye have made it 'a den of
thieves. '

636   Act III. iv. 584-85   Allusion
'Tis your son that speaks, / Your long-lost, late-found
son.
Luke 15:24
For this my son was dead, and is alive again; he was
lost, and is found. And they began to be merry.

637   Act IV. i. 67-72   Allusion
And she [Ida of Stralenheim], no doubt, will soften what-
soever / Of fierceness the late long intestine wars / Have

given all natures, ... sprinkled, as it were, / With
blood even at their baptism.
Hebrews 11:28

Through faith he [Moses] kept the passover, and the
sprinkling of blood, lest he that destroyed the firstborn
should touch them.

638   Act IV. i. 70-72
                                    Reference: Subject
Bred up upon / The knees of Homicide; sprinkled, as it
were, / With blood even at their baptism.
I Peter 1:2

[To the] Elect according to the foreknowledge of God the
Father, through sanctification of the Spirit, unto obedi-
ence and sprinkling of the blood of Jesus Christ.

639   Act IV. i. 460-62
                                    Quote: Exact
There is everlasting wail and woe, / 'Gnashing of teeth, '
and tears of blood, and fire / Eternal, and the worm
which dieth not!
Matthew 13:41-42

The Son of man shall send forth his angels, and they ...
shall cast them into a furnace of fire: there shall be
wailing and 'gnashing of teeth. '

640   Act IV. i. 460-62
                                    Quote: Approximate
There is everlasting wail and woe, ... and 'the worm
which dieth not'!
Mark 9:43-44

Hell ... where 'their worm dieth not, ' and the fire is
not quenched.

641   Act IV. i. 493
                                    Quote: Exact
Best of all! for this is 'pure religion'!
James 1:27

'Pure religion' and undefiled ... is this, To visit the fa-
therless and widows ... , and to keep himself unspotted
from the world.

642   Act V. i. 154
                                    Allusion
I [Siegendorf] have sought you, and have found you.
Matthew 7:7

Ask, and it shall be given you; seek, and ye shall find;
knock, and it shall be opened unto you.

643   Act V. i. 330-32
                                    Reference: Subject
Within an antechamber, / The door of which was half
ajar, I saw / A man who wash'd his bloody hands.
Matthew 27:24

When Pilate saw that he could prevail nothing, ... he took
water and washed his hands before the multitude, saying,
I am innocent of the blood of this just person.

The Cross Index

OLD TESTAMENT

Bible Passage	Poetry Reference	Bible Passage	Poetry Reference
GENESIS		(Genesis)	
			742, 743, 747, 749,
1:1	115, 169, 288, 356, 543		761, 832, 844, 847,
1:2	133, 151, 373, 436,		890, 956, 989
	551, 553, 606, 662,	2:7-8	334
	883	2:8	304
1:3	336, 899	2:9	734
1:3-4	675	2:16-17	510, 597
1:13-2:2	272	2:17	167, 1015
1:14	250	2:19-27	758
1:16	770	2:21	464
1:20	549	2:21-22	287
1:21	273	2:21-24	402
1:22	137	2:23-24	240, 486
1:26	583, 730, 1021	2:24	18, 103, 122, 413,
1:26-28	104, 929		414
1:26-2:25	441	2-3	124, 299, 388, 488,
1:27	852		496, 555, 674, 686,
1:28	224, 784, 978		825, 990
1:29	468	3:1	622
1	193, 548, 576, 579	3:1-7	378, 591
1-2	139, 396, 585, 609,	3:1-24	19, 41, 170, 236,
	610, 611, 765, 766		242, 281, 282, 300,
1-2; 3:8	586		313, 319, 320, 325,
1-3	337, 506, 595		331, 374, 377, 381,
1-4	24, 560		385, 386, 400, 435,
1-5	550		443, 448, 526, 539,
1; 6-9	544		596, 599, 612, 709,
2:1	604		715, 782, 837, 838,
2:1-24	78		855, 856, 900,
2:2	92		1020, 1052
2:7	116, 131, 161, 165,	3:6	33, 196, 286, 366,
	174, 177, 181, 192,		367, 429, 446, 455
	285, 297, 384, 459,	3:7	445, 1026
	491, 492, 504, 509,	3:14	699
	552, 615, 556 741,	3:14-15	359

Bible Passage	Poetry Reference	Bible Passage	Poetry Reference
(Genesis)		(Exodus)	
20:9	731	12:39	6, 12
21:22	660, 831	13:13	219, 220
22:16	794	13:21	811, 827, 967
24:7	964, 1042	14:8	326
25:22	503, 735	14:21	1047
25:30-34	312	14:27-28	903
25:33-34	876	14-21	861
27:28	123, 307	15:2	43
28:10-15	341	18:16	437
28:17	905, 1017	19:9	200
29:35	665	19:16	481, 259
31:40	275	20:1-17	255, 451, 912
32:2	653	20:3	216
32:24-25	9	20:4	885
32:24-32	146, 774	20:5	1038
32:30	188, 981	20:7	476
34:30	125	20:8	469, 478
37:5	330	20:8-10	90, 93
37:19	577	20:11	28
37:22	290	20:12	1057
39:7-20	321	20:16	257
39:10-13	254	20:17	256, 409, 479, 877, 883
41:43	140, 795	21:23	202, 997
43:23	197	21:23-25	127, 882
45:10	154	21:24	781
49:18	862	22:29	379
		23:16	32
		24:12	194, 904
EXODUS		25:8	101, 637
		26:10-22	186
1-14	914	26:31-33	360
2:22	114	26:33	189
3:5	105, 110, 113, 423, 664	28:29	980
3:8	13, 16, 102, 1046	29:33-37	763
3:14	764	30:34	308
4:8	263	32:15-16	644
4:9	371	32:29	382
4:22	34	33:11	187, 739, 888
5:13	262	33:20	646, 893
6-13	171	34:29-35	645
7:17	67, 128, 156, 902		
7:19	984		
7:11	77	LEVITICUS	
10:1-20	74		
10:19	277	1-7	60, 777
10:29	49	1-10	778
11:4-12:36	2	2:2-3	88
12:23	30	5:2	785

Bible Passage	Poetry Reference			
(Psalms)				
90:2	874			
90:10	407			
90:12	621,	771,	878	
91:5	280			
91:12	728			
92:12	361			
95:4	372			
100	1034			
102:11	68			
102:27	223			
104:15	487, 1044			
104:20	970			
104:31	36			
110:2	822			
119:160	542			
123:1	894			
126:5	226			
129:6-7	973			
129:8	310, 399			
137:1	266, 624, 636			
137:1-3	692			
137:2-3	910			
137:3	638			
137:5	264, 267			
137:6	702			
137	623, 635			
143:3	147			
145:17	887			
148:1	867			
149:6	793, 803			
Entire book 463, 628, 691				

PROVERBS

Bible Passage	Poetry Reference
4:9	982
10:17	744
11:12	866
11:14	420
13:14	936
16:18	1059
16:32	416
19:12	258, 460
20:8	879
22:1	365
23:6	490
27:7	454
30:20	820
31:10	241, 244, 245, 426

ECCLESIASTES

Bible Passage	Poetry Reference
1:1	466
1:2	235, 333, 619, 620
1:3	911, 1027
1:9	309
1:14	408
1:18	733
2:14	129
3:10	471
3:15	875
5:12	431
9:11	82
10:20	354
11:1	261, 433, 853
12:1	50
12:5	1060
12:7	38, 42, 62, 94, 95, 144, 152, 208, 380, 494, 661, 694, 714, 759, 843
12:12	1025

SONG OF SOLOMON

Bible Passage	Poetry Reference
4:15	663
Entire book 677	

ISAIAH

Bible Passage	Poetry Reference
1:9	716
1:13	99
1:22	270
1:24	756
2:4	927
2:19	351
4:6	172
6:10	301
7:14	295, 1011
8:7	963
9:4	418
9:6	906, 950
11:6	340, 707
11:6-7	536
14:12	26, 27, 47, 98, 217, 218, 298, 489, 508, 547, 589, 590, 673, 689, 696, 700, 729,

Bible Passage	Poetry Reference
DANIEL	
2:31-35	839
2:31-45	846
2:33-42	84
2:48	474
2, 4	332
3:1	425
3:5	924
3:23	727
4:14	792
4:19-37	657, 849
4:33	315
4:34	750
5:17-31	292
5:24	1029
5:25-30	362
5:25-31	857
5:27	48, 160, 757, 776, 799, 986, 1053, 1058
6:7	327, 1043
6:15	521
6:16	318, 323, 383, 520
6:21-22	316
7:2	20, 427, 704
7:9 (7:22)	96
8:10	324
11:7	338
HOSEA	
8:7	168, 370

Bible Passage	Poetry Reference
JOEL	
1:4	390
2:31	148
AMOS	
5:26	5, 797, 835, 1056
JONAH	
1:5	998
2:10	678
3:1-2	397
3:4	357, 925
MICAH	
6:15	480
6:16	814
HABAKKUK	
1:3	203
2:9	726
3:10	155
ZECHARIAH	
14:8	710
MALACHI	
4:1	339

Part II continued

NEW TESTAMENT

Bible Passage	Poetry Reference	Bible Passage	Poetry Reference
MATTHEW		(Matthew)	
		7:3-4	532
1:18	136, 197, 293, 495, 498, 507	7:7	98, 571, 642
		7:9	325, 499
1:18-25	417	7:12	521
1:21	199	7:14	572, 584
1:23	282, 318	7:16	19
2:11	565, 573	7:16-18	88
2:12	393	7:17-18	94
2:23	11, 252, 290, 371, 569	8:9	192, 216
		8:12	168, 433
3:9	259	8:20	395
3:11	173	8:31-32	520
3:12	370	9:2	313, 477, 560
3:16	200	9:17	158
4:5	50, 452	9:20	203, 222
4:9	21, 553	9:37-38	131
4:10	137, 445, 563	10:2	449, 596
4:19	174, 250	10:2-5	156
5:6	32	10:8	104
5:7	466	10:14	111, 124
5:8	50	10:28	631
5:16	402	10:29	126, 266, 267, 473
5:17	441	10:37	23
5:39	338	10:39	297
5:45	142	10:42	481a
6:2	114	11:7	67, 254, 255
6:9-13	146	11:29-30	568
6:10	511, 581	11:30	60
6:11	360, 423	12:25-26	460
6:13	16	12:32	162
6:14-15	454	12:38-39	428
6:22	622	12:50	240
6:24	52, 422	13:1-23	388
6:29	385	13:3-30	341
6:34	418	13:11	343
7:2	416	13:14	201
7:3	223, 232	13:19	248

CONCLUSION

Explanation of Data

Frequency of the Eight
Classifications

Table One, of the Appendices that follow, indicates the frequency with which the compendium's eight classification of biblical material appeared in Byron's poetry. This research showed a total of 1,704 uses of the Bible throughout the poetry. Of those uses 1,063 were from the Old Testament, and 641 were from the New Testament. Byron's use of nearly twice as much Old Testament material as New Testament is indicative of his major interest; however, the quantity of New Testament matter exceeds what one who is familiar with Old Testament-oriented works like Cain and Heaven and Earth might have expected. The largest classification was "Reference: Subject" with a total of 486 occurrences or over 28 percent of the total. The next largest category was "Quote: Exact" with 264 occurrences, almost exactly the same as the 261 "Allusions." The three categories of quotations accounted for over 36 percent of the total number of references while both reference categories accounted for more than 41 percent of the total. The smallest groups were "Parallelism" and "Allusion: Parodic," the two together being some 7 percent of the total.

Frequency of References
to the Old Testament

Tables One and Two indicate the frequency with which Byron included Old Testament material in his poetry. Of the 1,704 total number of occurrences of biblical material in Byron's poetry, 1,063 (over 62 percent) are from the Old Testament. Table Two shows that a full 50 percent of the Old Testament matter is from the Pentateuch, and over 35 percent of the Old Testament material is from one book of the Pentateuch, Genesis. In addition, Table Two suggests that Byron made considerable use of Old Testament wisdom and poetic literature, particularly Psalms; over 18 percent of all Old Testament matter is drawn from this area. Portions of the Old Testament, such as the prophets, however, were used only incidentally in Byron's Poetry, except for Isaiah with its account of Lucifer. Hoxie Neale Fairchild was correct perhaps in saying, in the "Byron" section of Religious Trends in English Poetry (5 vols., New York: Columbia University Press, 1949, 3:449), "Prophecy ... leaves him cold."

Frequency of References to the New Testament

Tables One and Three point out the frequency with which material from the New Testament appeared in the poetry. The 641 uses from the New Testament represent 38 percent of the whole. Table Three indicates that nearly 54 percent of the New Testament materials is drawn from the gospels. The 218 uses from Matthew account for some 34 percent of the New Testament matter. Of the 641 New Testament references, 157 or over 40 percent are drawn from the epistles of Paul. In addition, Byron seems to have relied rather heavily at times on the book of Revelation, which is used 54 times for 8 percent of the total New Testament material. He makes little or no use of some shorter epistles such as Titus, Philemon, and III John.

Distribution of Old Testament References

Table Four presents those poems in which Byron made the greatest use of the Old Testament. Byron's longer poems account for a great number of his uses of the Old Testament: Don Juan contains over 22 percent of the Old Testament material used; Childe Harold, over 11 percent. Those poems with primarily biblical themes

contain great quantities of Old Testament material: Heaven and
Earth has 122 references to the Old Testament, one more than the
much longer Childe Harold; Cain, obviously dependent as a whole
on Genesis 1-4, has in addition 49 other references to the Old Test-
ament.   All of Byron's major poetry makes at least some use of
the Old Testament.

Distribution of New Testament
References in the Poetry

          Table Five points out the poetry in which Byron makes
use of the New Testament.   As with the Old Testament, Byron
uses the New Testament primarily in his longer works: some 33
percent of the New Testament material is found in Don Juan; ano-
ther 10 percent is in Childe Harold. The only poem which might
be said to have a New Testament basis, The Vision of Judgment,
has some 6 percent of the New Testament material.   Old Testament
poems such as Cain and Heaven and Earth contain a significant
number of anachronistic New Testament references; such New Test-
ament themes as the afterlife and the atonement are essential to
the poet's full development of the historical reaches of the Genesis
accounts.   Otherwise, the New Testament uses are scattered rather
equally throughout Byron's poetry; and no significant poem fails to
use the New Testament at all.

Variations in Biblical Use
Throughout Byron's Life

          Byron seems to have used the Bible in his major poetry[*]
with varying degrees of frequency at different periods of his life,
which may be conveniently placed into four periods: birth to 1809,
1809 to the 1816 separation, 1817 to his 1821 departure from Ra-
venna, 1822 to his death in 1824.   As Table Six indicates, before

---

[*]For this computation only major poetry has been used.   Omitted
are 73 biblical references in the poems included under "Miscellan-
eous Poems," "Domestic Pieces," and "Ephemeral Verses."

1809 Byron used the Bible 36 times in 4,365 lines of poetry. That is, 2.2 percent of the total number of instances of biblical material is used in 7.3 percent of his poetry, a relatively small figure in either case. From 1809 to 1816 he used the Bible 306 times in 13,672 lines of poetry, indicating an increasing use of the Bible in his maturity in that 18.8 percent of the total biblical uses are in 22.8 percent of the poetry. From 1817 to 1821 Byron used the poetry 694 times in 23,367 lines of poetry: 42.5 percent of his biblical material is in 39 percent of the poetry. From 1822 to his death in 1824 Byron used the Bible 595 times in 18,505 lines of poetry: 36.5 percent of the instances of biblical matter are in 30.9 percent of his poetry. The suggestion arises that as Byron matured he wrote more poetry and increased his use of the Bible. The last few years of his life show 79 percent of his use of the Bible in nearly 70 percent of his poetry. Although Table Six indicates the greatest use of the Bible as well as the most poetry in the years from 1817 to 1821, one must note the relative productivity in the two years immediately before the poet's death. Recognizing the brevity of this fourth period, one must grant that Byron not only wrote increasing amounts of poetry as he grew older but that each successive period showed a continuing increase in the instances of biblical usage.

Themes or Subjects from the Bible As Found in Byron's Poetry

Old Testament Subjects Favored by Byron

Table Seven is suggestive of the Old Testament subject matter favored in Byron's poetry. A full 40 percent, or 200 of 438 occurrences classified as "Reference: Subject" and "Reference: Parodic," is from Genesis. Over 71 percent of those 200 cases of Genesis material is from the first four chapters of Genesis, indicating Byron's preoccupation with the accounts of the creation, the Eden story, and the saga of Cain. Byron seems to have relied most heavily upon those portions of the Old Testament which are narrative or historical in nature, using the familiar stories of the flood, Moses and the Israelites, Saul and David. Except for a number of references to Daniel and Isaiah 14, he generally omits historical material following the reign of David, such as that concerned with the divided kingdom. Historically, the Job story, used considerably by Byron, also pre-dates the divided kingdom. Byron uses much Old Testament material in passing, always returning to a handful of favorite stories and using some of them as the basis for significant poems like Cain and Heaven and Earth.

New Testament Subjects
Favored by Byron

Table Eight shows those New Testament subjects favored by Byron in his poetry. He relies on the parables for over 22 percent of all references to the New Testament, parables such as that concerning the rich man and Lazarus, and the parable of the sower. Incidents from the life of Jesus, with frequent references to his position as redeemer, account for 16 percent of the New Testament material. The Apostle Peter, largely because of his place in The Vision of Judgment, looms large in the frequency figures. Other characters, particularly Paul and Judas, receive only slightly less attention. Over 10 percent of Byron's references from the New Testament are from the book of Revelation, particularly accounts such as those of the Babylonian harlot and the millennium. Little use is made of accounts of the miracles or of material in minor epistles. As in his use of the Old Testament, Byron seems to prefer the narrative portions of the New Testament.

Types of References for
Old Testament Subjects

Byron uses all types of references when incorporating Old Testament subjects into his poetry, a fact best seen in Table Two. Over 32 percent of all Old Testament materials is classified there as "Reference: Subject." When that category is added to "Reference: Parodic," over 45 percent of the Old Testament references is included. In addition, as shown in Table One, Byron used

quoted matter of one type or another over 36 percent of the time.
In light of Byron's reputation for satire, it is interesting to note
that he uses the three types of parody for more than 20 percent of
his Old Testament references, a substantial figure but smaller than
might have been expected.

Types of References for
New Testament Subjects

Byron employs a variety of methods when using the New Test-
ament in his poetry, as may easily be seen in Table Three.   Quot-
ed matter accounts for 36 percent of New Testament material, just
as it did for Old Testament material.   The poet, however, makes
less use of the general type of material indicated by "Reference:
Subject" in the New Testament (21 percent of the New Testament
total) than he does of such material in the Old Testament (32 per-
cent of the Old Testament total). Nearly a quarter of Byron's New
Testament material is parodic in nature, approximately the same
as for the Old Testament.   Byron uses, as Table One shows, phras-
ings parallel to those in the New Testament 53 times, but only 15
times for the Old Testament, an unforeseen reversal of the usual
Old Testament dominance in Byron's poetry.

Biblical Phrases in Byron's Poetry

Recurrent Phrases
from the Old Testament

Table Nine points to a number of Old Testament phrases
repeatedly employed by Byron as part of his rhetorical style.   By-
ron's training in classical rhetoric is reflected in a number of ba-
lanced, three-syllable iambic phrases like "face to face" and "holy
ground."   Some of these phrases appear as many as five times.
Several short phrases such as "milk and honey" appear repeatedly,
as do a few longer phrases: "weighed in the balances," "a virtuous
woman," "to me belongeth vengeance."   One is reminded of Byron's
preface to Cain in which he claims that in his biblical phrases he
"made as little alteration, even of words, as the rhythm would permit."

Recurrent Phrases
from the New Testament

Table Ten indicates some of Byron's favorite New Testament phrases; three phrases employ the same rhythm found in the phrases from the Old Testament. As he did with the Old Testament, Byron often used balanced three-syllable phrases from the New Testament: "flesh and blood," "den of thieves," and "God is love." A given phrase, however, may not be found in the poetry more than three or four times. There is also an occasional longer New Testament expression like "prince of the power of the air" that Byron uses repeatedly. Other than the poet's use of classical rhetoric, and some few intermediate and longer phrases that are occasionally repeated, Table Ten shows no significant patterns.

Concluding Statement

This research confirms the heretofore unverified but general belief that Byron used the King James Version of the Bible. All former studies dealing with Byron's use of the Bible, including that of Harold Ray Stevens, "Byron and the Bible: A Study of Poetic and Philosophic Development," have assumed without supporting comment Byron's use of the King James Bible; but this research uncovered no previous attempt to verify that assumption. Correspondence with Byron's publishing house, heirs, and critics, along with the evidence of the compendium itself, confirms that Byron did use the King James Version in his poetry.

This research also confirms the generally held opinion regarding Byron's use of the Old Testament. Goethe once remarked that Byron should have lived to dramatize the entire Old Testament.* Most scholars have been acutely aware of Byron's debt to the Old Testament: Marchand says that Byron was "fascinated by the Old Testament" (Byron's Poetry, p. 84), and Murray Roston in Prophet

---

* As quoted in Henry Crabb Robinson, On Books and Their Writers, ed. Edith J. Morley, I, 372. This quotation may be found in Leslie A. Marchand, Byron's Poetry: A Critical Introduction (Boston: Houghton Mifflin, 1965), p. 85.

and Poet: The Bible and the Growth of Romanticism (Evanston, Ill.:
Northwestern University Press, 1965) speaks of Byron's very deep
admiration and affection for "the old Testament itself" (p. 18). The
great number of Old Testament uses shown by the tables serves to
reinforce these judgments.

A correction of the common view of Byron's use of the
New Testament is now in order, in light of the research. Seldom
has this usage been remarked upon, and then not at length or in
specific terms. Scholarship has proposed by silence and by overt
statement that Byron made no significant use of the New Testament.
Hoxie Neale Fairchild in Religious Trends in English Poetry (3:396)
says flatly, after speaking of Byron's preference for the Old Testa-
ment, "the New Testament, significantly, seems to have meant
little to him." Murray Roston fails to see the important influence
of the New Testament on Byron when he quotes,

> The wild dove hath her nest, the fox his cave,
> Mankind their country--Israel but the grave!

Roston says that the stanza "has no biblical indebtedness worthy of
note" (Prophet and Poet, p. 190), but the passage is clearly derived
from Matthew 8:20, "And Jesus saith unto him, The foxes have
holes, and the birds of the air have nests, but the Son of man hath
not where to lay his head." Byron lends some authority to state-
ments downplaying his use of the New Testament. In his preface
to Cain he writes, "It is to be recollected that my present subject
has nothing to do with the New Testament, to which no reference
can be here made without anachronism." Table Five, however,
shows 34 anachronistic references in Cain to the New Testament,
15 of them some type of quoted matter.

Even as critics have neglected Byron's use of the New
Testament, they have largely overlooked his reliance on biblical
language itself. Leslie Marchand in Byron's Poetry (p. 85) takes
at face value the poet's statement in his preface to Cain that he
had only rarely and with little alteration "taken from actual Scrip-
ture" the precise language of the Bible. Tables One, Four, and
Five, however, are indicative of the many instances in which Byron

took his words from the scripture. In the three categories of quo-
tations and in the "parallelisms," all of which emphasize Byron's
use of biblical phraseology, one can find over 40 percent of Byron's
total uses of the Bible.

Suggestions for Future Study

This research suggests further related studies. Addi-
tional insight into Byron's intellectual processes might be obtained
through a study of biblically related matter important to Byron:
commentaries, sermons, pamphlets, philosophies, and other pub-
lished materials. A study of Byron's way with biblical cadences
and rhythms should reveal much about his technique. Finally, ser-
ious detailed study should be made of Byron's use of the New Test-
ament in order to discover the ways it influenced his attitudes to-
ward his Old Testament subjects and to reveal in detail the place
of New Testament doctrines and concepts in his Old Testament
world.

APPENDICES

Appendix A: Major Tables

1. Biblical References in Byron's Poetry
2. Old Testament References in Byron's Poetry
3. New Testament References in Byron's Poetry

Appendix B: Frequency Tables

4. Old Testament References in Specific Poems
5. New Testament References in Specific Poems
6. Variations in Biblical Use Throughout Byron's Life
7. Old Testament Subject Matter in Byron's Poetry
8. New Testament Subject Matter in Byron's Poetry
9. Old Testament Phrases in Byron's Poetry
10. New Testament Phrases in Byron's Poetry

TABLE ONE. BIBLICAL REFERENCES IN BYRON'S POETRY

Classification	Old Testament	New Testament	Totals
Quote: Exact	166	98	264
Quote: Approximate	163	85	248
Quote: Parodic	57	49	106
Reference: Subject	348	138	486
Reference: Parodic	135	83	218
Allusion	149	112	261
Allusion: Parodic	30	23	53
Parallelism	15	53	68
Totals	1063	641*	1704

*Though the last reference in the N. T. part of the compendium is numbered 643, the total is actually 641; all tables are based on the actual total.

297

TABLE TWO. OLD TESTAMENT REFERENCES IN BYRON'S POETRY

Classification	Genesis	Exodus	Leviticus	Numbers	Deuteronomy	Joshua	Judges	Ruth	I Samuel	II Samuel	I Kings	II Kings	I Chronicles	II Chronicles	Ezra	Nehemiah	Esther	Job	Psalms	Proverbs
Quote: Exact	35	20	2	5	7	-	4	-	3	8	8	3	-	2	2	1	-	5	24	9
Quote: Approximate	24	15	3	2	10	3	1	2	1	4	4	1	1	-	1	1	1	8	28	1
Quote: Parodic	9	7	1	-	2	-	-	-	2	1	3	-	1	-	-	-	-	4	9	3
Reference: Subject	141	22	9	6	4	1	4	2	11	5	6	8	3	3	-	1	1	16	20	3
Reference: Parodic	67	9	1	4	1	1	2	1	2	1	4	2	1	-	-	-	-	5	7	1
Allusion	82	8	2	2	4	9	-	-	-	-1	1	1	-	-	-	-	-	1	12	1
Allusion: Parodic	14	4	2	-	1	-	-	-	-	-	-	-	-	-	-	-	-	-	3	-
Parallelism	5	3	-	-	-	-	-	-	-	1	-	-	-	-	1	-	-	-	1	-
Totals	377	89	20	19	29	14	11	5	19	20	26	15	6	5	4	3	2	39	104	18

298

(TABLE TWO Continued)

Classification	Ecclesiastes	Song of Solomon	Isaiah	Jeremiah	Lamentations	Ezekiel	Daniel	Hosea	Joel	Amos	Obadiah	Jonah	Micah	Nahum	Habakkuk	Zephaniah	Haggi	Zechariah	Malachi	Totals
Quote: Exact	5	-	11	2	-	2	6	-	-	-	-	-	-	-	1	-	-	1	-	166
Quote: Approximate	16	1	14	8	3	2	6	1	-	-	-	-	-	-	1	-	-	-	-	163
Quote: Parodic	2	-	7	1	-	2	2	1	-	-	-	-	-	-	-	-	-	-	-	57
Reference: Subject	9	-	44	7	1	5	7	-	1	2	1	3	2	-	-	-	-	-	1	348
Reference: Parodic	-	1	9	-	-	-	13	-	1	1	-	1	-	-	-	-	-	-	-	135
Allusion	2	-	14	3	-	-	5	-	-	1	-	-	-	-	1	-	-	-	-	149
Allusion: Parodic	-	-	4	1	-	-	-	-	-	-	-	1	-	-	-	-	-	-	-	30
Parallelism	3	-	1	-	-	-	-	-	-	-	-	-	-	-	-	-	-	-	-	15
Totals	37	2	104	21	4	11	39	2	2	4	0	5	2	0	3	0	0	1	1	1063

TABLE THREE. NEW TESTAMENT REFERENCES IN BYRON'S POETRY

Classification	Matthew	Mark	Luke	John	Acts	Romans	I Corinthians	II Corinthians	Galatians	Ephesians	Philippians	Colossians	I Thessalonians	II Thessalonians
Quote: Exact	26	2	9	16	10	-	4	3	1	-	2	-	1	1
Quote: Approximate	24	5	6	9	9	4	5	-	-	5	-	2	1	-
Quote: Parodic	17	3	4	2	5	2	4	-	-	1	-	1	-	-
Reference: Subject	50	4	13	6	7	5	11	3	2	2	1	2	3	1
Reference: Parodic	34	1	8	7	2	3	9	2	1	-	-	1	1	-
Allusion	40	1	9	14	8	5	2	1	-	4	-	1	-	-
Allusion: Parodic	9	-	1	-	-	4	1	-	-	1	-	-	1	-
Parallelism	18	2	5	2	1	2	5	3	-	5	-	-	-	-
Totals	218	18	55	56	42	25	41	12	4	18	3	7	7	2

(TABLE THREE Continued)

Classification	I Timothy	II Timothy	Titus	Philemon	Hebrews	James	I Peter	II Peter	I John	II John	III John	Jude	Revelation	Totals
Quote: Exact	1	–	–	–	5	6	1	2	3	–	–	1	4	98
Quote: Approximate	3	–	–	–	3	–	1	–	4	1	–	–	3	85
Quote: Parodic	2	1	–	–	2	–	–	1	2	–	–	–	2	49
Reference: Subject	–	–	–	–	5	–	1	1	2	–	–	3	16	138
Reference: Parodic	–	–	–	–	2	1	1	–	–	–	–	–	10	83
Allusion	2	–	–	–	4	3	2	–	1	–	–	2	13	112
Allusion: Parodic	–	–	–	–	3	1	–	–	–	–	–	–	2	23
Parallelism	3	–	–	–	2	–	–	–	1	–	–	–	4	53
Totals	11	1	–	–	26	11	6	4	13	1	–	6	54	641

301

TABLE FOUR. OLD TESTAMENT REFERENCES IN SPECIFIC POEMS

Classification	Ephemeral Verses	English Bards	Don Juan	Domestic Pieces	Deformed Transformed	Curse of Minerva	Corsair	Childe Harold	Cain	Bride of Abydos	Blues	Beppo	Age of Bronze
Quote: Exact	-	2	23	2	1	1	1	22	14	-	-	1	3
Quote: Approximate	-	5	23	4	5	2	1	20	10	1	-	-	-
Quote: Parodic	-	3	30	-	-	-	1	7	2	-	1	1	-
Reference: Subject	1	3	33	3	7	1	-	37	19	3	1	-	2
Reference: Parodic	1	5	86	-	1	-	-	10	2	-	-	-	-
Allusion	-	1	21	-	3	1	2	20	2	1	-	-	1
Allusion: Parodic	-	-	15	-	1	-	-	2	-	-	-	-	7
Parallelism	-	-	4	-	-	-	-	3	-	-	-	-	1
Totals	2	19	235	9	18	5	5	121	49	5	2	2	14

302

(TABLE FOUR Continued)

Classification	Morgante Maggiore	Miscellaneous Poems	Mazeppa	Marino Faliero	Manfred	Lara	Lament of Tasso	Island	Hours of Idleness	Hints from Horace	Hebrew Melodies	Heaven and Earth	Giaour
Quote: Exact	3	6	–	13	10	–	3	3	4	–	3	14	2
Quote: Approximate	4	3	2	6	7	2	1	4	6	–	8	17	1
Quote: Parodic	–	1	–	–	2	–	–	1	–	2	–	1	–
Reference: Subject	4	15	1	17	15	1	4	2	6	4	36	72	5
Reference: Parodic	–	6	2	1	1	–	–	2	1	2	–	–	–
Allusion	3	–	–	6	8	–	3	2	5	1	5	18	2
Allusion: Parodic	–	1	–	–	–	–	–	–	–	1	–	–	–
Parallelism	1	1	1	2	–	1	–	–	–	–	–	–	–
Totals	15	33	5	45	43	4	11	14	23	10	52	122	10

(TABLE FOUR Continued)

Classification	Totals	Werner	Waltz	Vision of Judgment	Two Foscari	Sonnet on Chillon	Siege of Corinth	Sardanapalus	Prophecy of Dante	Prisoner of Chillon	Poems on Various	Parisina	Ode on Venice
Quote: Exact	166	8	-	4	5	1	3	5	5	-	-	3	1
Quote: Approximate	163	4	-	4	6	1	4	4	6	-	-	2	-
Quote: Parodic	57	1	-	2	-	-	-	1	1	-	-	-	-
Reference: Subject	348	9	1	4	6	-	3	15	16	-	-	2	-
Reference: Parodic	135	-	2	13	-	-	-	-	-	-	-	-	-
Allusion	149	4	1	1	5	-	1	26	3	-	-	1	2
Allusion: Parodic	30	-	-	3	-	-	-	-	-	-	-	-	-
Parallelism	15	-	-	-	-	-	-	-	-	-	-	1	1
Totals	1063	26	4	31	22	2	11	51	31	-	-	9	3

304

TABLE FIVE. NEW TESTAMENT REFERENCES IN SPECIFIC POEMS

Classification	Age of Bronze	Beppo	Blues	Bride of Abydos	Cain	Childe Harold	Corsair	Curse of Minerva	Deformed Transformed	Domestic Pieces	Don Juan	English Bards	Ephemeral Verses
Quote: Exact	3	–	–	1	9	10	3	–	1	–	30	–	–
Quote: Approximate	1	1	–	–	5	16	1	2	3	–	23	–	–
Quote: Parodic	1	–	1	–	1	–	–	–	–	–	32	3	–
Reference: Subject	–	–	–	–	10	15	2	–	5	2	23	1	–
Reference: Parodic	1	–	1	–	–	1	–	–	1	–	50	5	2
Allusion	1	–	–	2	7	19	1	1	2	2	20	–	1
Allusion: Parodic	–	–	–	–	–	–	–	–	–	–	16	–	–
Parallelism	–	–	–	2	2	5	–	–	1	–	17	2	–
Totals	7	1	2	5	34	66	7	3	13	4	211	11	3

Classification	Giaour	Heaven and Earth	Hebrew Melodies	Hints from Horace	Hours of Idleness	Island	Lament of Tasso	Lara	Manfred	Marino Faliero	Mazeppa	Miscellaneous Poems	Morgante Maggiore
Quote: Exact	2	4	1	-	1	1	-	1	1	4	-	7	5
Quote: Approximate	2	3	1	-	-	-	-	-	5	2	-	2	4
Quote: Parodic	-	-	-	2	-	-	-	1	-	-	-	1	-
Reference: Subject	1	3	4	-	4	1	1	1	4	6	2	5	15
Reference: Parodic	-	-	-	1	-	-	-	-	-	2	-	2	-
Allusion	1	6	2	-	6	-	1	1	7	4	-	3	6
Allusion: Parodic	-	-	-	-	-	-	-	-	-	-	-	-	-
Parallelism	-	1	-	-	1	-	1	2	6	3	-	2	2
Totals	6	17	8	3	12	2	3	5	23	21	2	22	32

(TABLE FIVE Continued)

Classification	Ode on Venice	Parisina	Poems on Various ...	Prisoner of Chillon	Prophecy of Dante	Sardanapalus	Siege of Corinth	Sonnet on Chillon	Two Foscari	Vision of Judgment	Waltz	Werner	Totals
Quote: Exact	–	–	–	1	–	5	1	1	1	3	–	2	98
Quote: Approximate	2	–	–	–	2	2	1	–	2	3	–	2	85
Quote: Parodic	–	–	–	–	–	1	–	–	1	5	–	–	49
Reference: Subject	–	1	1	1	9	4	4	–	2	6	–	5	138
Reference: Parodic	–	–	–	–	1	–	–	–	–	15	1	–	83
Allusion	–	1	–	–	3	3	2	–	–	3	–	8	112
Allusion: Parodic	–	–	–	–	–	–	–	–	–	7	–	–	23
Parallelism	–	1	–	–	1	1	1	–	–	1	–	1	53
Totals	2	3	1	2	16	16	9	1	6	43	1	18	641

TABLE SIX. VARIATIONS IN BIBLICAL USE THROUGHOUT BYRON'S LIFE

Dates	Number of Lines	Percentage of Total Lines	Biblical References	Percentage of Total References
Birth-1809	4,365	17.3	36	02.2
1810-1816	13,672	22.8	306	18.8
1817-1821	23,367	39.0	694	42.5
1822-1824	18,505	30.9	595	36.5
Totals	59,909	100.0	1,631*	100.0

*See note, p. 289

TABLE SEVEN. OLD TESTAMENT SUBJECT MATTER IN BYRON'S POETRY

Subject	Reference: Subject	Reference: Parodic	Totals
Creation story (Genesis 1-2)	28	8	36
Eden story (Genesis 2-3)	45	41	86
Cain (Genesis 4)	20	1	21
Giants (Genesis 6)	8	-	8
Noah and flood (Genesis 6-9)	20	4	24
Nimrod (Genesis 10)	7	6	13
Babel (Genesis 11)	3	-	3
Abraham (Genesis 11-25)	5	-	5
Sodom (Genesis 19)	3	1	4
Lot's wife (Genesis 19)	-	1	1
Jacob (Genesis 32)	1	2	3
Joseph (Genesis 37-50)	-	2	2
Moses and Israel (Exodus 1-20)	22	6	28
Ten Commandments (Exodus 20)	4	5	9
Levitical Laws (Leviticus)	9	-	9

308

Subject	Reference: Subject	Reference: Parodic	Totals
Balaam (Numbers 22-24)	3	2	5
Ruth (Ruth)	2	1	3
Saul (I Samuel)	7	-	7
David (I and II Samuel)	6	3	9
Solomon (II Samuel; I Kings)	-	2	2
Captivity of Israel (II Kings)	6	-	6
Bruised reed (II Kings 18)	3	-	3
Job (Job)	16	5	21
Evil eye (Proverbs 23:6)	2	-	2
Lucifer (Isaiah 14)	25	3	28
Daniel (Daniel)	7	15	22
Jonah (Jonah)	3	1	4
Miscellaneous	92	25	177
Totals	347	134	481

TABLE EIGHT. NEW TESTAMENT SUBJECT MATTER IN BYRON'S POETRY

	Classification		
Subject	Reference: Subject	Reference: Parodic	Totals
Virgin Mary (Matthew 1)	9	2	11
Life of Jesus			
Jesus and sacrament (Matthew 26)	2	-	2
Jesus as atonement (Romans 25)	4	-	4
Jesus as forgiver (Mark 14)	9	-	9
Crown of thorns (Matthew 27)	1	-	1
Jesus misunderstood (Matthew 16)	1	-	1
Pilate's reaction (Matthew 27)	1	1	2
Rending of veil of temple (Matthew 27)	3	-	3
Resurrection and second coming (Acts 1)	6	-	6
Miracles			
Raising of Lazarus (John 11-12)	3	-	3
Parables			
Seed and fruit (Matthew 7)	5	2	7
Mote and beam (Matthew 7)	1	2	3
Sparrow's fall (Matthew 10)	1	2	3
The sower (Matthew 13)			
The tares (Matthew 13)	-	1	1
Lost sheep (Matthew 18)	1	1	2
Eye of needle (Matthew 19)	-	1	1
Ten virgins (Matthew 25)	1	-	1
Widow's mite (Mark 12)	2	1	3
Good Samaritan (Luke 10)	1	2	3
Prodigal son (Luke 15)	2	-	2
Rich man and Lazarus (Luke 16)	6	3	9
Importunate widow (Luke 18)	1	-	1
New Testament characters			
Peter	2	13	15
Judas	1	-	1
Paul	2	1	3
Pharisees	1	-	1
Centurion	2	-	2
Herodias	-	1	1
Luke	-	1	1

| | Classification | | |
Subject	Reference: Subject	Reference: Parodic	Totals
Jerusalem	8	-	8
Predestination	4	-	4
Charity	-	3	3
The Trinity	-	3	3
Marriage	-	2	2
Resurrection and judgment	9	-	9
Eternal reward and punishment	1	14	15
Book of Revelation			
Seven-headed dragon	1	-	1
Pale horse	2	-	2
Wormwood	2	-	2
Seven vials	1	1	2
Gates of Heaven	2	-	2
Millennium	3	1	4
Babylonian harlot	2	2	4
Book	-	2	2
Devil			
Prince of darkness	2	-	2
Wandering stars	2	-	2
Michael and devil	2	-	2
Totals	112	63	175

TABLE NINE. OLD TESTAMENT PHRASES IN BYRON'S POETRY

Biblical Phrase	Quote: Exact	Quote: Approximate	Quote: Parodic	Parallelism	Totals
Face to face (Genesis 32:30)	5	-	-	-	5
Milk and honey (Exodus 3:8)	3	-	2	-	5
Holy ground (Exodus 3:5)	3	1	1	-	5
Weighed in the balances (Daniel 5:27)	2	3	-	-	5
A virtuous woman (Proverbs 31:10)	3	-	1	-	4
The valley of the shadow of death (Psalm 23:4)	-	3	1	-	4
My son, my son! (II Samuel 18:33)	2	1	1	-	3
Get thee hence (I Kings 17:3)	2	1	-	-	3
All is vanity (Ecclesiastes 1:2)	2	1	-	-	3
To me belongeth vengeance (Deuteronomy 32:35)	-	2	1	-	3
Number our days (Psalm 90:12)	-	3	-	-	3
Eye for eye (Exodus 21:24)	-	-	-	3	3
Dust unto dust (Genesis 3:19)	-	-	-	3	3
Totals	22	15	6	6	49

TABLE TEN. NEW TESTAMENT PHRASES IN BYRON'S POETRY

Biblical Phrase	Quote: Exact	Quote: Approximate	Quote: Parodic	Parallelism	Totals
Flesh and blood	4	–	–	–	4
Prince of the power of the air	–	4	–	–	4
In word ... in deed	–	3	1	–	4
Get thee hence	2	1	–	–	3
From my youth up	–	2	1	–	3
A rushing mighty wind	–	2	1	–	3
Den of thieves	2	1	–	–	3
God is love	–	–	2	–	2
Totals	8	13	5	–	26

BIBLIOGRAPHY

BIBLIOGRAPHIES

"Annual Bibliography. " MLA International Bibliography of Books
   and Articles. New York: Modern Language Association,
   1921-1973. 52 vols.

The Cambridge Bibliography of English Literature. Cambridge,
   England: Cambridge University Press, 1957. 5 vols.

"Current Bibliography. " Keats-Shelley Journal. New York: Keats-
   Shelley Association of America, 1952-1975.

Downs, Robert B. American Library Resources: A Bibliographic
   Guide. Chicago: American Library Association, 1951.

Elkins, A. C. , and Forstner, L. J. , eds. The Romantic Movement
   Bibliography, 1936-1970. Ann Arbor, Mich. : Pierian
   Press, 1973. 7 vols.

Modern Humanities Research Association. Annual Bibliography of
   English Language and Literature (1920-1973). 13 vols.
   Cambridge, England: Cambridge University Press, 1937-
   1949.

Munby, A. N. L. , ed. Sale Catalogues of Libraries of Eminent
   Persons. London: Mansell with Sotheby Parke-Bernet
   Publications, n. d. 6 vols.

The New Cambridge Bibliography of English Literature. Cambridge, ·
   England: Cambridge University Press, 1972. 4 vols.

"The Romantic Movement: A Selective and Critical Bibliography. "
   English Language Notes, Supplement. Boulder: Univer-
   sity of Colorado, 1965-1973.

"The Romantic Movement: A Selective and Critical Bibliography. "
   Philological Quarterly. Iowa City: State University of
   Iowa, 1950-1964. 5 vols.

Santucho, Oscar José. George Gordon, Lord Byron: A Compre-
   hensive Bibliography of Secondary Materials in English,
   1807-1974. With a Critical Review of Research by Clem-

ent Tyson Goode, Jr. Metuchen, N.J.: Scarecrow Press, 1977.

Union List of Serials in Libraries of the United States and Canada. Edited by Winifred Gregory. New York: H. W. Wilson, 1943.

Wise, Thomas. A Bibliography of the Writings of George Gordon Noel, Baron Byron. London: privately printed, 1932-1933. 2 vols.

EDITIONS AND LETTERS

Byron, George Gordon Noel, Lord. Byron: A Self-Portrait: Letters and Diaries, 1798 to 1824. Edited by Peter Quennell. London: John Murray, 1950. 2 vols.

_____. The Complete Poetical Works of Lord Byron. Edited by Paul Elmer More. Boston: Houghton Mifflin (Riverside Press), 1905.

_____. Lord Byron's Correspondence. Edited by John Murray. London: John Murray, 1898-1901. 2 vols.

_____. The Works of Lord Byron: Letters and Journals. Edited by Rowland E. Prothero. London: John Murray, 1898-1901. 6 vols.

_____. The Works of Lord Byron: Poetry. Edited by Ernest Hartley Coleridge. London: John Murray, 1898-1904. 7 vols.

BIOGRAPHIES AND BIOGRAPHICAL STUDIES

Kennedy, James. Conversations on Religion with Lord Byron and Others, Held in Cephalonia, a Short Time Previous to His Lordship's Death. London: John Murray, 1830.

Lovell, Ernest J., Jr., ed. His Very Self and Voice: Collected Conversations of Lord Byron. New York: Macmillan, 1954.

Marchand, Leslie A. Byron: A Biography. New York: Knopf, 1957. 3 vols.

CRITICAL ESSAYS AND STUDIES

Bradford, Gamaliel. "The Glory of Sin: Byron" in Saints and Sinners. Boston: Houghton Mifflin, 1932.

Calvert, William J. Byron: Romantic Paradox. Chapel Hill: University of North Carolina Press, 1935.

Chew, Samuel C. "Byron" in The English Romantic Poets: A Review of Research. New York: Modern Language Association, 1950.

Fairchild, Hoxie Neale. "Byron" in Religious Trends in English Poetry. New York: Columbia University Press, 1939-1958. 5 vols.

Gleckner, Robert. Byron and the Ruins of Paradise. Baltimore: Johns Hopkins University Press, 1967

Joseph, Michael Kennedy. Byron the Poet. London: V. Gollancz, 1964.

McGann, Jerome J. "Editing Byron's Poetry." The Byron Journal 1 (1973): 5-6.

_____. Fiery Dust: Byron's Poetic Development. Chicago: The University of Chicago Press, 1968.

Marchand, Leslie. Byron's Poetry: A Critical Introduction. Boston: Houghton Mifflin, 1965. (Riverside Studies in Literature.)

Marjarum, Edward Wayne. Byron as Skeptic and Believer. Princeton, N. J. : Princeton University Press, 1938

Pönitz, Arthur. "Byron und die Bibel." Ph. D. dissertation, University of Leipzig, 1906.

Roston, Murray. Biblical Drama in England from the Middle Ages to the Present Day. Evanston, Ill. Northwestern University, 1968.

_____. Prophet and Poet: The Bible and the Growth of Romanticism. Evanston, Ill. : Northwestern University Press, 1965.

Stavrou, C. N. "Religion in Byron's Don Juan." Studies in English Literature 3 (1963): 567-94.

Steffan, Truman Guy. Lord Byron's Cain: Twelve Essays and a Text with Variants and Annotations. Austin: University of Texas Press, 1968.

Stevens, Harold Ray. "Byron and the Bible: A Study of Poetic and Philosophic Development." Ph. D. dissertation, University of Pennsylvania, 1964.

BIBLICAL MATERIALS

The Bible. King James Version.

Black, Matthew, ed. The Cambridge History of the Bible. Vol. 3. Cambridge, England: Cambridge University Press, 1963.

Bruce, F. F. The Books and the Parchments. London: Pickering & Inglish, 1950.

Cruden, Alexander. Complete Concordance to the Old and New Testaments. Edited by A. D. Adams, C. H. Irwin, and S. A. Waters. New York: Holt, Rinehart, and Winston, 1949.

Dakin, A. Calvinism. Philadelphia: Westminster Press, 1946.

Price, Ira Maurice. The Ancestry of Our English Bible. New York: Harper & Brothers, 1956.

Young, Robert. Analytical Concordance to the Bible. Grand Rapids, Mich.: Wm. B. Eerdmans, n. d.

HANDBOOKS AND DICTIONARIES

The Compact Edition of the Oxford English Dictionary. New York: Oxford University Press, 1971.

Fowler, H. W. A Dictionary of Modern English Usage. Oxford: Clarendon Press, 1934.

Shipley, Joseph Twadell, ed. Dictionary of World Literature. New York: Philosophical Library, 1943.